A BASIC COURSE

IN

ENGLISH

A First Dictionary

A First English Companion

A First Encyclopædia

Talking of Teaching

Can You Tell Me?

ARE ALSO BY
Walter D. Wright

ILLUSTRATED BY
CHRISTOPHER SANDERS, R.A.

PUBLISHED BY
JAMES NISBET & CO. LTD., DIGSWELL PLACE, WELWYN, HERTS.

MADE AND PRINTED IN GREAT BRITAIN BY
WILLIAM CLOWES & SONS, LIMITED, LONDON, BECCLES AND COLCHESTER

FIRST PUBLISHED 1961

0 7202 0949 8

A BASIC COURSE IN

ENGLISH

by Walter D. Wright

DIGSWELL PLACE

JAMES NISBET AND COMPANY LTD

PREFACE

THE design of this book springs from a number of personal convictions that I believe to be axioms in the teaching of English:

¶ Most children learn the basic skills only by systematic study and disciplined practice; proficiency cannot be left to come of its own accord.

¶ To understand the correction of errors, and to follow the teacher's advice on rules and usage, the pupil must have an adequate stock-in-trade of grammatical and technical terms; these terms must be made thoroughly familiar to him by frequent use in meaningful context, not thrust at him as abstract definitions.

¶ Habits, both good and bad, become ingrained by repetition; most of the time used in teaching the groundwork of the language should be spent not on testing (which stresses ignorance without increasing knowledge) but on good example and copious practice.

¶ Self-tuition and self-correction should be much encouraged and practised; the ability to use dictionaries and other reference books not only helps to ensure a high degree of accuracy in the pupil's answers but lays the foundation for independent enquiry and correction in adult life.

¶ The main emphasis in the teaching of the subject as a whole should be on expression, creation and appreciation; this being so, drill and practice in the basic skills should be carried out with the greatest possible economy of time.

¶ Teaching is best left to the teacher; the most useful function of text-books is to provide abundant material for illustration and exercise, so conceived and organized that whatever is needed is available instantly.

With these considerations in mind I have planned *A Basic Course in English* as a book to be used flexibly throughout the secondary school, at various stages of age and ability. That is to say, an elementary exercise might be suitable for bright children in the first year, for less able children in the second year, and for children in need of remedial work in (say) the fourth year. The division of the book into clearly-defined sections, and the availability of a comprehensive index, give the teacher complete and easy freedom of choice according to his needs. The sets in each section are in logical sequence, and the exercises in each set are graded; but it is for the teacher to pick and choose as he thinks fit for any particular group of pupils.

I have treated grammar as a tool and as an aid to correct usage, not as inert knowledge, and have refrained from including anything solely because custom seems to demand it. The touchstone for every exercise has been the question: Will it improve the pupil's understanding and use of English? As for spelling, I have confined myself to whatever simple and helpful rules there are, avoiding confusing the pupil with exceptions. For those teachers who wish to improve their pupils' spelling and understanding of words in a most rewarding way I offer the section on Word Study, at the same time expressing the opinion that no secondary school should regard the lack of a foreign language in the syllabus as sufficient grounds for neglecting the study of simple etymology.

The exercises called *Mark These Yourself* are intended as a reward and a challenge to the bright pupils who finish their work first and who need to be given profitable employment that will not add still further to the teacher's burden of marking; they can of course be used effectively in other ways also. The idea behind the *Look These Up* questions is that pupils shall be encouraged to seek out things for themselves, be given interesting and sometimes entertaining glimpses of topics in other sections and be reminded that they are in fact studying not a number of subjects but one complete whole.

To Mr. H. J. Mackenzie Wood, who has helped me to keep the book in focus during its long period of preparation, I am most grateful, as I am to my wife for her advice and her work on the proofs. I am indebted also to colleagues, among whom Mr. H. D. Brookes should be mentioned in particular, for encouragement and helpful criticism.

If any errors or inconsistencies have escaped my notice I shall be glad to have my attention drawn to them so that they can be corrected in later editions.

Cannock   W. D. W.
Staffordshire
1961

CONTENTS

FOREWORD TO SECTION ONE

HOW do people become first-class craftsmen or designers? They may have a knack or a flair for their work. But almost certainly they have learned a great deal about the materials and the tools they use. By study and experiment they have found out how to achieve the best results, and how to avoid mistakes. Their fine workmanship does not happen of its own accord; it is the outcome of patient attention to detail.

How do people become expert writers and speakers of English? In the first place they take their example from others. But sooner or later they must study the language in detail—the ways in which words and sentences are built, and the rules and customs by which English is governed.

Imagine how difficult it would be to understand lessons in woodwork or domestic science if you did not know the meanings of words such as *chisel* and *omelette*. Who ever heard of a chemist who did not know the difference between glycerine and strychnine, or of a railway engine-driver who did not understand the signals? How could anyone discuss the working of a motor car unless he knew the names of the various parts and how they fit together?

The English language is made up of many parts. There are rules to be obeyed and mistakes to be avoided. For all these there are special names. Unless we are familiar with them we cannot discuss the language intelligently; neither can anyone else explain clearly to us where we may have gone wrong.

In this section on Grammar you will learn many of the most important names and rules that you need to know for the writing and speaking of good English.

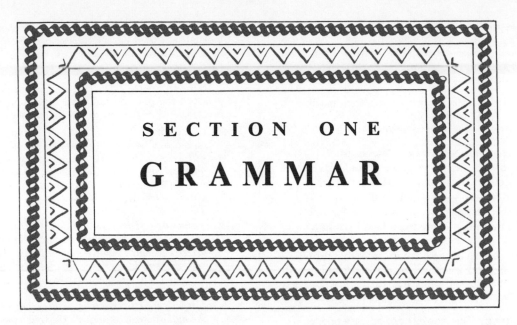

SECTION ONE
GRAMMAR

1. PHRASES AND SENTENCES

1. If a person says *I am going home* we know perfectly well what he means, but if he suddenly says *On my way home* we wait to hear what else he is going to say. *I am going home* is a sentence, because it makes sense and has a complete meaning. *On my way home* is not a whole statement, and is called a phrase.

Say which of the following are sentences and which are phrases.

(*a*) Down by the bridge
(*b*) Peter said nothing
(*c*) All the day long
(*d*) The sea is salt
(*e*) Next to the doctor's
(*f*) Nelson was wounded
(*g*) Grass grows
(*h*) As cold as ice
(*i*) Up the hill he went
(*j*) Go to your places

2. Dictionary definitions are given in the form of phrases, thus:—

> **diadem.** A crown.
> **heart.** The blood-pump of the body.

Here is the same information given in the form of sentences:

> A diadem is a crown.
> The heart is the blood-pump of the body.

Look up the following words in your dictionary, and define them in complete sentences:

(*a*) tarpaulin
(*b*) delta
(*c*) eel
(*d*) borax
(*e*) oboe
(*f*) sky
(*g*) elbow
(*h*) tinfoil
(*i*) whale
(*j*) honey
(*k*) pliers
(*l*) dinosaur

3. Turn these phrases into sentences by making suitable additions.

(*a*) Behind a hedge . . . . .
(*b*) On the stroke of twelve . . . . .
(*c*) A few days ago . . . . .
(*d*) Since yesterday . . . . .
(*e*) At the foot of the cliff . . . . .
(*f*) In spite of his tiredness . . . . .
(*g*) Farther along the road . . . . .

4. Turn these phrases into sentences by putting not less than four words in front of each.

(*a*) . . . . . a most interesting book.
(*b*) . . . . . inside the cave.
(*c*) . . . . . a horse without a rider.
(*d*) . . . . . at the water's edge.
(*e*) . . . . . throughout the day.
(*f*) . . . . . at regular intervals.

5. It is possible to remove a phrase from each of the following sentences and leave a complete sentence. Write out the sentences that remain when these phrases are removed, and make sure that they convey the main sense of the originals.

> EXAMPLE: He sprang to his feet, blazing with anger.
> ANSWER: He sprang to his feet.

(a) She crept into a back seat, late as usual.
(b) Delighted at our success, we held a party.
(c) With pieces of string he repaired the net.
(d) There he stood, hands on hips.
(e) The men, fearing an explosion, ran for safety.
(f) Each morning, before breakfast, I go for a swim.

6. Re-arrange each of these sentences so that the phrase now at the end is moved near the beginning, with commas before and after it. In the first two sentences the phrases to be moved are printed in italics.

> EXAMPLE: This book is not an easy one, *even for adults.*
> ANSWER: This book, even for adults, is not an easy one.

(a) Every pupil has passed the examination, *without exception.*
(b) The fox walked away in disgust, *tired of trying to reach the grapes.*
(c) No man could move that boulder, however strong.
(d) Jim kept one eye open, hoping to see Santa Claus.
(e) Mary put her head under the clothes, afraid of the thunder and lightning.
(f) The peasant killed the goose that laid the golden eggs, hoping to get rich quickly.

7. **How not to do it.** Some journalists, trying to appear brisk and conversational, avoid long sentences in which several phrases are separated by commas. They put them between full stops as though they were sentences. For example:

> *The Government should act now. Before it is too late.*

This is thoroughly bad English, and you should not imitate it in your own writing.

Another kind of bad English sometimes used by journalists leaves out the verbs, as we sometimes do in conversation. For example:

> *Quite a good idea.*

In the following extracts from newspaper columns pick out the phrases and parts of sentences that are printed as though they are complete sentences.

(a) *In Cornwall they order another small, privately-owned bus company to raise its fares. So that it will keep in line with the higher fares of the big undertakings. The Government should make up its mind whether it really wants to bring prices down. Or whether that is just talk.*
(b) *They came in their thousands to see the great motorway. The week-end driver with the children in the back. The young sports-car enthusiast with his girl friend. And the pedestrians, the cyclists, and the coach parties who thronged the fly-over bridges. They came to pay a spontaneous tribute to the new motorway.*
(c) *Fifty thousand pounds is to be spent on tests for the hull of a new America's Cup challenger. A lot of money to spend before a yacht is even started. But not too much.*
(d) *From the Chancellor of the Exchequer, good news. And better advice. Production has risen by eight per cent. in a year. A stable cost of living has been achieved in Britain.*
(e) *This man knows what it is like to endure failure and misfortune. Because he has known fame and glory. Ten years ago he was a celebrity. Today he is almost forgotten.*

2. COMMON NOUNS

1. In the following unfinished phrases the words in italics are common nouns. Complete each phrase by adding another common noun that is suitable. You may find a dictionary helpful.

> EXAMPLE: The *hilt* of a ——
> ANSWER: The hilt of a sword

(a) The *spokes* of a ——
(b) The *keel* of a ——
(c) The *pendulum* of a ——
(d) The *rungs* of a ——
(e) The *fuselage* of an ——
(f) The *kernel* of a ——

(g) The *jamb* of a ———
(h) The *radius* of a ———
(i) The *pistil* of a ———
(j) The *estuary* of a ———

2. In the following statements the words in italics are common nouns. Complete each statement by adding another common noun (one word only) that is suitable.

   EXAMPLE: *Polo* is a ———.
   ANSWER: Polo is a game.

   (a) A *cello* is an ———.
   (b) A *lizard* is a ———.
   (c) An *antelope* is an ———.
   (d) *Spinach* is a ———.
   (e) An *aster* is a ———.
   (f) A *quail* is a ———.
   (g) *Granite* is a ———.
   (h) A *pomegranate* is a ———.
   (i) A *doublet* is a ———.
   (j) *Badminton* is a ———.

3. A common type of definition in the dictionary is that in which we are told:
   1. the class or group to which a thing belongs;
   2. the use to which it is put.

   Here is the pattern:

   A/An | Class or group | for | Use or purpose

   For example, we can define a *hammer* as

   A | tool | for | driving in nails

   Write short definitions of the following words. Underline every noun.

   EXAMPLE: **hammer.** A <u>tool</u> for driving in <u>nails</u>.

   (a) dynamo
   (b) bucket
   (c) pincers
   (d) camera
   (e) putty
   (f) wardrobe
   (g) catapult
   (h) telegraph

4. In each of the following sentences the word in italics is a common noun. Substitute another common noun that means the same (or nearly the same) thing.

   EXAMPLE: This soap has a pleasant *perfume*.
   ANSWER: This soap has a pleasant smell.

   (a) It was only a mischievous *prank*.
   (b) They found that the *sepulchre* was empty.

(c) This is forbidden by an ancient *statute*.
(d) His *respiration* became weaker.
(e) Many thermometers contain *quicksilver*.
(f) People said that he was a *sorcerer*.
(g) The barrel is full of *molasses*.
(h) These stoves burn *kerosene*.

5. All the words in the two lists below are common nouns. Each person referred to in List A is often associated with one of the persons in List B. Pair them off like this:

   employer and *workman*

   List A: employer, doctor, king, host, nobleman, governess, mayor, editor, lawyer
   List B: patient, client, workman, pupil, retainer, journalist, subject, guest, alderman

6. **Same word, different meaning.** Use each of these common nouns twice, in two sentences, to show that it can mean two quite different things. Be sure that you use the words as nouns—that is, as the names of *things*.

   EXAMPLE: sash.
   SUGGESTED ANSWER: (1) She wore a white sash round her waist. (2) The sash of the kitchen window is jammed.

sole	plane	mail	riddle
smack	tip	file	rent
	scales	race	

7. **What is he called?** A person who *travels* is called a traveller, and one who *assists* is an assistant. Using your dictionary to make sure of the correct spelling, say what the following persons are called:

   A PERSON WHO . . .

   (a) . . . *begs* for food
   (b) . . . *competes* against others in a race
   (c) . . . *applies* for something
   (d) . . . *represents* a firm
   (e) . . . *studies* for an examination
   (f) . . . *corresponds* with you by post
   (g) . . . *conspires* to commit a crime
   (h) . . . *brags* about his skill
   (i) . . . *deputizes* for his master
   (j) . . . *criticizes* a theatrical play
   (k) . . . *saves* his nation from disaster
   (l) . . . *depends* on others for a living

3

8. Make a list of any twenty of the common nouns contained in this passage from *The Black Arrow*.

> *Upon the very margin of the ditch, not thirty feet from where they crouched, an iron cauldron bubbled and steamed above a glowing fire; and close by, in an attitude of listening, as though he had caught some sound of their movements among the ruins, a tall, red-faced, battered-looking man stood poised, an iron spoon in his right hand, a horn and a formidable dagger at his belt. Plainly this was the singer; plainly he had been stirring the cauldron, when some incautious step among the lumber had fallen upon his ear. Near by another man lay slumbering, rolled in a brown cloak, with a butterfly hovering above his face.*

3. PROPER NOUNS

1. The word *country* is a common noun, but *Australia* is a proper noun. Similarly, *girl* is a common noun and *Joan* is a proper noun.

The following list contains ten common nouns and ten proper nouns. Write them out in two columns in your ordinary handwriting—not in block capitals. Head the columns *Common* and *Proper*.

PLYMOUTH	COLLAR	FEMALE	SCHUBERT
ROSETTE	CONGO	COLUMBUS	EARTHQUAKE
ANNE	CHARLES	ASIA	TELEPHONE
PLUMBER	KENT	HYDRANT	MUSHROOM
VENUS	PIRATE	EASTER	CONUNDRUM

2. The following words are common nouns. For each one, find a corresponding proper noun.

For example, you could begin with *Amazon, January, France*; but think of other answers to the first three for yourself.

If you write them out, arrange them in two columns with the common nouns on the left and the proper nouns on the right.

river	month	country	town
ocean	boy	girl	mountain
county	continent	island	newspaper
language	inn	ship	aeroplane
religion	planet	theatre	goddess

3. Does it need a capital letter? A word can be either a common noun or a proper noun according to the sense in which it is used. For example, if we say

> *No museum is better known than the British Museum*

we use the word *museum* first as a common noun to refer to museums in general and then as a proper noun to mean one particular museum.

Write the following in your usual handwriting, putting in capital letters wherever necessary.

(*a*) THE NAME OF HER SCHOOL IS ST. MARY'S HIGH SCHOOL.

(*b*) THE FINE EARTHENWARE CALLED CHINA IS SO NAMED BECAUSE IT WAS BROUGHT INTO EUROPE FROM CHINA.

(*c*) THE HOTEL ROYAL IS THE ONLY HOTEL I CAN RECOMMEND.

(*d*) THE MAIN GATE OF THE PARK IS AT THE END OF PARK ROAD.

(*e*) THE CANARY IS A SONG-BIRD THAT ORIGINATED IN THE CANARY ISLANDS.

(*f*) MERTON COLLEGE IS THE OLDEST COLLEGE IN OXFORD.

(*g*) THE BLACK FOREST IS ONE OF THE MOST BEAUTIFUL FORESTS IN EUROPE.

(*h*) IT WAS IN 1922 THAT BROADCASTING WAS BEGUN BY THE BRITISH BROADCASTING COMPANY.

(*i*) IN 'THE MERCHANT OF VENICE' HE TOOK THE PART OF ANTONIO THE MERCHANT.

(*j*) NORTH OF COUNTY DURHAM IS THE COUNTY OF NORTHUMBERLAND.

4. Surnames. The following words are the surnames of people, and are therefore proper nouns. Some of these words can also be used as common nouns; for example, the word HILL can mean either *Hill* (a person) or *hill* (a small mountain).

Pick out from this list those words that can be used only as proper nouns, and *not* as common nouns (e.g., *Pearson*)

HILL	CLAY	PEARSON	KNIGHT
ATKINS	ARCHER	BISHOP	HEATH
DAVIES	BIRD	TAYLOR	EDGE
LLOYD	NIGHTINGALE	PRICE	DIXON
FARMER	CARR	BARBER	DEAN
CLARKE	BOND	KNOTT	BELL
COATES	MASON	GAY	DRAKE

5. Common nouns from proper nouns. Some common nouns are made from proper nouns—that is, taken from the names of persons and places. Say which common nouns were adopted in this way as the names of the things described below.

Pages 160–1 of *A First English Companion* will help you.

EXAMPLE: Fine earthenware from China
ANSWER: china

(a) A garment made in Jersey
(b) Food served as the Earl of Sandwich liked it
(c) A flower named after the botanist Dahl
(d) Woollen yarn from Worstead
(e) A machine suggested by Dr. Guillotin
(f) A wine from Oporto in Portugal
(g) Fine linen from Cambray
(h) A kind of mountain that was supposed to be the workshop of the god Vulcan

Other exercises on the use of capital letters appear on pages 61–62.

4. VERBS

1. Suggest a verb. It is possible to say in one word what certain things *do*. For example, fish *swim* and dogs *bark*. The words *swim* and *bark*, as used here, are verbs.

Add a suitable verb (a single word) to each of the following so as to make a sensible statement.

(a) Mountaineers ——.   (j) Dynamite ——.
(b) Vegetables ——.   (k) Elastic ——.
(c) Fuels ——.   (l) Iron ——.
(d) Choristers ——.   (m) Diamonds ——.
(e) Bees ——.   (n) Authors ——.
(f) Farmers ——.   (o) Reptiles ——.
(g) Water ——.   (p) Rodents ——.
(h) Ice ——.   (q) Petrol ——.
(i) Cork ——.   (r) Orators ——.

2. A common type of definition in the dictionary is that in which we are told the occupation of a particular class of person. Here is the pattern:

A | Person | who | Occupation |

For example, we can define a *tailor* as

A | man | who | makes clothes |

Write short definitions of the following words. In each one, under!ine the verb.

EXAMPLE: **tailor.** A man who <u>makes</u> clothes.

(a) plumber   (e) sorcerer
(b) milkmaid   (f) nun
(c) sentinel   (g) authoress
(d) landlord   (h) aviator

3. Find the verb. Pick out all the verbs in the following sentences. Copy the sentences and underline the verbs.

(a) The little dog laughed.
(b) The last straw breaks the camel's back.
(c) The mouse ran up the clock.
(d) Good King Wenceslas looked out.
(e) Drink this medicine.
(f) They fought the dogs, and killed the cats,
     And bit the babies in the cradles.
(g) A peck of pickled peppercorns Peter Piper picked.
(h) Up you go!

4. Supply the verb. In each of the following exercises replace the phrases in italics by a verb (one word only) that means as nearly as possible the same. Use your dictionary, and be guided by the clues given in brackets.

EXAMPLE: He allowed his television licence
to *end and become useless.*
(*lap*——)
ANSWER: He allowed his television licence
to lapse.

(a) The producer told me to *walk in a shuffling manner* like an old man. (*sham*——)
(b) We shall have to *cut down expenses.* (*econ*——)
(c) The vessel began to *roll about* in the waves. (*wal*——)
(d) She is going to Bournemouth to *get well again.* (*recu*——)
(e) We heard the noise *echo to and fro* among the cliffs. (*rever*——)
(f) We saw him *pull a face* as though he had felt a sharp pain. (*grim*——)
(g) He *dressed up in disguise* as a woman. (*masqu*——)
(h) The bandits went out to *lie in wait for* the mail coach. (*way*——).

5

5. Some verbs tell us that things or persons *are* (or *were*) something. Some verbs tell us that things *become* (or *became*) something. Pick out all such verbs in the following sentences.

> EXAMPLE: Today is Tuesday.
> ANSWER: is

(a) I am late for school.
(b) These cakes are rather dry.
(c) My cousin's dog is a spaniel.
(d) Scott and Amundsen were explorers.
(e) Last night's concert was most enjoyable.
(f) Butter becomes soft in the sun.
(g) The night grew cold and stormy.
(h) The leaves turned yellow.
(i) We get excited at Christmas.

6. **Strangers.** In each of these sets of three verbs there is one 'stranger'—a verb quite unlike the other two in meaning. Find it, and then use it in a sentence.

Begin the sentence with the words shown in brackets, and try to show that you know the *meaning* of the chosen verb. For example, in the first one (a) it is not sufficient to say *Why did you hesitate?* It is better to say *Why did you hesitate before you answered me?*

(a) determine, hesitate, resolve. (*Why did you . . . . ?*)
(b) conclude, expire, begin. (*At what time . . . . ?*)
(c) arrange, disturb, confuse. (*When the books arrive . . . . .*)
(d) connect, detach, uncouple. (*I shall need a screwdriver . . . . .*)
(e) construct, dismantle, erect. (*A gang of men arrived . . . . .*)
(f) detest, cherish, revere. (*The reason why I . . . . .*)
(g) soothe, provoke, console. (*If you speak to Fred like that . . . . .*)

7. Pick out the verbs in these sentences. If you write out the sentences in full, underline the verbs.

(a) I wander'd lonely as a cloud.
(b) The mirror cracked from side to side.
(c) The ploughman homeward plods his weary way.
(d) Buy my English posies!
(e) Like a yawn of fire from the grass it came.
(f) Now the great winds shoreward blow.
(g) How solitary gleams the lamplit street.
(h) The North wind powders me with snow.
(i) But in the purple pool there nothing grows.
(j) Blow, blow, thou winter wind.

8. **Synonyms.** In each of these sentences, find the main verb. When you have done this, choose another verb (one word only) that can be put in place of it without changing the sense. Then write out the sentence with its new verb. Your dictionary will help you.

> EXAMPLE: The acrobats astonished us with their skill.
> SUGGESTED ANSWER: The acrobats amazed us with their skill.

(a) He brandished a cudgel above his head.
(b) During the night the Indians encircled the camp.
(c) The concrete is reinforced with steel bars.
(d) We are menaced by floods in this valley.
(e) The accident has not impaired his sight.
(f) Did she decline the invitation?
(g) Commend him for his gallantry.
(h) Along the hedgerows, cattle browsed.
(i) He gnashed his teeth in anger.
(j) The enemy capitulated without a fight.

9. If a person is in *agreement* with you he is said *to agree*; if he shows *obedience* he is said *to obey*. Keeping to this pattern, reply to each of the following questions by giving the corresponding verb. Each answer should consist of two words, as shown above (*to agree*, etc.).

WHAT IS A PERSON SAID TO DO IF HE . . . .

(a) gives an *explanation*?
(b) is full of *admiration*?
(c) is quick in *recognition*?
(d) gives a *subscription* to a fund?
(e) makes a *division* of prize-money?
(f) gives *notification* of a meeting?
(g) gives the *pronunciation* of a word?
(h) orders the *suspension* of a player?
(i) gives *permission* for a holiday?
(j) makes a valuable *acquisition*?

For further exercises on verbs see pages 22–23.

✓ MARK THESE YOURSELF

The answers are on page 144

What is the difference between:

(a) a pole and a Pole;
(b) a swede and a Swede;
(c) a vandal and a Vandal;
(d) may and May;
(e) mercury and Mercury;
(f) a jersey and Jersey?

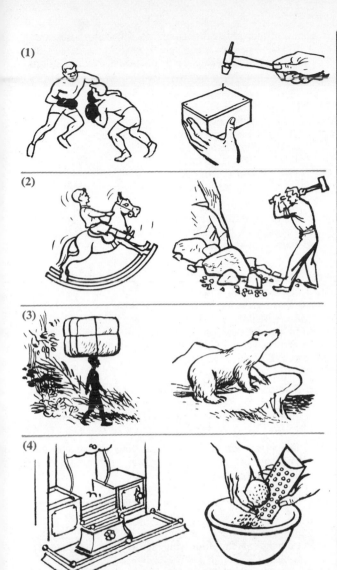

(1)

(2)

(3)

(4)

Noun or Verb? Here are four pairs of pictures. Each pair represents two words that happen to be spelt and pronounced exactly alike but are not connected in meaning. One of each pair is used as a noun, and the other as a verb. When you have decided what the words are, write them out for each picture, and show whether they are used as nouns or as verbs.

5. ONE WORD, TWO USES

1. In each of these pairs of sentences the word in italics is used once as a noun and once as a verb—but not always in that order. Say which is which.

> EXAMPLE: 1. How often do you *weed* the garden?
> 2. This plant is a *weed*.
> ANSWER: 1. verb.
> 2. noun.

(a) Keep it under *lock* and key.
(b) Be sure to *lock* it up safely.

(c) *Float* on your back until help comes.
(d) He saw that his *float* had sunk.

(e) The noise *echoes* in the valley.
(f) They set the *echoes* ringing.

(g) This cave is big enough to give *shelter* to all of us.
(h) This cave is big enough to *shelter* us all.

(i) I was asked to *report* on the meeting.
(j) Who wrote this *report* on the meeting?

(k) The captain's cruelty led to *mutiny*.
(l) The crew decided to *mutiny*.

2. In each of these sentences one word is printed in italics. Say whether it is used as a noun or as a verb.

(a) This is a *test* of skill.
(b) How can I *claim* a refund?
(c) *Pickle* the beetroot in vinegar.
(d) *Heat* should be applied gradually.
(e) The prize was almost within my *grasp*.
(f) Did he *remark* on your new hat?
(g) He was driven from pillar to *post*.
(h) She pays little attention to *dress* or appearance.

3. Use each of the following words first as a verb and then as a noun, in two separate sentences.

> EXAMPLE: run
> SUGGESTED (a) Run as quickly as
> ANSWER: you can.
> (b) We need one more run to win.

| walk | jump | play | swim | dance |
| step | kick | talk | taste | smell |

4. Here, as in Exercise 3, use each word as a verb and then as a noun. Notice here, however, that each word's meaning when used as a verb is quite different from its meaning when used as a noun; for example, a *moor* is not a place where we *moor* a boat.

moor	prune	grate	bear	shed
refrain	till	don	quail	brook

6. SUBJECT AND PREDICATE

From the table below you will see that:—

(a) the part of a sentence that explains what person or thing we are talking about is called the *subject*;

(b) whatever is said about the subject is called the *predicate*. The predicate must contain a verb, as shown by the words in italics.

SUBJECT	PREDICATE
Birds	*fly*.
My brother Charles	*writes* detective stories.
A soldier, in full kit,	*ran* ten kilometres.
The man next door	*is digging* his garden.

Here is an easy way of finding the subject:

1. Pick out the verb. (e.g. *fly*, or *writes*)
2. Ask yourself *What?* or *Who?* (e.g., *What flies?* or *Who wrote?*)
3. The answer to the question is the subject of the sentence.

---

1. Write out the following sentences. Then separate the subject from the predicate with a vertical line, and underline the verb.

EXAMPLE: My brother Charles | writes detective stories.

(a) Peter drove the car.
(b) Wax melts easily.
(c) Birds of a feather flock together.
(d) This motor works by electricity.
(e) Thousands of people perished.
(f) Mr. Jones, the insurance collector, called today.
(g) Two large trees were obstructing the line.
(h) He is waiting for Trevor.

2. Supply suitable subjects for the following predicates. If your answers are given in writing, write out the completed sentences in full. Some of the subjects should consist of *several* words.

(a) . . . . . is my favourite game.
(b) . . . . . are found in Africa.
(c) . . . . . flow into the sea.
(d) . . . . . went up the hill.
(e) . . . . . had left her nest.
(f) . . . . . is a large building.
(g) . . . . . are visiting Norway.
(h) . . . . . has been shown on television.

3. Supply a suitable predicate of more than one word for each of the following subjects. Underline the main verb in each predicate.

(a) The cowboy . . . . .
(b) My home . . . . .
(c) New York . . . . .
(d) The trees at the top of the hill . . . . .
(e) A light on a tall tower . . . . .
(f) Snowdrops and crocuses . . . . .
(g) The whole of the money . . . . .
(h) His excuse . . . . .

4. **Find the subject.** The subject is not bound to be at the beginning of a sentence; it can be in the middle, at the end, or anywhere at all. For example:
After the lightning came a crash of thunder.

The verb here is *came*. Ask yourself *what* came? The answer is *a crash of thunder*. The subject of this sentence is therefore *a crash of thunder*. The sentence could in fact be re-arranged like this:
A crash of thunder came after the lightning.

In each of the following sentences, pick out the subject.

(a) Behind the bush a leopard crouched.
(b) In her hair was a blue ribbon.
(c) Between the rows of trees runs a narrow cart-track.
(d) Under this stone lie the bodies of two crusaders.
(e) Like wildfire the news spread through the village.
(f) In spite of the blizzard the climbers reached the summit.
(g) Sometimes the milkman forgets to call.

5. Supply suitable subjects for the following predicates, and then re-arrange the sentences so that the subjects come first.

> EXAMPLE: Into the room came .....
> SUGGESTED ANSWER: A little child came into the room.

(a) In the undergrowth crouched .....
(b) Behind them was .....
(c) At the foot of the hill stands .....
(d) In the manger lay .....
(e) Last week ..... was wrecked.
(f) Tomorrow ..... shall go shopping.
(g) On each wall ..... was hung.
(h) Disappointed, ... returned home.

6. Using the rule you have been given, pick out the subject in each of these sentences. Then re-arrange the sentence so that the subject is at the beginning.

(a) From the window hung a flag.
(b) Behind the bushes lies a ditch.
(c) In the grate a fire burned brightly.
(d) At the cross-roads a policeman stands.
(e) Alone she cuts and binds the grain.
(f) By fairy hands their knell is rung.
(g) All alone went she.
(h) High on the shore sat the great god Pan.
(i) Ten thousand saw I at a glance.
(j) Down swung the sound of the far-off bell.

7. Re-arrange each of these sentences so that the subject is at the end. In the first three you can do this by using the word in italics as the first word; in the others you must decide for yourself which word comes first.

> EXAMPLE: Long creepers hung *from* the trees.
> ANSWER: From the trees hung long creepers.

(a) A mouse jumped *out* of his pocket.
(b) A policeman stood *on* each side of him.
(c) The Pied Piper stepped *into* the street.
(d) Open country lies beyond the town.
(e) Fifty prisoners were kept in this dungeon.
(f) Two statues stood at the head of the stairs.
(g) Thick ropes were tied around the trunk of the tree.
(h) Ragged breakers roared around the bay.
(i) The princess stepped out of the car.
(j) The wedding bells rang out.

7. SINGULAR AND PLURAL

In most of these exercises you will find a dictionary very helpful.

1. Write out each of these phrases, replacing the dash by the plural form of the word in brackets.

> EXAMPLE: Several ——— (*fox*)
> ANSWER: Several foxes

(a) Many ——— (*wolf*)
(b) Various ——— (*key*)
(c) A few ——— (*giraffe*)
(d) Crowds of ——— (*woman*)
(e) Some ——— (*fly*)
(f) Numerous ——— (*mosquito*)

2. **Words ending in o.** Arrange the plurals of these nouns in two columns according to whether they end in *s* or *es*.

> piano, potato, echo, photo dynamo, hero, volcano, curio, tomato, soprano.

3. **Words ending in y.** Using your dictionary, write out the plurals of these words:

> penny, valley, pulley, ruby, remedy, donkey, story, storey, journey, pastry, melody, kidney.

When you have done this you will notice that some of the plurals still contain the letter *y*. What letter comes *before* the *y* in each of these words? What is the rule for forming the plurals of nouns ending in *y*? (See Set 44 on page 77.)

4. Some nouns, including the names of several kinds of fish, are the same in the plural as in the singular; e.g., *salmon*. Find as many of these words as you can.

5. **What is the singular?** In the following phrases substitute *A* or *An* for the words in italics, and put the remaining words in their singular forms.

> EXAMPLE: *Two* armies
> ANSWER: An army

(a) *Ten* toes
(b) *A set of* dominoes
(c) *Numerous* wolves
(d) *Many* caves
(e) *Three* ladies
(f) *Several* pig-sties
(g) *A number of* alleys
(h) *A shoal of* mackerel
(i) *A few* children
(j) *A team of* oxen
(k) *A fleet of* buses
(l) *Four* men-servants
(m) *Two different* radii
(n) *A host of* cherubim

6. The plural of *cupful* is *cupfuls* (not *cupsful*). Following the same rule, complete the following phrases. Clues to the missing words are given in brackets.

Two ————— of medicine (*teaspoon*)
Three ————— of conkers (*pocket*)
Four ————— of broth (*basin*)
Five ————— of sherry (*wineglass*)
Six ————— of water (*bowl*)
Seven ————— of waste paper (*bag*)
Eight ————— of milk (*jug*)
Nine ————— of apples (*basket*)
Ten ————— of sand (*shovel*)
Eleven ————— of coal (*bucket*)
Twelve ————— of nuts (*hand*)

7. **Words that are always plural.** Several pairs of plural nouns are set out below. One of the plural nouns in each pair has no singular. For example, treacle is called *molasses*, but there is no such thing as a *molass*. Say which of these words are always plural.

(*a*) fans and bellows
(*b*) pincers and spanners
(*c*) pliers and chisels
(*d*) needles and scissors
(*e*) rakes and shears
(*f*) tweezers and nail-files
(*g*) shovels and tongs
(*h*) trousers and waistcoats
(*i*) measles and pimples
(*j*) lumps and mumps
(*k*) oats and peas
(*l*) soap-suds and bubbles

8. Rewrite these sentences so that the words in italics are in plural form.

EXAMPLE: The *handkerchief was* crumpled.
ANSWER: The handkerchiefs were crumpled.

(*a*) The *bus is* late.
(*b*) My *sister-in-law has* returned.
(*c*) The *deer was* caught alive.
(*d*) The *goose is* ready for market.
(*e*) The *mongoose has* killed two snakes.
(*f*) *Was* the *army* defeated?
(*g*) *Is* the *kangaroo* fully grown?
(*h*) *Has* your *tooth* stopped aching?

9. **Are you sure?** Arrange these words in two columns according to whether they are singular or plural. Head the columns accordingly. Use your dictionary, and do not guess.

lens	gladioli	strata	terminus
fungi	topaz	aphis	larvae
plateaux	bureau	dice	axis

✓MARK THESE YOURSELF

The answers are on page 144

1. Each of these words has *two* plural forms; what are they?

(*a*) penny   (*d*) cherub   (*g*) gladiolus
(*b*) hoof   (*e*) seraph   (*h*) brother
(*c*) formula   (*f*) aquarium   (*i*) cow

2. (*a*) What is this?

(*b*) What are these?

3. Arrange these verbs in two columns according to whether they mean *to move into* or *to move out of*. Head the columns *In* and *Out*.

enter	emerge	intrude	issue
discharge	penetrate	escape	invade
evacuate	immigrate	insinuate	emanate

4. Pair off each of the verbs in list A with a verb in list B that has the opposite sense.

A. accept   advance   gratify   amplify   commend
B. diminish   bestow   recede   chide   displease

5. What is the difference between:

(*a*) two spectacles and a pair of spectacles;
(*b*) two compasses and a pair of compasses;
(*c*) physic and physics?

6. Punctuate this sentence so that it cannot be misunderstood:

She is too young to marry her father thinks

10

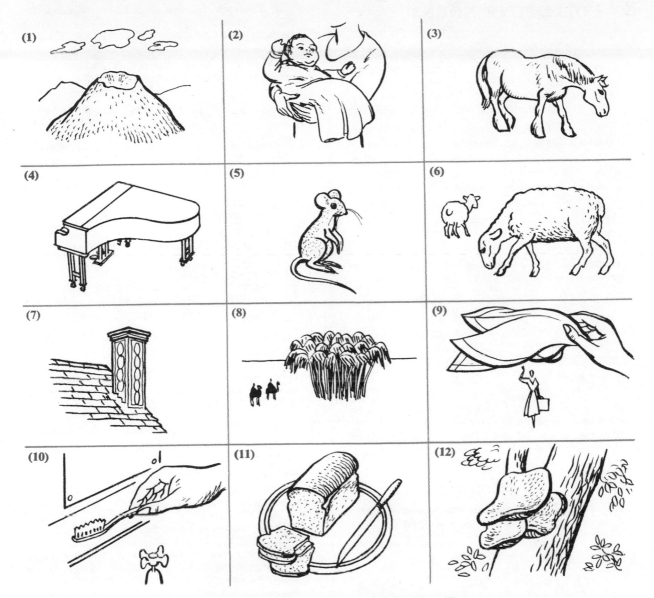

(1)   (2)   (3)

(4)   (5)   (6)

(7)   (8)   (9)

(10)   (11)   (12)

Singular and Plural. The names of the things illustrated above are nouns that form their plurals in different ways. Write down each noun, together with its plural form.

8. COLLECTIVE NOUNS

1. The noun *newspapers* is plural, but if we refer to the papers under a newsboy's arm as a *bundle* we are using a noun that is singular. Words of this kind— singular nouns as the names of *groups* of things—are called collective nouns.

Supply suitable collective nouns for the following.

(a) A ——— of wolves   (g) A ——— of rifle-shots
(b) A ——— of thieves   (h) A ——— of loaves
(c) A ——— of sheep   (i) A ——— of porpoises
(d) A ——— of buffaloes   (j) A ——— of partridges
(e) A ——— of puppies   (k) A ——— of stairs
(f) A ——— of savages   (l) An ——— of poems

Pages 158–9 of *A First English Companion* will help you.

2. What would you expect people to be *doing* in the groups named below?

EXAMPLE: a choir
ANSWER: singing

(a) A crew   (e) A queue
(b) An orchestra   (f) A troupe
(c) A chorus   (g) A congregation
(d) An audience   (h) A mob

3. When we use the word *library* we know that it must refer to a collection of books, so it is unnecessary to say *a library of books*. But the word *bunch* can mean a group of keys, or flowers, or grapes, etc.

In the following list of collective nouns some are like *library* and refer to one kind of thing only; others are like *bunch*, and can refer to several things. Arrange them in two columns, and begin like this:

ONE KIND		SEVERAL KINDS	
library		bunch	
menagerie	bundle	flock	congregation
forest	herd	orchestra	archipelago
team	bouquet	gang	constellation
band	swarm		

4. (a) Find three collective nouns that can be used in referring to a group of *people*.

In the same way find three collective nouns for each of the following:

(b) A group of *soldiers*
(c) A group of *trees*
(d) A group of *picked flowers*
(e) A group of *stars*

✅ MARK THESE YOURSELF

The answers are on page 144

1. Each of the things named below belongs to a different class or group. Study the examples given, and then carry on in the same way with the others, giving one word for each. A dictionary will help you.

EXAMPLES: 1. trout   2. screwdriver
ANSWERS: 1. fish   2. tool

(a) lizard   (h) polo   (o) waistcoat
(b) hornet   (i) loganberry   (p) nettle
(c) nitrogen   (j) water   (q) curate
(d) rhododendron   (k) rye   (r) yen
(e) granite   (l) morphia   (s) teak
(f) microphone   (m) diphtheria   (t) copper
(g) waggon   (n) pinnace   (u) brass

2. Can you think of a well-known verb of four letters that ends with ENY?

3. If your name is *Baker* it is probable that one of your ancestors was a baker by trade. See if you can think of at least ten more names of this kind.

4. Supply suitable verbs to complete the following.

EXAMPLE: A thief *steals*.

(a) A vocalist ———.   (e) A donor ———.
(b) A combatant ———.   (f) A vendor ———.
(c) A pugilist ———.   (g) A debtor ———.
(d) A glutton ———.   (h) A vagrant ———.

5. Arrange these names in the order in which you would find them in a telephone directory. Remember the rule of indexing, that "nothing comes before something" (e.g., *Jones, E.* comes before *Jones, Ernest*).

Morgan, J.   Morgan, S.   Morgan, S. J.
Morgan, Charles   Morgan, John
Morgan, Samuel   Morgan, J. W.

6. What is the subject of this sentence?

On the top shelf is a large box.

Plural and Collective. The pictures below illustrate twelve things, each of which can be described either by a plural noun (such as *cricketers*) or by a collective noun (such as *team*).

Name each picture in both ways, giving a plural noun and a collective noun for it.

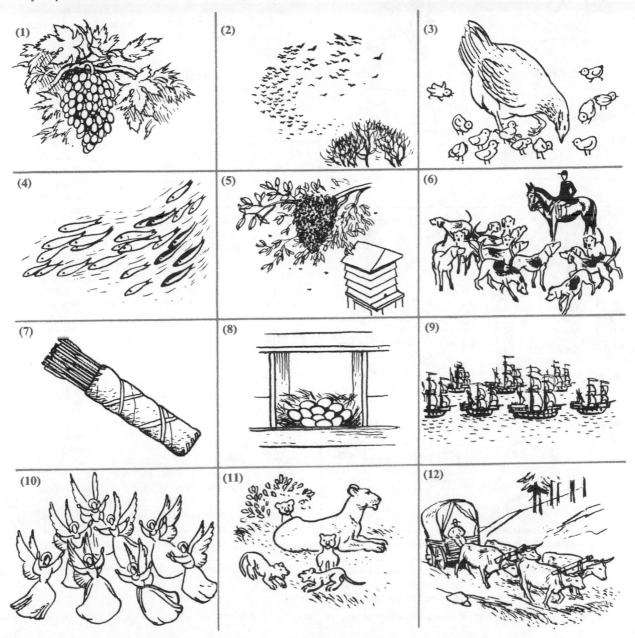

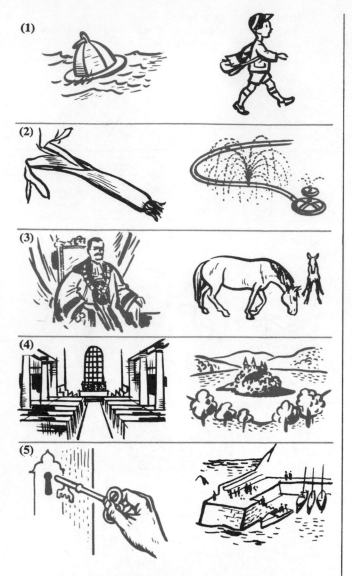

Nouns often confused. Do you sometimes make mistakes over pairs of words such as *beach* and *beech*, *maize* and *maze*, etc.? Five such pairs of common nouns are illustrated. When you have decided what they are, write them out so that the word illustrated in black comes first, and the one in red second.

Pages 163–170 of *A First English Companion* will help you.

PASSAGE FOR REVISION

On the next page and in later exercises you will be asked questions about this extract from *Travels with a Donkey in the Cevennes*, by Robert Louis Stevenson. For the moment, however, read it for your own enjoyment.

Night is a dead monotonous period under a roof; but in the open world it passes lightly, with its stars and dews and perfumes, and the hours are marked by changes in the face of Nature. What seems a kind of temporal death to people choked between walls and curtains, is only a light and living slumber to the man who sleeps afield. All night long he can hear Nature breathing deeply and freely; even as she takes her rest, she turns and smiles; and there is one stirring hour unknown to those who dwell in houses, when a wakeful influence goes abroad over the sleeping hemisphere, and all the outdoor world are on their feet. It is then that the cock first crows, not this time to announce the dawn, but like a cheerful watchman speeding the course of night. Cattle awake on the meadows; sheep break their fast on dewy hill-sides, and change to a new lair among the ferns; and houseless men, who have lain down with the fowls, open their dim eyes and behold the beauty of the night.

When that hour came to me among the pines, I wakened thirsty. My tin was standing by me half full of water. I emptied it at a draught; and feeling broad awake after this internal cold aspersion, sat upright to make a cigarette. The stars were clear, coloured, and jewel-like, but not frosty. A faint silvery vapour stood for the Milky Way. All around me the black fir-points stood upright and stock-still. By the whiteness of the pack-saddle, I could see Modestine walking round and round at the length of her tether; I could hear her steadily munching at the sward; but there was not another sound, save the indescribable quiet talk of the runnel* over the stones.

* *brook*

14

★ REVISION

On the opposite page is an extract from Stevenson's *Travels with a Donkey in the Cevennes*. The first four of the following questions are set on this passage.

If necessary, turn back to earlier pages to refresh your memory.

1. (*a*) Find ten common nouns in lines 1–5.
   (*b*) Pick out all the proper nouns in the whole passage.
   (*c*) Find seven plural nouns in lines 18–22.

2. Say whether the following words are used in this passage as nouns or as verbs.

(*a*) slumber	(line 7)	(*d*) tether	(line 34)
(*b*) rest	(line 10)	(*e*) talk	(line 37)
(*c*) smiles	(line 10)	(*f*) change	(line 19)

3. Name the subject of the sentence beginning
   (*a*) with the word *My* in line 24;
   (*b*) with the word *All* in line 30;
   (*c*) with the word *When* in line 23.

4. From lines 32–38 extract three statements of five words each. Separate them by full stops, and be sure that they are complete sentences.

5. Say which of the following are sentences and which are phrases:
   (*a*) When the swan returned to its nest
   (*b*) When he talks he smiles
   (*c*) Now he knew that he had won
   (*d*) Now that he knew he had won
   (*e*) Not to worry

6. Rewrite this eighteenth-century recipe, using capital letters only where they would be considered necessary nowadays.

   To fry Cucumbers for Mutton Sauce:

   You must brown some Butter in a Pan, and cut the Cucumbers in thin Slices; drain them from the Water, then fling them into the Pan. When they are fried brown, put in a little Pepper and Salt, a bit of Onion and Gravy, and let them stew together. Squeeze in some juice of Lemon; shake them well, and put them under your Mutton.

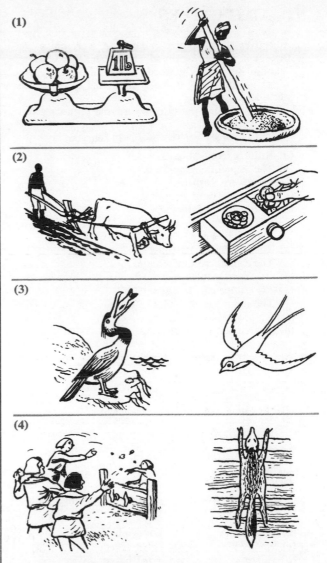

(1)

(2)

(3)

(4)

Noun or Verb? These pictures, like those on page 7, can be paired to represent two words which happen to be spelt and pronounced exactly alike, but which are not connected in meaning. One of each pair is used as a noun, and the other as a verb. When you have decided what the words are, write them out so as to show whether they are used here as nouns or as verbs.

9. ADJECTIVES

1. Adjectives from proper nouns. A car made in Britain is a *British* car; silk from China is *Chinese* silk, and so on. The words *British* and *Chinese* are adjectives that tell us more about the car and the silk respectively.

Following this pattern, reword the phrases given below.

Page 186 of *A First Dictionary* will help you.

(*a*) Rubber from Malaya
(*b*) The Alps of Switzerland
(*c*) Fiords in Norway
(*d*) The railways of Belgium
(*e*) A village in Holland
(*f*) Coffee from Brazil
(*g*) The Civil War in Spain
(*h*) The history of Portugal
(*i*) The architecture of Poland
(*j*) Oil from Mexico
(*k*) Tribesmen of Morocco
(*l*) The language of Malta
(*m*) Cotton grown in Peru
(*n*) The customs of Ceylon

2. Many words are defined in the dictionary according to this pattern:

| A/An | Adjective | Adjective | Class or group |

For example, we can define *cauldron* as

| A | large | deep | boiling-pan |

Write suitable definitions for the following words, following the same pattern. Underline the adjectives.

EXAMPLE: **cauldron.** A large deep boiling-pan.

(*a*) tusk   (*e*) mud
(*b*) pebble   (*f*) minuet
(*c*) emerald   (*g*) silver
(*d*) gauze   (*h*) banjo

3. Synonyms. In each of the following groups of words there are four adjectives that are similar in meaning. The words in the first group could be used to describe an injury, and those in the second group might describe a bride; but as these words have different shades of meaning they cannot all be used in exactly the same circumstances.

In each group there is one word that has a stronger and more emphatic meaning than the others (just as *wicked* is more emphatic than *naughty*).

Say which is the strongest word in each group.

(*a*) painful, uncomfortable, agonizing, sore
(*b*) attractive, exquisite, pretty, charming
(*c*) large, great, massive, immense
(*d*) irate, resentful, infuriated, indignant
(*e*) luscious, palatable, savoury, appetizing
(*f*) good, incomparable, valuable, beneficial

4. In each of these sets of four adjectives there is one word that is opposite, or nearly opposite, in meaning to the other three. Pick out this word in each set.

(*a*) Careful, cautious, reckless, prudent
(*b*) abundant, plentiful, meagre, copious
(*c*) destitute, rich, wealthy, affluent
(*d*) industrious, energetic, diligent, indolent
(*e*) polite, brusque, courteous, chivalrous
(*f*) miniature, colossal, diminutive, puny
(*g*) sturdy, robust, stalwart, infirm
(*h*) trivial, petty, momentous, paltry

5. In the following phrases pick out all the adjectives. (The words *a*, *an*, and *the* are adjectives, but should not be counted for the purpose of this exercise.)

(*a*) An oily liquid
(*b*) A tall, tapering tree
(*c*) A cold, untidy, dismal room
(*d*) A stupid and unkind remark
(*e*) The brightest light I ever saw
(*f*) Bigger plums and cherries
(*g*) A heavy chest with iron handles
(*h*) Pink pills for pale people
(*i*) A square peg in a round hole
(*j*) Home-cured bacon, new potatoes and garden peas.

6. Suggest suitable adjectives. Enlarge the meanings of the following nouns by adding two adjectives to each. (Do not count the words *a*, *an*, and *the*.)

EXAMPLE: fire
SUGGESTED ANSWER: A large, crackling fire

valley	dog	mountain	footballer
town	wind	dream	adventure
castle	dancer		

Pages 174–82 of *A First English Companion* will be found helpful.

16

7. **Avoiding the word NICE.** In this exercise you are asked to think of twenty ways of avoiding the use of *nice*—which is a much overworked word and one that has little meaning unless it is used with great care.

Rewrite these phrases, replacing the word *nice* in each one by a more suitable adjective. Change *A* to *An* wherever necessary. Try not to use any adjective more than once.

EXAMPLE: A *nice* book
SUGGESTED ANSWER: An interesting book

(*a*) A *nice* pear
(*b*) A *nice* man
(*c*) A *nice* woman
(*d*) A *nice* tune
(*e*) A *nice* armchair
(*f*) A *nice* sunset
(*g*) *Nice* handwriting
(*h*) A *nice* garden
(*i*) A *nice* frock
(*j*) A *nice* party
(*k*) A *nice* meal
(*l*) *Nice* manners
(*m*) A *nice* smell
(*n*) A *nice* cathedral
(*o*) A *nice* dance
(*p*) A *nice* pianist
(*q*) A *nice* neighbour
(*r*) A *nice* gift
(*s*) *Nice* weather
(*t*) A *nice* cat

If you are using *A First English Companion*, turn to pages 179–82. The following groups of words may be helpful: 4, 14, 17, 23, 36, 37, 40, 41, 57, 64, 90.

8. **Is it forceful enough?** Find a suitable adjective to describe each of the following persons or things. The adjectives in brackets are given as clues, but they are not strong enough; they only *suggest* words similar in meaning, such as those given on pages 174–82 of *A First English Companion*.

EXAMPLE: An earthquake that kills ten thousand people (*bad*)
ANSWER: disastrous

(*a*) A motorist who drives through a busy street at a hundred kilometres an hour (*careless*)
(*b*) A man who sees his dog being kicked and thrashed (*annoyed*)
(*c*) A most remarkably clever scholar (*intelligent*)
(*d*) A sound so great that it re-echoes (*loud*)
(*e*) A coronation ceremony (*grand*)
(*f*) A person whose entire possessions have been destroyed by fire (*sad*)
(*g*) A germ (*small*)
(*h*) A wind that uproots large trees (*rough*)
(*i*) A person who finds himself confronted by a tiger (*frightened*)

9. **Is it too forceful?** Most of us are guilty of exaggeration from time to time. We complain about a *freezing* wind that is really only *cool* or *chilly*. Some of the phrases below are obvious exaggerations, while others could be true in certain circumstances. Suppose that they are all exaggerations; now find, for each one, two other adjectives that are less forceful.

EXAMPLE: A furious father
SUGGESTED ANSWER: cross, angry

(*a*) A filthy pinafore
(*b*) A brilliant child
(*c*) An idiotic question
(*d*) A colossal slice of cake
(*e*) A microscopic helping of trifle
(*f*) An interminable speech
(*g*) A prehistoric bicycle
(*h*) Abusive behaviour
(*i*) A squalid beggar
(*j*) A priceless horse
(*k*) A hideous vase
(*l*) A shocking headache

10. **Opposites.** Each of the following phrases contains an adjective. Decide which word it is (not counting *a*, *an*, or *the*) and replace it by an adjective that has approximately the opposite meaning.

EXAMPLE: A beautiful building
SUGGESTED ANSWER: An ugly building

(*a*) Truthful men
(*b*) A courageous soldier
(*c*) Modern tools
(*d*) Nimble fingers
(*e*) A greedy person
(*f*) A distant relation
(*g*) People who are wealthy
(*h*) The glossy side of the paper
(*i*) An experience that was delightful
(*j*) Sufficient meat for a week.

11. Suppose that you had to write dictionary definitions of the following names of animals. Find *one* suitable adjective that could be used for each one. Try not to repeat yourself.

EXAMPLE: Weasel
SUGGESTED ANSWER: nimble

(*a*) tiger
(*b*) fox
(*c*) zebra
(*d*) rhinoceros

(e) cat   (h) badger
(f) mammoth   (i) lynx
(g) bear   (j) unicorn

12. More synonyms. Find three adjectives that can be used to describe each of the things mentioned below.

If you have *A First English Companion*, use the words in brackets as clues that will help you to choose suitable synonyms (that is, words of similar meaning) from the lists on pages 174–82.

EXAMPLE: The latest design in cars
     (*new*)
SUGGESTED ANSWER: modern, new-fashioned,
     up-to-date

(a) An old hat   (*dirty*)
(b) A prize-winning bloom at a flower show   (*good*)
(c) A champion tennis-player   (*quick*)
(d) A disease for which there is no cure   (*bad*)
(e) The roar of a great crowd   (*loud*)
(f) A person who feels too tired and drowsy to work (*idle*)

13. Adjectives from nouns. Here is a dictionary definition:

poetic. Concerning poetry.

There are twelve similar definitions of adjectives in the list below, but the adjectives themselves have been omitted. Using a dictionary, you should have little difficulty in supplying the missing adjectives; they are easy to recognize, because they are formed from the nouns in italics. Be sure that every word you give as an answer can be used to *describe* something.

EXAMPLE: Concerning a *volcano*
ANSWER: volcanic

(a) Done as an *experiment*
(b) Given as a *compliment*
(c) So tiny that it cannot be seen without a *microscope*
(d) Showing *skill*
(e) Having or needing *intellect*
(f) Concerning a *metropolis*
(g) Showing *courtesy*
(h) Showing *charity*
(i) Making a grand *spectacle*
(j) Done according to a *system*
(k) Behaving with *chivalry*
(l) Like a *tempest*

14. More adjectives from nouns. In this exercise, follow the instructions given in Exercise 13.

(a) Concerning a *scholar*
(b) Shaped like a *cylinder*
(c) Producing *discord*
(d) Concerning *matrimony*
(e) Guilty of *negligence*
(f) Showing *apathy*
(g) Regarded as a *burden*
(h) Subject to attacks of *asthma*
(i) Fond of *argument*
(j) Good for *nutrition*
(k) Treating someone with *derision*
(l) In the same direction as a line of *longitude*

See also Exercise 10 on p. 87.

15. Three kinds of adjectives. Arrange these adjectives in three columns according to whether they answer the following questions:

1. Of what sort?
2. How much or how many?
3. Which?

NOTE. These three kinds of adjectives are called: 1. adjectives of quality; 2. adjectives of quantity; 3. demonstrative adjectives.

high	six	this	several	proud
these	few	those	sharp	ugly
that	some	all	clean	his
famous	my	both		

16. Adjective or noun? If we speak of *cold weather* we use the word *cold* as an adjective; if we say that someone has *a cold* we use it as a noun.

All the words printed in italics below can be used either as adjectives or as nouns. Say how each of them is used here.

(a) Can cats see in the *dark*?
(b) I prefer a *liquid* polish.
(c) He is an *expert* violinist.
(d) The *secret* has been well kept.
(e) The meat turned to *gold* in his mouth.
(f) I enjoy a *novel* experience.
(g) A *solid* has three dimensions.
(h) Deliver us from *evil*.
(i) He lacks *moral* courage.
(j) Fierce raged the tempest o'er the *deep*.

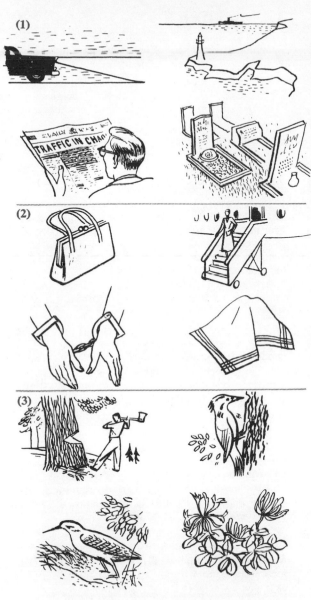

(1)

(2)

(3)

4. Compound nouns. These pictures illustrate three groups of compound nouns. There are four words, all with the same beginning, in each group: for example, all the words in the top group begin with *head*. Without any more help than this, see if you can identify all the words.

10. COMPOUND WORDS

1. Compound nouns. From each of the nouns given below, several compound nouns can be made by adding other nouns to it.

For example, by adding *drop* to the word *rain* we get *raindrop*. By adding *coat* to *rain* we get *raincoat*.

The word *rainiest* would not count as a correct answer because it is not a noun; besides, *-iest* is not a complete word.

Find two more compound words beginning with *rain*, and then see how many you can make in the same way from the others. Use your dictionary.

(a) rain	(f) snow	(k) farm
(b) fire	(g) sea	(l) book
(c) sun	(h) day	(m) neck
(d) post	(i) foot	(n) road
(e) bed	(j) play	(o) butter

2. In this exercise follow the instructions given in Exercise 1.

(a) night	(e) sky	(i) house
(b) moon	(f) air	(j) back
(c) water	(g) land	(k) stair
(d) life	(h) hedge	(l) eye

3. In Exercises 1 and 2 you have been given the beginnings of compound nouns and asked to supply appropriate endings. You are now required to work the other way round.

The words given below are the endings of compound nouns, and you are asked to supply appropriate beginnings. For example, using *man* as an ending we may have *postman*, *milkman*, etc.

(a) man	(e) stone	(h) berry
(b) work	(f) fly	(i) yard
(c) house	(g) flower	(j) side
(d) light		

5. Compound adjectives. A callous person is said to be *hard-hearted*. The adjective *hard-hearted* is called a compound adjective because it is made up of two words joined by a hyphen.

Use suitable compound adjectives to describe the ten persons referred to below. The first part of each compound adjective is supplied in brackets; the second part should refer to one of the following parts of the body.

brain   eye   face   finger   fist
hand   head   heart   knee   neck   skin

EXAMPLE: A deceiver   (*two*)
ANSWER: two-faced

(*a*) A coward   (*chicken*)
(*b*) A watchful person who misses nothing   (*eagle*)
(*c*) A generous benefactor   (*open*)
(*d*) A miser   (*tight*)
(*e*) A reckless mad-cap   (*hare*)
(*f*) An obstinate and stubborn person   (*stiff*)
(*g*) A thief   (*light*)
(*h*) Someone who is not easily insulted or offended   (*thick*)
(*i*) A timid, spiritless person   (*weak*)
(*j*) A keen business-man who has no time for sentiment   (*hard*)

6. **More compound adjectives.** In Exercise 4 you found compound adjectives to describe different kinds of persons. You are now to find compound adjectives that can be applied to events, experiences, emotions, etc. You are again given the first part of each compound adjective in brackets, but you will have to find the second half of each word for yourself.

(*a*) A terrifying experience   (*hair*)
(*b*) A day on which something specially important happens   (*red*)
(*c*) A price that is as low as it can possibly be   (*rock*)
(*d*) A desire for revenge that one has experienced for many years   (*deep*)
(*e*) Wages paid for difficult and prolonged work   (*hard*)
(*f*) A murderous attack committed deliberately and without anger   (*cold*)
(*g*) The guilty and furtive appearance of a scoundrel   (*hang*)
(*h*) An investment that can be relied upon   (*gilt*)
(*i*) A custom that has existed for centuries   (*time*)
(*j*) A distressing account of a great tragedy   (*heart*)
(*k*) A grievance that has been felt for many years   (*long*)
(*l*) A pompous speech   (*high*)

See also the Exercises on *Hyphens* (page 70).

11. GENDER

1. **Feminine to masculine.** These nouns are of feminine gender; give their masculine forms.

mare	doe	niece	duchess
mistress	lass	witch	she-goat
sow	madam	nun	maidservant

2. **Masculine to feminine.** These nouns are of masculine gender; give their feminine forms.

earl	colt	mayor	host
sultan	bachelor	ram	tom-cat

3. **Say which gender.** In this exercise you will need to bear in mind that nouns which can refer equally well to males or females (e.g., *doctor*) are said to be of *common* gender, and that the names of lifeless things (e.g., *bottle*) are of *neuter* gender.

Arrange the following nouns in four columns under the headings MASCULINE, FEMININE, COMMON, NEUTER.

drake	pullet	cloud	singer	heifer
puppy	vase	window	tabby-cat	
gander	passenger	player	ship	ewe
heir	assistant	moon	Jew	peer
filly	spectator	belle	blond	tulip

From the nouns of neuter gender in your fourth column see if you can pick out two that are the names of things often referred to as *she*.

4. **Common gender.** Without using any of the words given in Exercise 3, make a list of at least six (and as many more as you can) nouns of common gender. Do not include any names of animals; all the words you choose should refer to human beings.

5. **Words ending in -ESS (i).** Find five nouns of feminine gender that are formed by adding **ess** to the masculine noun without any other alteration; for example, *countess* (but not *tigress*).

6. **Words ending in -ESS (ii).** Find five nouns of feminine gender that are formed by altering the ending of the masculine noun and adding **ess**; for example, *tigress*, which is formed by dropping the **e** from *tiger* and adding **ess**.

7. Masculine and feminine. In these illustrations there are six *pairs*. In each pair there is one masculine and one feminine. Identify them all by name.

8. Many feminine nouns are formed from the corresponding masculine nouns; for example, *princess* is formed from *prince*. Others are quite different words, such as *wife* and *husband*. Find five other pairs that are not alike in any way.

9. What are they called? Give the masculine name and the feminine name for each of the persons in the list below.

> EXAMPLE: A person who *governs*
> ANSWER: governor, governess

(*a*) A person who *conducts*
(*b*) A person who *instructs*
(*c*) A person who *hunts*
(*d*) A person who *manages*
(*e*) A person who *prophesies*
(*f*) The head person in an *abbey*
(*g*) A person who owns *land*
(*h*) A person who claims to use *sorcery*
(*i*) A person who *waits* on diners
(*j*) A person who is *heroic*
(*k*) A person who rules over an *empire*

10. In French, all nouns are either masculine or feminine, even when they are the names of such things as plants and buildings, as you will see from the following extracts from a French–English dictionary.

Taking each English word in turn, say whether (in our own language) it is of masculine, feminine, common, or neuter gender. There is no need to write out the French words, but you may find it interesting to see if any of them remind you of some English words.

crayon, *m.*, pencil
dame, *f.*, lady
docteur, *m.*, doctor
femme, *f.*, woman
fleur, *f.*, flower
matin, *m.*, morning
mer, *f.*, sea
monsieur, *m.*, gentleman
mouton, *m.*, sheep
personne, *f.*, person
plume, *f.*, pen
pont, *m.*, bridge
porte, *f.*, door
prairie, *f.*, meadow
renard, *m.*, fox
sorcière, *f.*, witch
taureau, *m.*, bull
terre, *f.*, earth
victime, *f.*, victim
vin, *m.*, wine

Which of the above words are of the same gender in both languages?

See also the Exercises on *Personification* (page 128).

21

12. TENSE

1. Past or present? In the following sentences the verbs are printed in italics. Say which of them are in the present tense and which are in the past tense.

    (*a*) Mr. Hake *sells* fish.
    (*b*) Fred *met* Jim.
    (*c*) Joan *slept* soundly.
    (*d*) Elizabeth *is* ten today.
    (*e*) Christopher and Gillian *have* a rabbit.
    (*f*) Stephen *cut* his knee.

2. Present to past. All the sentences in this exercise begin with the words *At the present moment* as a reminder that they are in the present tense. Say how they would be worded in the past tense, if each one began with the word *Yesterday* . . . . .

    AT THE PRESENT MOMENT . . . . .

    (*a*) she plays the piano.
    (*b*) we speak softly.
    (*c*) I am very happy.
    (*d*) the snow falls thickly.
    (*e*) children feed the swans.

3. Past to present. All the following sentences begin with the word *Yesterday*, as a reminder that they are in the past tense. Say how they would be worded in the present tense, if each one began with the words *At the present moment* . . . . .

    YESTERDAY . . . . .

    (*a*) they wore scarves.
    (*b*) I had no money.
    (*c*) Jill went up the hill.
    (*d*) she sold sea-shells on the sea-shore.
    (*e*) Jack Horner ate his pudding.

4. Headlines. Newspaper headlines are often written in the present tense, so that reports shall seem to be 'up-to-the-minute'. For example, a paragraph about a girl climber who has died on a mountain might be headed like this:

GIRL DIES ON MOUNTAIN

Write similar headlines of *not more than four words*, in the present tense, about

(*a*) a trawler that sank in the Channel;
(*b*) an officer who lost a secret document;
(*c*) a gang that stole £15,000;
(*d*) two brothers who fell from a scaffold;
(*e*) a railway engine that plunged down an embankment;
(*f*) a flash of lightning that struck a steeple;
(*g*) an earthquake that shook the city of Athens;
(*h*) a swarm of bees that stung shoppers in a city street.

5. Auxiliary verbs. To form the *future* tense we must use the auxiliary verbs *shall* and *will*:

    I *shall* go home.
    They *will* go home.

An auxiliary verb helps the principal verb to make its tense. Here are other examples:

    He *was* going home. (PAST)
    He *is* going home. (PRESENT)

The auxiliary verb and the principal verb are not always next to each other:

    Has he gone yet?

In each of the following sentences pick out the auxiliary verb and the principal verb, and say whether the sentence is in the past, present, or future tense.

    EXAMPLE: Were the boys wearing coats?
    ANSWER: were wearing; *past tense*

(*a*) The handle of the jug was cracked.
(*b*) In July I shall go to Cornwall.
(*c*) My brothers will help you.
(*d*) The pigeons are eating the crops.
(*e*) Shall I bring my fishing-rod?
(*f*) Is the mill still working?

6. Past, present, or future? (i) Write sentences beginning with the words and phrases set out below. After each one say in brackets whether the sentence is in the past, present, or future tense.

    EXAMPLE: Yesterday . . . . .
    SUGGESTED ANSWER: Yesterday I bought a diary. (*Past*)

(*a*) Tomorrow . . . . .
(*b*) At the present time . . . . .
(*c*) Next week . . . . .
(*d*) Last night . . . . .
(*e*) Someday . . . . .
(*f*) Once upon a time . . . . .
(*g*) At this very moment . . . . .
(*h*) One of these days . . . . .

7. Past, present, or future? (ii) Write out these sentences, and underline the verbs. After each sentence, in brackets, put the word *Past*, *Present*, or *Future* to indicate the tense of the verb you have underlined.

EXAMPLE: Next week I shall be fourteen.
ANSWER: Next week I <u>shall</u> be fourteen. (*Future*)

(*a*) The wheel runs on ball bearings.
(*b*) George will tell you the way.
(*c*) The walls and shelves are grey.
(*d*) Crinolines were fashionable in those days.
(*e*) Father will go with me to the station.
(*f*) I eat my food too quickly.
(*g*) We shall swim in the river.
(*h*) The Vicar read the first lesson.
(*i*) One of these stamps cost ten pence.
(*j*) I expect a snowstorm.

8. The hymn *Now thank we all our God* ends:

> *For thus it was, is now,*
> *And shall be evermore.*

What do you notice about the tenses used in these lines?

9. The following description of an industrial town is taken from a guide-book published in 1838. Re-word it in the past tense—that is, as you would re-tell it to a friend after having read it.

> *The place is extremely black and dirty, and the people are rough and uneducated. The men earn a good deal of money, but they spend it upon eating and drinking. On Saturday the market is one of the noisiest exhibitions imaginable, and the so-called amusement of bull-baiting still exists. There are no schools; the children play in the streets from the time that they can run till they go to the factory, and there they work till they have children themselves to do the same thing again.*

10. The following extract is taken from a guide to the Grand Junction Railway, which was opened in 1837. Re-word it in the past tense—that is, as you would tell it to a friend after having read it.

> *The mixed trains consist of both first-class and second-class coaches; the latter have no cushions, or divisions of the compartments. Both kinds have seats on the roof for the accommodation of those who prefer riding outside. Each passenger's luggage is placed on the roof of the coach in which he takes his place; carpet bags go underneath the seat opposite that which the owner occupies.*
>
> *Every train is provided with Guards, and a Conductor, who is responsible for the order and*

> *regularity of the journey. No smoking is allowed in the Station-houses, or in any of the coaches, even with the consent of the passengers.*
>
> *Trains run from Birmingham to Liverpool twice daily, and the journey takes a little over five hours.*

11. This extract from a tale of mystery is written in the past tense. Make it more dramatic by re-writing it in the present tense.

> *I pushed open the door and went inside. The house was in darkness. Upstairs a door creaked. I stood stock still, but silence fell again. I took out a match and struck it, but before I could light the candle a gust of wind from the doorway blew out the flame. In the grounds an owl hooted. A shiver ran down my spine, and I could neither move nor speak.*

12. Mixed tenses. The following passage illustrates a common mistake, the careless mixing of tenses. Re-write the passage either wholly in the past tense or wholly in the present tense.

> *We see a light shining at the foot of the cliff, so we pick our way down the narrow path towards it. Brambles scratched our legs, and our feet slip on the wet clay. A stiff breeze that blew from the sea carried salt spray to our lips, and brought to our ears the sound of rowlocks. There was no moon, but in the last remnant of twilight we could see figures moving on the beach, though we could not make out who they were. Determined to find out what is going on we quicken our pace, hoping that we shall not be heard.*

See also the Exercises on *Past Tense or Past Participle?*
(page 108).

13. ABSTRACT NOUNS

A *thief* can be caught, but his crime of *theft* can only be thought of and talked about.   The word *thief* is a *concrete* noun; the word *theft* is an *abstract* noun. Abstract nouns denote those qualities, etc., which cannot be pointed out as objects but which have to be understood in the mind.

---

1. Complete each of the following statements by adding an abstract noun formed from the concrete noun printed in italics.   Use your dictionary.

   EXAMPLE: A *patriot* is known for his ———.
   ANSWER: A patriot is known for his patriotism.

   (a) A *hero* is praised for his ———.
   (b) A *friend* is valued for his ———.
   (c) A *child* goes to school during his ———.
   (d) A *slave* has to endure ———.
   (e) A *tyrant* is hated for his ———.
   (f) A *robber* is arrested for ———.
   (g) An *infant* has to be nursed during its ———.
   (h) A *coward* is despised for his ———.

2. Complete each of the following statements by adding an abstract noun related to the adjective printed in italics.

   EXAMPLE: An *angry* man shows his ———.
   ANSWER: An angry man shows his anger.

   (a) A *kind* person pleases others by his ———.
   (b) A *skilful* acrobat displays his ———.
   (c) An *active* volcano shows signs of ———.
   (d) A *famous* man is one who has achieved ———.
   (e) A *determined* pupil works with ———.
   (f) A *generous* person is noted for his ———.
   (g) An *elegant* woman is admired for her ———.
   (h) A *stupid* person should be pitied for his ———.

3. Complete each of the following statements by adding an abstract noun related to the verb shown in italics.

   EXAMPLE: To *suspect* is to show ———.
   ANSWER: To suspect is to show suspicion.

   (a) To *hate* a person is to show ———.
   (b) To *free* a prisoner is to give him his ———.
   (c) To *grieve* is to experience a feeling of ———.
   (d) To *please* one's mother is to give her ———.
   (e) To *satisfy* one's teachers is to give them ———
   (f) To *encourage* a boy is to give him ———.
   (g) To *exaggerate* is to be guilty of ———.
   (h) To *deceive* people is to practise ———.

4. For each of the abstract nouns in the following list find the corresponding adjective.

   EXAMPLE: generosity.
   ANSWER: generous.

   To test your answers, make sure that each one can be used to complete this sentence:

   Mr. Jones is a(n) ——— man.

jealousy	friendliness	courage	pride
wisdom	insolence	poverty	hopefulness
vanity	humility	heroism	envy
patriotism	gratitude		

5. All the answers in this exercise are abstract nouns, and the clues to them are given in brackets.   Use your dictionary, and be sure that your answers are in fact *nouns*—not adjectives or verbs.

   Say what quality or characteristic is shown by A PERSON WHO.....

   (a) is rude and insulting   (*inso———*)
   (b) praises people more highly than they deserve (*flat———*)
   (c) is careful and wise in all he does (*pru———*)
   (d) is entirely faithful and loyal (*fid———*)
   (e) is alert and watchful (*vig———*)
   (f) is willing to let others do and think as they please (*tol———*)
   (g) is shrewd and intelligent (*sag———*)
   (h) has feelings of hatred and enmity (*ani———*)
   (i) is candid and outspoken (*cand———*)
   (j) is very lively and sprightly (*viv———*)
   (k) always expects the worst to happen (*pess———*)
   (l) is very sorry for having done wrong (*peni———*)
   (m) is cross and peevish (*pet———*)
   (n) is gentle and merciful (*len———*)
   (o) is shouting joyfully (*jub———*)
   (p) behaves like a humble slave (*serv———*)
   (q) is common and coarse (*vul———*)
   (r) is quiet and humble (*mod———*)
   (s) looks on the bright side of life (*opt———*)
   (t) is moderate in his habits (*temp———*)
   (u) is careful in speech and actions (*discr———*)

   See also Exercise 9 on page 87.

14. CONJUNCTIONS

1. And or but? It is often possible to combine two *closely-related* sentences into one by using the word *and* as a conjunction:

> The horse-chestnut bears flowers that are often called candles, *and* its nuts are well-known as 'conkers'.

When we join two sentences that are *contrasted* with each other we may use the conjunction *but*:

> The alder grows well on high river-banks, *but* it does not like low and swampy ground.

Using *and* or *but* each time, join the following pairs of sentences in the same way.

(a) The walnut was brought into Britain by the Romans.   Its original home was Persia.

(b) The beech is a magnificent tree with a massive trunk.   Its timber is very useful for many purposes.

(c) The branches of the oak twist about in zig-zag fashion.   The thick bark is deeply furrowed.

(d) In towns the lime is usually a stunted tree.   In the country it rivals even the elm in appearance.

(e) In winter the hornbeam can be mistaken for the beech.   It is far less picturesque.

(f) The long trunk of the elm usually has one or two large horizontal limbs.   The corky bark is very rugged.

(g) We think of conifers as evergreen trees.   The larch loses its leaves in winter.

(h) The osier can be found on river-banks.   It can generally be recognized by its long and upward-thrusting branches.

In the following exercises (2, 3, 4, 5, 6, 7) choose the most suitable conjunctions from the following list:

after	and	although	as
because	but	for	or
so	though	until	when
	while	yet	

2. Choosing the right conjunction. Join each of the following pairs of sentences into one longer sentence, using a different conjunction for each pair.

> EXAMPLE: Dutch roads are straight and level.   The land is flat.
> ANSWER: Dutch roads are straight and level because the land is flat.

(a) The sun came out.   The birds sang again.

(b) There are thousands of bees in the hive.   Only the queen lays eggs.

(c) Penguins cannot fly.   They have wings.

(d) Will you have tea?   Do you prefer coffee?

(e) The wind became stronger.   The captain decided to seek shelter.

(f) The tower is called the Eiffel Tower.   A man named Eiffel designed it.

(g) The nurse bandaged my leg.   The doctor had stitched the wound.

(h) The electricity was cut off.   Mother was cooking the dinner.

(i) The story is a strange one.   It is true.

(j) I cannot help you.   I should very much like to do so.

3. It is a bad mistake to write like this:

> *It rained all day we had to play indoors.*

This should either be written as two sentences:

> *It rained all day.   We had to play indoors.*

or, better still, like this:

> *It rained all day, so we had to play indoors.*

In each of the following statements, two sentences have been wrongly telescoped into one.   Use conjunctions to join the pairs properly.   Do not use *and* more than once.

(a) The lighthouse-keepers cannot be relieved heavy seas are still breaking over the rock.

(b) After covering half the course he was still walking strongly his feet were badly blistered.

(c) The ice suddenly closed in the ship became jammed between two floes.

(d) Thieves stole luggage and clothing from his car he was calling on friends near by.

(e) The mouse kept on nibbling at the net at last the lion was able to escape.

(f) More than ten thousand people attended the show the organizers are doubtful whether the event will make a profit.

4. Look at these two short sentences:

I still cannot swim.   I have tried very hard.

They can be made into one longer sentence by using the conjunction *although*:

I still cannot swim, although I have tried very hard.

Another method is to reverse the order of the two sentences and begin with the conjunction:

Although I have tried very hard I still cannot swim.

———————

Choosing suitable conjunctions, combine each of the following pairs of sentences as shown above.   Use first one of the above methods and then the other—that is, give two different answers each time.

(*a*) They were late for school.   The bus broke down.
(*b*) She writes beautifully.   She is blind.
(*c*) Mary cut the bread and butter.   Joy was making the tea.
(*d*) They huddled closer together.   The night grew colder.
(*e*) I replaced the shoes on the shelf.   I had cleaned them.
(*f*) Paper is cheap. It is plentiful.

Now turn back to Exercise 2, and look at your answers to (*c*), (*f*), (*g*), and (*h*).   Re-arrange each one so that it begins with the conjunction.

5. Then ... then ... then ...   It is clumsy to string a number of sentences together, and join them one after another by the word *then*:

The rain stopped, then the people flocked back to the show-ring, then the judges decided not to cancel the parade after all.

It is usually much better to begin the first sentence with a suitable conjunction, leave out *then* at the beginning of the second sentence, and replace *then* at the beginning of the third sentence by a more appropriate conjunction:

When the rain stopped, the people flocked back to the show-ring, *so* the judges decided not to cancel the parade after all.

———————

Use this method to correct the following badly-arranged sentences.

(*a*) The cowboy rode round the ring, then two clowns were trying to lasso him, then he galloped away without being caught.

(*b*) The piston reaches the top of the cylinder, then a spark fires the mixture of air and petrol-vapour, then the piston is forced downwards again.
(*c*) The king had been killed in battle, then there was a long period of strife and unrest, then the young prince was old enough to ascend the throne.
(*d*) The rudder was jammed, then the boat went round in circles, then the captain was compelled to stop the engines.
(*e*) The sun rose by degrees above the horizon, then slender tongues of flame began to reach across the fields, then at last the whole valley was aglow with the morning light.

6. You have seen how two simple sentences can be combined by using a conjunction.   In the example below, only the second sentence is given; the first sentence is represented by dots, and the conjunction by a dash:

.... ——— the grass is wet.

Complete the sentence in four different ways, using a different beginning and conjunction for each.   For example, one answer could be

You may play on the lawn unless the grass is wet.

7. You are now given only the first of two sentences. Complete the combination in four different ways by supplying conjunctions and second sentences.

The car stopped ——— ....

15.   THE OBJECT

On page 8 you were given an easy way of finding the subject of a sentence.   Make sure you know it.

To find the *object* of a sentence, proceed as follows:

Pick out the verb, and put the question *What?* or *Whom?* after it.

EXAMPLES: 1. Charles wrote a letter.
            2. The electors chose Mr. Simpson.

By asking the questions *Wrote what?* and *Chose whom?* we see that the objects of these sentences are:

ANSWERS: 1. a letter
            2. Mr. Simpson

1. In the following sentences, say which is the verb; then pick out the subject; finally, name the object.

Put a box round the verb, a single line under the subject, and a double line under the object, like this:

The electors ⎡chose⎤ Mr. Simpson.

(a) The rocket hit the moon.
(b) The geese chased us.
(c) Mr. Deakin keeps cocker spaniels.
(d) A fierce gale uprooted many trees.
(e) The gipsies made pegs and baskets.
(f) During the holiday I read *Heidi*.
(g) In four matches he scored five hundred runs.
(h) Robert caught, without any help, a large salmon.

2. You have already seen that the subject of a sentence is not bound to be at the beginning of the sentence. Similarly, the object is not always placed at the end.

In the example given below, the verb is *caught*, the subject is *our dog*, and the object is *a rat*.

Last week, *our dog caught a rat* in the cellar.

With the following sentences, carry out the instructions given in Exercise 1.

(a) Brian cut his finger with a chisel.
(b) Mother called me at eight o'clock.
(c) I sold my stamp album for fifty pence.
(d) A thousand people lost their homes in the flood.
(e) Stanford, with the greatest ease, turned the ball past Hollins for a single.
(f) Yesterday we met uncle in the park.
(g) In a fork of the tree the boys built a small hut as an observation post.

3. **Transitive verbs and intransitive verbs.** A verb that takes an object is called a *transitive* verb:

Spiders *catch* flies.

A verb that does not take an object is called an *intransitive* verb:

Water *flows*.

Remember than an object must be either a noun or the equivalent of a noun. If we say that *water flows quickly*, or *water flows under the bridge*, there is still no object and the verb is therefore still intransitive.

In each of the following sentences pick out the verb and say whether it is used transitively or intransitively. Write out the verbs and put either (T) or (I) after them.

EXAMPLE: Tortoises sleep during the winter.
ANSWER: sleep (I)

(a) Suddenly the engine started.
(b) Mr. Spooner sold his golf-clubs.
(c) Joan spilt a jugful of milk.
(d) Butter melts easily.
(e) Scrub the floor thoroughly.
(f) Can I borrow six pence from you?
(g) Very soon the plaster set hard.
(h) Children were running to and fro.

4. **Transitive or intransitive?** Many verbs can be used either transitively (with an object) or intransitively (without an object).

In each pair of the following sentences a verb is used first in one of these ways and then in the other. Say which is transitive and which is intransitive.

(a) 1. On windy days Stephen *flies* his kite.
    2. The kite *flies* well in the wind.
(b) 1. He *shook* like a man with a fever.
    2. He *shook* his fist at the trespassers.
(c) 1. Did your ears *burn* last night?
    2. You are foolish to *burn* the candle at both ends.
(d) 1. The blacksmith *bends* the red-hot iron.
    2. A thin copper rod *bends* easily.
(e) 1. Mother says that I *spread* the butter too thickly.
    2. The wet patch gradually *spread* across the ceiling.

5. Some verbs are always intransitive; that is, they cannot take an object. For example, one cannot *dwell* anything, or *kneel* anything, or *cling* anything.

Ten of the verbs below are always intransitive; say which they are.

strive	slink	freeze	lie	fall
ebb	meet	die	remain	blossom
sink	consent	drink	appear	

6. Some verbs are always transitive; that is, they must always have an object. For example, it is nonsense to say *He neglected* unless we go on to say *what* he neglected (e.g., *He neglected his horse*).

Ten of the verbs below are always transitive. Say which they are.

purify	burst	encourage	annoy
invite	feel	defeat	amaze
possess	sing	afford	disturb
	correct	shut	

7. **Three unusual verbs.** There are several intransitive verbs that undergo a change of spelling and pronunciation when we use them transitively. You will find three of them below. Complete the unfinished sentences.

(a) ⎰ Where does the village *lie*?
    ⎱ Please —— the table.

(b) ⎰ When does the sun *rise*?
    ⎱ They could not —— the slab.

(c) ⎰ We watched the tree *fall*.
    ⎱ We saw the foresters —— the tree.

8. Each of the six verbs given below has two definitions, because each verb can be used either transitively or intransitively. Say which definition refers to the transitive use of the verb, and which to its intransitive use.

Remember: A transitive verb takes an object.
An intransitive verb does not take an object.

(a) **boil.** 1. To bubble up and give off steam or gas.
2. To heat a liquid until it gives off steam or gas.

(b) **fly.** 1. To make a kite, etc., rise in the air.
2. To move through the air with wings.

(c) **grow.** 1. To increase in size.
2. To produce crops, etc., by cultivation.

(d) **keep.** 1. To retain something in one's possession.
2. To remain in a certain state.

(e) **melt.** 1. To turn a solid into a liquid by means of heat.
2. To become liquefied by heat.

(f) **spoil.** 1. To go bad.
2. To damage something or make it useless.

★ REVISION

1. What is the difference between

(a) a green house and a *greenhouse*?
(b) a blue bottle and a *bluebottle*?
(c) a red skin and a *redskin*?
(d) a black bird and a *blackbird*?
What do we call the words in italics?

2. Rewrite these sentences in the past tense by changing the verbs printed in italics.

Pages 172–3 of *A First English Companion* will help.

(a) I *know* that he *has* a bicycle.
(b) I *write* to him each week while he *is* away.
(c) We *sit* and *freeze*.
(d) He *sings* as he *digs*.
(e) The dog *runs* until he *catches* a hare.
(f) I *choose* my own books when I *go* there.

3. Define these *in complete sentences*:

(a) spanner	(d) lichen	(g) rodent
(b) gourd	(e) weevil	(h) radium
(c) nomad	(f) talcum	(i) placard

The following questions are about the extract from *Travels with a Donkey* on page 14.

4. (a) Pick out five adjectives in lines 28–29.
(b) Pick out two adjectives in line 7.
Which noun do they refer to?
(c) Read lines 8–14. In what tense are they written?
(d) Find the verb *emptied* on line 25.
What is its subject, and what is its object?
(e) Find an abstract noun in lines 30–34.
(f) Rewrite the sentence that begins with the word *Cattle* (line 17) in the past tense.
(g) Find two conjunctions in lines 1–5.
(h) Find the verb *open* in line 21. In single words give its subject and its object.

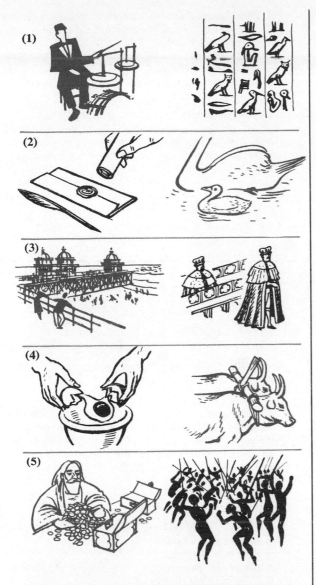

Nouns often confused. Here are five more pairs of words that have the same sound but different spelling. They are all common nouns. Write them down, putting the word illustrated in red first, and the word illustrated in black second.

As with the picture on page 14, you will find pages 163–70 of *A First English Companion* helpful.

📖 LOOK THESE UP

Even if you have not yet been told anything about the things referred to in this column you can easily find out all you need to know to get the answers right. After each question you are given a reference number in red; this tells you which page and set or exercise to turn to for information that will help you to answer the question.

For example, 85 Ex. 12 means *Page 85, Exercise 12;* 80 **51** means *Page 80, Set 51,* and so on.

1. Write down the following words, and then put a sign over the first vowel in each one to show whether it is long or short.

pot	hold	mind	den
cap	spade	duty	but
senior	dip	pack	right

85 Ex. 12

2. Give five prefixes that mean *not*. 86 Ex. 3

Choosing prefixes from those you have just found, give words that mean

not natural	not mortal
not movable	not noticed

80 **51**

3. (*a*) Why is there a double *n* in *unnecessary* but not in *uncertain*?

(*b*) There is no double *s* in *disappear*; give a word beginning with *dis* that *does* have a double *s* in this position.

80 **51**

4. Look at these pairs of words:

      highway, highways
      chimney, chimneys

Why is the *y* not changed to *i* when we add *s*, as it is in *cherry, cherries*?

77 **44** Ex. 1

5. Look at these pairs of words:

      uncoil, uncoiled
      avail, availed

Why is the *l* not doubled when we add *ed*, as it is in *shovel, shovelled*?

79 **48**

6. A picture in *Punch* showed a London taxi-driver in dispute with a woman driver at a busy cross-roads. The taxi-driver shouted

    "Sound your 'orn!"

The woman's retort was

    "Sound your aspirates!"

What is the point of this joke? 85 Ex. 10

16. PRONOUNS

The early exercises in this set contain pronouns from the following list:

I	you	he	she	it	they
me	him	her	we	us	them

I. What do they stand for? Pick out all the personal pronouns in the sentences given below, and say to which nouns they refer.

> EXAMPLE: John and Clive caught a hedgehog. They put it in a box.
> ANSWER: they = John and Clive
> it = the hedgehog

(a) Alan and Margaret picked some blackberries. They found them in the hedgerow.

(b) Tinker is a spaniel. He is only a puppy. The children are very fond of him.

(c) Anne said to Roger, "I will knit a pullover if you will wear it."

(d) Brian said to Martin, "Shall we ask mother if she will take us to the circus?"

(e) Father said to the nurse, "If Sheila Foster is in this ward will you please take me to her?"

(f) Philip had not seen Jane's aquarium. He asked her to show it to him.

(g) When Mr. and Mrs. Jackson sent Audrey a handbag she wrote to thank them for it.

(h) Sylvia said to Frank, "If we worry the turkeys they may chase us."

2. What does it mean? Pronouns should be used carefully and in such a way that there is no doubt about the nouns to which they refer. Otherwise the results can be either confusing or ridiculous, as the following sentences show.

Say why these sentences are badly constructed, and how they could be improved.

(a) Fred told Clive that his father had met with an accident.

(b) Jill saw Judith while she was shopping with her mother.

(c) Carol and Trevor are in the field looking for their pet rabbits. Have you seen them?

(d) Stephen suggested to Stuart that it might be a good thing if he took over the duties of team manager.

(e) Tony reached for his camera to photograph the deer, but before he could pick it up it had darted back into the wood.

(f) When the trainers settled down for the night their horses were alive and well, but when they woke in the morning they were dead.

3. Subject and object. The short sentences listed below are all grammatically correct. You will see from them that some personal pronouns are always used as the *subject* of a sentence, while others are always used as the *object*. For example, it is correct to say *She amused us*, but wrong to say *Us amused she*.

Using these sentences as a guide, make out two lists:

1. *Pronouns used as the subject*
2. *Pronouns used as the object*

He met us	He knows them
She saw him	She nursed him
We like him	They interrupted me
I helped her	He taught her
She left us	We beat them
They caught him	I praised him
We told her	They pleased us

Keep the lists when you have made them, as you will need them for later exercises.

4. Choosing the right pronoun (i). In the following sentences replace the words in italics by personal pronouns. Use pronouns from the two lists that you compiled in Exercise 3, and ask yourself in each sentence what is the subject and what is the object.

> EXAMPLE: *David and Patrick* met *Tony.*
> ANSWER: They met him.

(a) *Patrick* met *David and Susan.*

(b) *Bridget* met *Tony.*

(c) *Tony* met *Bridget.*

(d) *Susan* met *Bridget.*

(e) *Susan and I* met *Bridget.*

(f) *Patrick* met *David and me.*

(g) *David and Patrick* met *Susan.*

(h) *David and Patrick* met *Susan and me.*

(i) *Bridget* met *Patrick and Susan.*

(j) *David and I* met *Patrick.*

(k) *Susan* met *David and me.*

(l) *Susan and I* met *Patrick and Bridget.*

5. **Choosing the right pronoun (ii).** In this exercise follow the pattern of Exercise 4. There are no italics to help you this time.

(a) Paul and I saw Helen.
(b) Paul saw Joyce and Helen.
(c) Helen saw Joyce.
(d) Paul saw Helen.
(e) Paul saw Helen and me.
(f) Helen saw Paul.
(g) Joyce saw Helen and Paul.
(h) Joyce and Paul saw Helen.
(i) Helen and I saw Paul.
(j) Helen saw Joyce and me.
(k) Joyce and Paul saw Helen and me.
(l) Joyce and I saw Helen and Paul.

See also the exercise on *I and me* (page 43).

6. **Possessive pronouns.** In each of these sentences replace the phrase in italics by a verb and a possessive pronoun (two words only) that mean the same thing. There should not be an apostrophe anywhere in your answers.

> EXAMPLE: Those jewels *belonged to her.*
> ANSWER: Those jewels were hers.

(a) This pen *belongs to you.*
(b) These coats *belong to us.*
(c) That handbag *belongs to her.*
(d) This house *belongs to them.*
(e) That cricket bat *belonged to me.*
(f) Two of the dogs *belonged to him.*

7. **Emphatic pronouns.** Consider this simple sentence:

Miss Carter lives in the village.

If we wish to emphasize the fact that it is Miss Carter (and not someone else about whom we have been talking) who lives in the village, we say

Miss Carter *herself* lives in the village.

If, on the other hand, we want to make it quite clear that Miss Carter's home is actually in the village (and not some distance from it), we say

Miss Carter lives in the village *itself.*

The words *herself* and *itself*, used in this way, are emphatic pronouns.

Now arrange each of the following sentences in two ways, emphasizing first one of the words printed in italics and then the other. When you have finished you will find that you have used seven different emphatic pronouns, all of them ending with *self* or *selves.*

(a) *We* took a photograph of *the Princess.*
(b) *I* will be responsible for buying all the food if *you* will prepare the meal.
(c) *The train* was badly damaged, but *the passengers* were not injured.
(d) Wait until *Miss Reeves* returns, and ask her if *she* is willing to present the prizes.
(e) *Mr. Arden* composed the music, but *he* did not take part in the performance.
(f) *He* was anxious to take the girls on the water chute, but *they* were not willing.

8. **In which person?** You will find the following table useful in this exercise:

I swim	... *First person singular*
You swim	... *Second person singular*
He swims ⎫	
She swims ⎬ ...	*Third person singular*
It swims ⎭	
We swim	... *First person plural*
You swim	... *Second person plural*
They swim	... *Third person plural*

Say in which person each of the following sentences is written, and then carry out the instructions given in brackets.

> EXAMPLE: He rides his bicycle.
> (*Change to first person plural.*)
> ANSWER: (i) Third person singular.
> (ii) We ride our bicycles.

(a) She washed her hands.
(*Change to first person plural.*)
(b) You are your own master.
(*Change to first person singular.*)
(c) They must learn to stand on their own feet.
(*Change to second person plural.*)
(d) I hung my head in shame.
(*Change to first person plural.*)
(e) It is a beautiful valley.
(*Change to third person plural.*)
(f) You must all remember to bring your raincoats.
(*Change to first person plural.*)
(g) I shall be glad to be on my own.
(*Change to third person plural.*)

9. In which person? When you talk about your father you use the pronoun *he*, which is the third person singular. In which person are you speaking when you refer to the following?

(*a*) Yourself   (*e*) Yourself and a friend
(*b*) The people of India   (*f*) Your pencil
(*c*) Your uncle   (*g*) Your shoes
(*d*) Your aunt   (*h*) Yourself and your family

10. Changing the person. (Oral exercise)

In the following sentences all the words in italics are personal pronouns. Re-arrange the sentences in different forms, keeping to the same person throughout each one. Begin with each of the pronouns given in brackets, and make any other changes that may be necessary.

For example, the first answer is

He loves his mother; his mother loves him.

(*a*) *I* love *my* mother; *my* mother loves *me*.
(Begin with *He, You, She, We, They*)

(*b*) *My* journey takes *me* near the place where *I* was born.
(Begin with *Your, His, Her, Our, Their*)

(*c*) *I* am taking *my* slippers with *me*.
(Begin with *He, She, We, They*)

(*d*) *He* failed *his* examination, as *his* teachers had expected *him* to do.
(Begin with *I, You, She, We, They*)

(*e*) *Our* skis are too big for *us*, but *we* shall have to manage as best *we* can.
(Begin with *My, Your, His, Her*)

11. Invitations and announcements (i). It is usual to write invitations and formal announcements in the third person. For example, instead of writing *I hope that all of you will pay your membership fees promptly* and then signing his name, the secretary of a society might put up this notice:

The Secretary hopes that all members will pay their membership fees promptly.

A statement of this kind should not be signed. The following three sentences are given as a guide; they contain (in italics) the only pronouns you should use when writing in the third person.

He thanks Mr. Jones for asking *him* to *his* party.

She thanks Mrs. Jones for asking *her* to *her* party.

They thank Mr. and Mrs. Jones for asking *them* to *their* party.

Complete the following by inserting the correct pronouns—all in the third person.

(*a*) Miss Anne Derry thanks Mr. and Mrs. L. J. Neville for inviting —— to —— son's coming-of-age party, and has much pleasure in accepting.

(*b*) The Directors wish all —— employees the compliments of the season, and hope that —— will enjoy —— Christmas holiday.

(*c*) Mr. Stanley Lovatt thanks the staff and pupils of Milford School for inviting —— to —— annual dance, but regrets that owing to a previous engagement —— will be unable to attend.

(*d*) Mr. and Mrs. L. W. Hayward thank Mrs. Bridgeman for inviting —— to the wedding of —— daughter on 10th May, but regret that owing to the fact that —— will be abroad at that time —— are unable to accept.

(*e*) James Burton assures —— customers that they will receive the same attention as in the past, and that —— will do —— best to have the rebuilding done before May.

(*f*) Mrs. S. B. Palmer wishes —— friends and neighbours to know how grateful —— is for the kindness —— have shown to —— during —— recent bereavement.

12. Invitations and announcements (ii). Imagine that you have written the following sentences about yourself, and that you now wish to rewrite them in the third person. Call yourself either *he* or *she*, and follow the pattern of the sentences in Exercise 11.

(*a*) I am grateful for the invitation.
(*b*) I hope to be present.
(*c*) I have much pleasure in accepting the invitation.
(*d*) I shall be happy to attend.
(*e*) It gives me much pleasure to accept.
(*f*) I regret that I shall not be able to attend the party.
(*g*) I should have liked to be present.

13. Invitations and announcements (iii). Mr. Richard Roe, a successful candidate at a council election, inserts the following letter in a local newspaper.

I wish to thank all those who voted for me on Tuesday, and to say how pleased I am to have the opportunity of representing you on the Council. I shall do my utmost to serve this district to the best of my ability, and I hope that I shall at all times be worthy of the trust that you have placed in me.

RICHARD ROE

He could have expressed himself differently by writing in the third person, beginning like this:

Richard Roe thanks all those electors . . . . .

Rewrite the letter for him in this way.

14. Notices and instructions. If it is necessary to say to hospital visitors *You should have your permit ready*, the printed notice may be worded (in the third person) like this:

VISITORS SHOULD HAVE THEIR PERMITS READY

Re-arrange the following instructions in the same way.

(*a*) (*To patients about to enter hospital*):
   You must bring your own soap and towel with you.

(*b*) (*To the members of a tennis club*):
   You are requested to pay your annual subscription before 31st January.

(*c*) (*To customers in a large store*):
   You should ask the supervisor to help you if you need advice.

(*d*) (*To hirers of river cruisers*):
   You will have your deposit returned to you when you bring back your boat in good condition.

(*e*) (*To the operator of a machine*):
   You should depress the knob with your thumb, and move the lever away from you until you can push it no farther.

15. Archaic pronouns. Some of the personal pronouns in these quotations from the Bible are no longer in ordinary use. There are also verb forms that are not commonly used nowadays. Rewrite the quotations in modern English.

(*a*) Hast thou found me, O mine enemy?
(*b*) Out of thine own mouth will I judge thee.
(*c*) If thine eye offend thee, pluck it out.
(*d*) Thou fool, this night thy soul shall be required of thee.
(*e*) When thou doest alms, let not thy left hand know what thy right hand doeth.

   See also the Exercises on *Relative Pronouns* (page 44) and on *Indirect Speech* (page 69).

17. ADVERBS

An adverb may tell us more about the meaning of

(*a*) a verb: (The fire burned *brightly*.)
(*b*) an adjective: (It was *very* heavy.)
(*c*) another adverb: (The train moved *quite* slowly.)

---

1. How was it done? In each of the following sentences replace the phrase in italics with a single adverb of the same meaning.

   The last word in each sentence is a clue to the required word, which can be found in your dictionary. Pay particular attention to spelling.

   EXAMPLE: He answered the questions *with intelligence*.
   ANSWER: He answered the questions intelligently.

(*a*) He played golf *with skill*.
(*b*) He answered me *with impudence*.
(*c*) She described her experiences *with humour*.
(*d*) They proceeded *with caution*.
(*e*) The victors marched into the city *with triumph*.
(*f*) We were urged to give *with generosity*.
(*g*) The appeal was received *with charity*.
(*h*) She nursed her patients *with devotion*.
(*i*) He made the model *with ingenuity*.

2. The adverbs that you are asked to supply in this exercise are a little more uncommon than those in Exercise 1. Again, replace the phrase in italics with a single adverb of the same meaning, using the last word as a clue.

(*a*) The diameter of the wheel was measured *with precision*.
(*b*) In his speech and actions he behaved *with discretion*.
(*c*) Mary looked at her broken doll *with dejection*.
(*d*) The old man treated the village children *with benevolence*.
(*e*) The birds sang *with melody*.
(*f*) He gave his opinion *with candour*.
(*g*) She blushed, and replied *with diffidence*.
(*h*) The bulldog held on *with tenacity*.
(*i*) She sewed it *with dexterity*.

3. Replace each of the phrases printed in italics below by an adverb that has the same meaning. You will find that your adverbs either begin with **un-** or end with **-lessly**.

> EXAMPLES: 1. To move *without noise*
> 2. To play *without fairness*
> ANSWERS: 1. To move noiselessly
> 2. To play unfairly

(a) To live *without happiness*
(b) To speak *without truth*
(c) To struggle *without help*
(d) To work *without skill*
(e) To jump *without fear*
(f) To act *without sense*
(g) To talk *without wisdom*
(h) To behave *without thought*

4. Replace each of the phrases printed in italics below by an adverb that has the same meaning; the adverb must begin with one of these prefixes:

> **dis-   im-   in-   ir-**

Use your dictionary.

> EXAMPLE: To behave *without honesty*
> ANSWER: To behave dishonestly

(a) To answer *without patience*
(b) To move *without regularity*
(c) To sew *without perfection*
(d) To count *without correctness*
(e) To behave *without loyalty*
(f) To measure *without accuracy*
(g) To speak *without respect*
(h) To talk *without reverence*

5. **Adverbial phrases.** In the following sentences the words in italics are adverbs. Look them up in the dictionary and find phrases that have the same meaning. (We call these *adverbial phrases*.)

Rewrite the sentences, using the adverbial phrases instead of the adverbs. Some slight re-arrangement in the order of the words may be necessary, but the meaning must remain unchanged.

> EXAMPLE: I *always* wear this ring.
> SUGGESTED ANSWER: I wear this ring at all times.

(a) *Why* are you crying?
(b) Hang your coat *here*.
(c) I looked for him *everywhere*.

(d) It must be *somewhere*.
(e) You will *soon* learn.
(f) *Now* do this exercise.
(g) I *often* go camping.
(h) She was *nowhere* to be seen.

6. The verbs *to trudge*, *to stride*, *to strut*, etc. can all be defined as particular ways of *walking*. For example:

stride. To walk with long steps.

Here is the pattern of the definition:

> To | Action | | In what manner |

The word in the first box is another verb, and the second box contains either an adverb or an adverbial phrase.

Write similar definitions of the following verbs, and underline the adverbs and adverbial phrases.

> EXAMPLE: **whisper.** To speak <u>very softly</u>.

(a) scamper   (e) prowl
(b) warble   (f) shatter
(c) smoulder   (g) waddle
(d) scribble   (h) vibrate

7. **Adverb or adjective? (i)** Some people make the mistake of using adjectives when adverbs are needed. For example, it is wrong to say, "I can see it *plain*"; the word should be *plainly*.

In each of the following pairs of sentences one dash should be replaced by an adjective and the other by an adverb formed from the adjective. The adjective is given in italics.

> EXAMPLE: Please be ——.
> Please come ——.   (*quick*)
> ANSWER: Please be quick.
> Please come quickly.

NOTE. In some pairs the adverb is in the first sentence.

(a) Why are you so ——?
   Why are you walking so ——?   (*slow*)
(b) She fell ——.
   The box was ——.   (*heavy*)
(c) Speak more ——.
   His speech is not very ——.   (*distinct*)
(d) You chose the —— one.
   You have nailed this ——.   (*wrong*)
(e) I did it ——.
   It was an —— mistake.   (*accidental*)
(f) In all his habits he is very ——.
   He does this ——.   (*regular*)

34

(*g*) This switch works ——.
This switch is ——.   (*different*)

(*h*) Be sure to make the gate ——.
Be sure to lock the gate ——.   (*secure*)

8. **Adverb or adjective?** (ii) In Exercise 7 you had the help of knowing that one sentence of each pair contained an adjective, and the other an adverb. Here there is no such helpful pattern, and you must decide whether to use the adjective or the adverb. You are again given the adjectives, in italics, as clues.

(*a*) She walked out —— for her prize.   (*proud*)

(*b*) His voice was loud and ——.   (*clear*)

(*c*) She referred —— to my parents.   (*scornful*)

(*d*) Why did he answer me so ——?   (*angry*)

(*e*) Fruit is —— this year.   (*plentiful*)

(*f*) Be sure to add these figures ——.   (*correct*)

(*g*) The infants danced ever so ——.   (*pretty*)

(*h*) The room had been made clean and ——.   (*tidy*)

9. **Adverbs from adjectives.** Unless you are careful you are liable to make spelling mistakes in forming adverbs from certain adjectives. Form adverbs from the following adjectives and check your spelling carefully.

EXAMPLES: quick, weary, playful
ANSWERS: quickly, wearily, playfully

secret	harsh	similar	regular	brave
close	active	angry	busy	clumsy
truthful	skilful	noble	feeble	graceful
humble	gentle	true	majestic	frantic
gay	full	whole	cool	sly

10. **Classification of adverbs.** In these sentences the words in italics are adverbs. Arrange the single words in five columns according to whether they are adverbs of *time*, *place*, *manner*, *number*, or *degree*. Put the appropriate heading at the top of each column.

I am coming *now*.
Put it *here*.
She bore the pain *bravely*.
The circus is held *twice* daily.

Stop *immediately*.
The boat rocked *violently*.
Occasionally we dance.
I must go *soon*.
Silently the door opened.
He is not *wholly* bad.

He was *slightly* injured.
Have you looked *everywhere*?
Then I went home.
He tried *repeatedly*.
He is *frequently* late.
I cannot find it *anywhere*.

There she goes!
The flash was *exceedingly* bright.
We were *courteously* received.
The rock *scarcely* moved.
He has *always* been an early riser.

11. **More adverbial phrases.** In each of the following sentences the words in italics (that is, the adverbial phrases) are to be replaced by an adverb—a single word. Suitable adverbs can be found among those used in Exercise 10.

EXAMPLE: I thought so *at that time*.
ANSWER: I thought so then.

(*a*) I was received *with courtesy*.

(*b*) He shouted for help *again and again*.

(*c*) He writes to me *from time to time*.

(*d*) We searched *in every possible place*.

(*e*) I want it done *at this very moment*.

(*f*) The car was *only just a little* damaged.

(*g*) They came in *without any noise*.

12. **Synonyms.** In the following phrases replace each of the adverbs by another adverb of approximately the same meaning.

Pages 174–82 of *A First English Companion* will help you, but take care that you form *adverbs* from the adjectives given there.

EXAMPLE: To behave bravely
SUGGESTED ANSWER: To behave courageously

(*a*) To reply indignantly

(*b*) To resist stubbornly

(*c*) To act senselessly

(*d*) To behave fraudulently

(*e*) To smile bashfully

(*f*) To grow abundantly

(*g*) To be furnished sumptuously

(*h*) To stand conspicuously

13. **Idioms.** By adding different adverbs to a verb we can make phrases (known as *idioms*) that have special meanings. For example, the engine of a car is run *in*, a race is run *off*, and a debt is run *up*.

In the following sentences replace the words in italics by an idiom of two words, consisting of a verb (which you are given) and an adverb.

NOTE. All these idioms can be found in *A First English Companion*.

In the first four sentences use the verb **turn**.

(*a*) If a policeman were to *arrive unexpectedly* those boys would be in trouble.
(*b*) At nine o'clock we decided to *go to bed*.
(*c*) When the last performance is over, everyone in the circus has to *set to work*.
(*d*) The way was blocked, so we had to *go in the opposite direction*.

In the next three sentences use the verb **fall**.

(*e*) Why did they *disagree*?
(*f*) The soldiers were ordered to *take their places in the ranks*.
(*g*) I hope our plans do not *come to nothing*.

In the remaining sentences use the verb **put**.

(*h*) If Mr. Charles is ill the concert will have to be *postponed*.
(*i*) The riot was *suppressed* quickly.
(*j*) The vicar lost the place in his notes, but was not at all *embarrassed*.

14. **Split infinitive.** When a verb is used in its infinitive form (*to run, to hope*), and an adverb is introduced between the word *to* and the verb (*to quickly run, to fondly hope*) we have what is known as a *split infinitive*. This is generally considered a fault, but there are rare occasions when it is permissible to split an infinitive in order to make one's meaning clear. (If a split infinitive is unavoidable, there should never be more than one word between *to* and the verb.)

NOTE. *to always be annoyed* is a split infinitive, but *to be always annoyed* is not. The infinitive here is *to be*.

What alterations would you make in these sentences?

(*a*) Our aim is to satisfactorily and efficiently carry out our customers' orders.
(*b*) I like to occasionally go to a play or to a concert.
(*c*) The best plan is to sometimes if not always finish off with a window-leather.
(*d*) To conscientiously do one's duty is better than to be selfishly indulgent.

18. COMPARISON OF ADJECTIVES

A day is *long*, a week is *longer*, and a year is *longest*. These three stages are known as degrees of comparison:

long ... *positive degree*
longer ... *comparative degree*
longest ... *superlative degree*

1. Copy the table of adjectives shown below, and complete it. Use your dictionary to make sure you have no spelling mistakes.

POSITIVE	COMPARATIVE	SUPERLATIVE
long	longer	longest
wet		
big		
shiny		
sad		
hot		
lonely		
thin		
slim		
dry		
sly		

2. The word *clumsier* means *more clumsy*, and *clumsiest* means *most clumsy*. It is a bad mistake to say *more clumsier* or *most clumsiest*. Bearing this in mind, say what the following words mean.

daintier	jolliest	loveliest
angriest	wealthier	wiser
cleverest	fiercer	noblest
gentler	gloomiest	sillier

3. Copy the table of adjectives shown below, and then complete it.

POSITIVE	COMPARATIVE	SUPERLATIVE
short		
noisy		
	more important	
peaceful		
		shabbiest
good		
shy		
	farther	
	elder	
		worst
much		
little		

36

4. Two, or more than two? The comparative degree refers to *two* things or persons; the superlative degree refers to *more than two*:

> The *sharper* of two knives; the *sharpest* of three.
> The *more famous* of two men; the *most famous* of all.

It is wrong to refer to the *sharpest* of *two* knives, or the *most* famous of *two* men.

———————

Complete each of the following sentences by inserting either the comparative or the superlative of the adjective given in brackets.

(*a*) The ——— of them all is Robin. (*jolly*)

(*b*) The ——— of the twins is David. (*tall*)

(*c*) Either steel or brass can be used; steel is the ———. (*cheap*)

(*d*) Bind it with string or wire, whichever is the ———. (*convenient*)

(*e*) The ——— girl in the class is Stella. (*dependable*)

(*f*) He was the ——— person I have ever met. (*friendly*)

(*g*) Weigh them both and tell me which is the ———. (*heavy*)

(*h*) Either of these frocks would suit you, but the pink one is the ———. (*pretty*)

(*i*) His was the ——— picture in the exhibition. (*striking*)

(*j*) My left eye is the ——— one. (*weak*)

(*k*) He was the ——— climber in the party. (*intrepid*)

(*l*) You will find two basins on the shelf; bring me the ———. (*small*)

5. More and most. The words *more* and *most* are the comparative and the superlative forms of the adjective *much*. Following the rule already given in Exercise 4, we see that the word *more* must refer to *two* things, and *most* to *more than two*.

Complete these sentences by putting either *more* or *most* in place of each dash.

(*a*) Who did ——— work; Jim, Carl, or Michael?

(*b*) Which gives you ——— satisfaction, classical music or jazz?

(*c*) Alan works harder than David, but David has the ——— intelligence.

(*d*) Look through all the sheds in the catalogue, and order the one with the ——— floor-space.

(*e*) When you have thought about every occupation that may suit you, choose the one that will bring you the ——— happiness in life.

(*f*) Which country has ——— coast-line, Norway or Sweden?

(*g*) Mark Elizabeth's homework as well as Oliver's, and tell me who has the ——— mistakes.

(*h*) Consider both possibilities, and ask yourself which offers the ——— chance of success.

6. Less and least. Complete these sentences by putting either *less* or *least* in place of each dash. *Less* refers to *two*, and *least* to *more than two*.

(*a*) Ask to see all the stoves they have in stock, and find out which one uses ——— fuel.

(*b*) Which motor cycle makes ——— noise, Ralph's or Leslie's?

(*c*) Which county has ——— rainfall, Lancashire or Norfolk?

(*d*) The children were fairly well-behaved, but Colin gave the ——— trouble of all.

(*e*) Which need ——— upkeep, steel window-frames or wooden ones?

(*f*) Of the two materials I prefer this one because it contains ——— cotton.

7. The more, the more. Some proverbs have a neat way of making comparisons:

> *The higher the plum tree, the riper the plum;*
> *The richer the cobbler, the blacker his thumb*

In everyday speech we may say

> *The softer the mattress, the more comfortable the bed*

> OR *The more watchful the police, the more cunning the thief*

Following this pattern, and using the adjectives in brackets as clues, complete the following phrases.

(*a*) ——— the knife, ——— the cut (*sharp, clean*)

(*b*) ——— the soil, ——— the crop (*rich, heavy*)

(*c*) ——— the light, ——— the exposure (*bright, short*)

(*d*) ——— the bone, ——— the meat (*near, sweet*)

(*e*) ——— the china, ——— the cup (*thin, fragile*)

(*f*) ——— the air, ——— the view (*clear, distant*)

(*g*) ——— the storm, ——— the damage (*violent, great*)

(*h*) ——— the supply, ——— the price (*plentiful, low*)

(*i*) ——— the crime, ——— the punishment (*wicked, severe*)

(*j*) ——— the nation, ——— the people (*industrious, prosperous*)

8. The more, the less. The pattern of the phrases in Exercise 7 was

The more ——, *the more* ——

In this exercise the phrases are similar in construction and contrast, but the pattern is

The more ——, *the less* ——

(*a*) —— the work, —— the results (*hurried, accurate*)

(*b*) —— the rooms, —— the house (*numerous, convenient*)

(*c*) —— the legs, —— the table (*thick, graceful*)

(*d*) —— the metal, —— the wire (*hard, pliable*)

(*e*) —— the scenery, —— the journey (*interesting, tiring*)

(*f*) —— the altitude, —— the air pressure (*great, little*)

9. Adjectives that should not be compared. Some adjectives should never be compared. For example, an *absent* pupil cannot be more absent than he is already, and an *everlasting* mystery cannot last longer than for ever. More than half the adjectives in the list below are of this kind; say which they are.

endless	square	invisible	afraid
painful	empty	dead	angry
daily	level	stupid	ceaseless
complete	silent	awkward	dangerous
parallel	true	final	disagreeable
perpetual	intelligent	handsome	immovable
innocent	identical	supreme	obstinate
punctual	infallible		

✓MARK THESE YOURSELF
The answers are on page 144

1. (*a*) How is the word *min r* spelt when it means (i) a mine-worker; (ii) a person under 18?

(*b*) When a boxer *feints*, does he need medical attention? (Say why or why not.)

(*c*) Complete this unfinished song-title:

Cockles and Mus . . . .

2. If you had to write these words partly on one line and partly on another, how would you hyphenate them?

surname	suitable	superhuman
underneath	undress	uniform

19. PREPOSITIONS

1. **Idioms.** A person who is displeased *with* your behaviour may say that he disapproves *of* it, objects *to* it, or frowns *upon* it. There are no rules for deciding which prepositions to use in such phrases; the sayings are idioms that have to be learned by hearing and using them.

See if you can supply the correct prepositions to complete the following sentences. You should not have to use any one preposition more than twice.

(*a*) I am surprised —— you.

(*b*) You may rely —— me to help you.

(*c*) The mongoose is not afraid —— snakes.

(*d*) Lacrosse is similar —— hockey.

(*e*) Who has been interfering —— these tools?

(*f*) I know I can depend —— you.

(*g*) She was accompanied —— her mother.

(*h*) I am accustomed —— heat.

(*i*) I was encouraged —— his praise.

(*j*) Please refrain —— smoking.

(*k*) Are you satisfied —— your new car?

(*l*) She cared —— the wounded.

(*m*) May I confide —— you?

(*n*) Never shrink —— your duty.

(*o*) You must be thankful —— your escape.

(*p*) He is not worthy —— such a reward.

2. **Idioms and popular sayings.** The English language is rich in idioms that depend for their meanings on the correct choice of prepositions. A person who is overcharged is said to pay *through* the nose; one who is made to do as we wish is led *by* the nose; and when we do something regardless of a person's displeasure we say that it is done *under* his very nose.

In the sentences given below you are to supply the correct preposition in place of each dash.

You will find *A First English Companion* helpful.

(*a*) She was unable to take part in the game because she was feeling —— colour.

(*b*) Have you an ear —— music?

(*c*) It goes —— the grain for me to have to lend him money.

(*d*) Strike out on your own, and do not be content to go —— the stream.

(*e*) He is a desperate character who would stick —— nothing.

(*f*) Tell me the truth, without beating —— the bush.

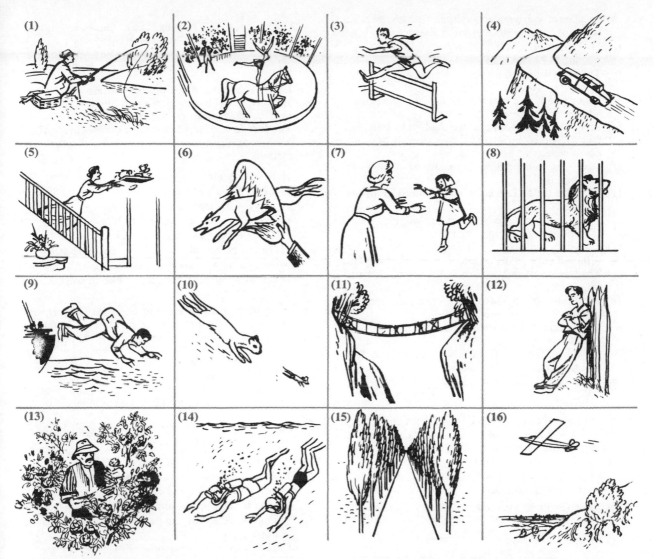

3. Choosing the right preposition. If a dog sees a pile of straw he might jump *over* it, run *round* it, or wriggle *through* it. The words *over*, *round*, and *through* are used here as prepositions to show the relationship between the dog's actions and the pile of straw.

In each of these pictures there are two or more things or persons that exist in a certain relationship to each other

For example, we could say about Nos. 1 and 2:

1. The angler sits *near* the stream.
2. The horse trots *in* the ring.

Find other suitable prepositions for Nos. 1 and 2 (instead of *near* and *in*) and then carry on in the same way with the other pictures. Write a simple sentence about each one, and underline the preposition. Try not to use any preposition more than once.

4. More idioms and popular sayings. In this exercise follow the instructions given in Exercise 2.

(*a*) His letter does not actually contain any complaints, but I can read —— the lines.

(*b*) The army attacked without warning, and took the city —— storm.

(*c*) You should have said that earlier; anyone can be wise —— the event.

(*d*) It is —— the cards that we shall go to Italy.

(*e*) Our village is —— the times; we still have no piped water.

(*f*) Give him your opinion fearlessly, straight —— the shoulder.

(*g*) You can trust him; he is —— board in all his dealings.

(*h*) If you live —— your means you will find yourself in difficulties sooner or later.

(*i*) He finally reduced the price of the caravan by £10, and gave us the crockery —— the bargain.

(*j*) The farmer offered the Scouts the use of his barn to tide them —— their difficulty.

(*k*) He admits his mistake, so there is no need to throw it —— his teeth.

(*l*) You should think carefully, and not jump —— conclusions.

(*m*) At the outbreak of war they had only a few thousand men —— arms.

(*n*) Do not go too far away; I want you to stay —— call.

5. It is often said that a sentence should not end with a preposition, but there is in fact no such rule. In conversational or idiomatic English we often use a preposition as the last word:

Where are you going to?
What is she looking at?

In serious writing, however, it is usually the custom to avoid ending with a preposition wherever possible.

———

This exercise (together with Exercise 6) will give you practice in re-arranging sentences from one form to the other, according to which is the more suitable for the occasion. First, let us see how to move the preposition away from the end.

EXAMPLE 1: This is the line ∧ to write your name *on*.
ANSWER: This is the line on which to write your name.

EXAMPLE 2: Do you know the boy ∧ my brother goes cycling *with*?
ANSWER: Do you know the boy with whom my brother goes cycling?

In the above examples the preposition is in italics, and a caret (∧) has been inserted to show you where to put the preposition, followed by *which* or *whom*. The first four of the following exercises are marked in the same way to help you to understand the method.

(*a*) Bring a knife ∧ to sharpen your pencil *with*.

(*b*) I was given a locker ∧ to keep my books *in*.

(*c*) It is the manager ∧ I wish to speak *to*.

(*d*) I could not see anything ∧ to hide *behind*.

(*e*) This is the chart they steered by.

(*f*) Tennis is the only game I am any good at.

(*g*) He is a man I have the greatest respect for.

(*h*) She is a person I should not like to work under.

6. The sentences in this exercise are expressed formally. They are to be re-arranged so as to be informal and conversational, with the prepositions at the end.

EXAMPLE: Here is the window-pane *through* which John put his hand.
ANSWER: Here is the window-pane that John put his hand through.

In the first four sentences you are helped by being shown the prepositions in italics.

(*a*) *At* which hotel are you staying?

(*b*) *In* which drawer have you put the thimble?

(*c*) Is this the book *about* which you were telling me?

(*d*) Was it you *with* whom she was angry?

(*e*) Patrick is a boy on whom I thought I could depend.

(*f*) He lent me the hose-pipe with which he washes the car.

(*g*) Flax is the plant from which linen is made.

(*h*) I will give you the address of the dealers from whom I had my stamps.

(*i*) The police asked us if he was the man for whom we had been looking.

(*j*) Tell me who it was to whom you spoke.

(*k*) There is the ledge along which we had to crawl.

(*l*) Is this the road by which we came in?

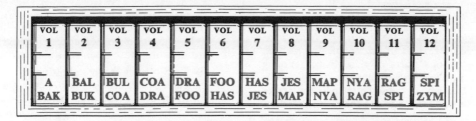

✅ MARK THESE YOURSELF: Using an encyclopedia

The answers are on page 144

The twelve volumes of an encyclopedia have their backs (or "spines") indexed as shown above. From this we see that information about *Canada* should be found in Vol. 3, and that we can expect to find *electricity* in Vol. 5.

Say in which volumes you will look for information on the following topics.

(*a*) rockets   (*c*) Livingstone   (*e*) steam
(*b*) dynamite   (*d*) India   (*f*) badminton

(*g*) chess   (*k*) Danube   (*o*) stalactites
(*h*) plastics   (*l*) fuels   (*p*) Bahamas
(*i*) banks   (*m*) Java   (*q*) nylon
(*j*) Mohammed   (*n*) clouds   (*r*) St. Lawrence

Remembering that to find information about Sir Walter Raleigh we must turn to *Raleigh* (Vol. 11), say where you would look for the following:

(*s*) William Caxton   (*u*) How to measure rainfall
(*t*) Queen Victoria   (*v*) The Battle of Britain

📖 LOOK THESE UP

See page 29 for instructions

1. Replace the dots in these sentences by prefixes that mean *not*.

   (*a*) He stood ·· resolute at the water's edge.
   (*b*) His writing is almost ·· legible.
   (*c*) A landslide has made the road ·· passable.
   (*d*) These ties are quite ·· expensive.   86 Ex. 3

2. If a boy says *I haven't brought nothing to eat*, meaning that he will have to go hungry, what mistake is he making?
   Give *two* ways in which he could have expressed himself correctly.   109 **80**

The following questions are about the extract from *Travels with a Donkey* on page 14.

3. Rewrite lines 23–25 in the third person, remembering that the author is a man.   32 Ex. 11

4. Say whether these words are used transitively or intransitively:

   (*a*) break (line 18)   (*d*) turns (line 10)
   (*b*) open (line 21)   (*e*) speeding (line 17)
   (*c*) wakened (line 24)   (*f*) passes (line 2)
                                    27 Ex. 3

5. (*a*) Find a simile in lines 28–29.
   (*b*) Find a simile in lines 14–20.   125 **108**

6. (*a*) Find an example of personification in lines 1–14.
   (*b*) Find an example of personification in lines 34–38.
                                    128 **109**

7. Find a relative pronoun in lines 18–22, and say to what or to whom it refers.   44 Ex. 2

8. Pick out two present participles used as adjectives in lines 8–13.   52 Ex. 1

9. Pick out two adverbial phrases in lines 17–20.
                                    51 Ex. 7

20. AGREEMENT

A young child who says *Me like it* or *I is tired* has not yet learned the rules of grammatical *agreement* between the various parts of a sentence. Young children are not the only offenders; many people who are old enough to know better make mistakes in such sentences as those in the following exercises.

---

1. In place of the dash in each of the following sentences put one of the words given in the table below. Take care that it agrees in number (that is, singular or plural) with the word printed in italics in the sentence.

SINGULAR	PLURAL
Is	*Are*
Was	*Were*
Has	*Have*

(a) —— there a *box* for these dominoes?
(b) —— there been a *reduction* in prices?
(c) —— there any *gloves* on the window-ledge?
(d) —— there *telephones* a hundred years ago?
(e) —— there *anyone* upstairs?
(f) —— there a hundred *pence* in a pound?
(g) —— there any *books* in the cupboard?
(h) —— there been any *wood-pigeons* in the garden?

2. Without changing the tense, re-arrange each of these sentences by using the following method:

1. Omit the word or words printed in italics.
2. If the subject of the sentence is in the singular, begin the sentence with *There is* or *There was*. If the subject of the sentence is in the plural, begin the sentence with *There are* or *There were*.

EXAMPLE: Eighty families *live* in this block of flats.
ANSWER: There are eighty families in this block of flats.

(a) A thousand pictures *hang* in this art gallery.
(b) A monastery *stood* here five hundred years ago.
(c) Sunflowers and hollyhocks *grew* in her garden.
(d) Gold *occurs* in these mountains.
(e) Concerts *take place* here several times a week.
(f) Six men *took part* in the expedition.
(g) A clump of trees *grows* on the hill-top.
(h) A crowd of people *stood* in the market-place.

3. **Each, every.** The words *each* and *every* refer to things separately (each *one*, every *one*). They must therefore be used with singular verbs and pronouns.

In the following sentences choose the correct words from those given (in italics) as alternatives.

(a) Each of us *was/were* questioned.
(b) Each of my brothers *are/is* taking a turn.
(c) Every one of you must behave like *a man/men*.
(d) Every one of these chisels *look/looks* blunt.
(e) Each of the hats *bears a label/bear labels* saying that *they have/it has* been reduced to half price.
(f) Each of the animals *has/have* been shut up in *their/its* own *pens/pen*.
(g) Every one of these envelopes *have/has* dirty marks on *them/it*.
(h) Every one of the boys *was/were* expected to make *their/his* own *bed/beds*.

4. **Either, neither.** The word *either* means *one or the other*. *Neither* means *not either one*. These words must therefore be used with singular verbs and pronouns:

Neither of the boys *was* able to reach *his* home.

In the following sentences choose the correct words from those given as alternatives.

(a) Either of these lamp-shades *are/is* suitable.
(b) Neither of these scarves *are/is* mine.
(c) Neither of my parents *has/have* yet seen my report.
(d) *Was/were* either of the applicants suitable?
(e) Neither of these *are/is* worth considering.
(f) I hope that neither of these ropes *breaks/break*.
(g) *Have/Has* either of these stair carpets any red in *it/them*?
(h) Neither of the grocers in our village *has/have* electric light in *his shop/their shops*.
(i) Call me when either of the bells *ring/rings*.
(j) *Do/Does* either of the girls make *her/their* own dresses?

5. **Singular or plural?** We have seen that in every sentence the verb must agree with its subject:

The *case* has been found.
The *cases* have been found.

If instead of using the single word *case* we use the phrase *case of jewels*, the subject is still *case* (not *jewels*), so the verb must still be in the singular:

The *case* of jewels has been found.

When the subject is in the plural it must of course be followed by a plural verb.

In the following sentences choose the correct words from those given as alternatives. In each of the first five sentences the subject is also picked out for you in italics.

(a) *One* of his eyes *was/were* injured.
(b) *The cupboard* under the stairs *are/is* dark.
(c) *The eggs* lying in the dry sand *are/is* almost invisible.
(d) *A photograph* of the prizewinners *have/has* been taken.
(e) *A copy* of the rules *was/were* pinned up.
(f) Many songs from this opera *is/are* still popular.
(g) This book of operatic songs *is/are* still popular.
(h) The tallest of the three boys *is/are* John.
(i) Pipes from the strainer *carry/carries* away the syrup.
(j) The movement of her arms *were/was* most graceful.

6. **Which is the subject?** Which is the correct word to use in this sentence?

Through the meadows *run/runs* a stream.

If you choose the wrong one it is probably because you have not noticed that the subject is at the end of the sentence. Moving it to the beginning we get this arrangement:

A stream *runs* through the meadows.
The correct version of the original sentence is therefore

Through the meadows *runs* a stream.

In the following sentences choose the correct words from those given as alternatives. Re-arrange each sentence in your mind (as shown in the above example) so as to make sure that the verb agrees with the subject.

(a) Among the trees *stand/stands* a statue.
(b) On the promenade *is/are* two kiosks.
(c) Behind the curtains *hangs/hang* a cord.
(d) On this bush *grows/grow* pale yellow flowers.
(e) In that mountain range *rise/rises* two well-known rivers.
(f) Which socks *are/is* Colin to have?
(g) At the end of three weeks *comes/come* a holiday of two days.
(h) What emotions *does/do* a man feel when faced by death?

7. In each of the following sentences the subject is enlarged by a phrase that distracts our attention from the subject and tends to make us use the wrong form of the verb—plural instead of singular, or vice versa. The phrases that may mislead you are between the commas in each sentence. Choose the correct words from the alternatives given in italics.

(a) All the animals, with the exception of one pony, *were/was* brought out before the roof collapsed.
(b) The festival, contrary to expectations, *have/has* made a profit.
(c) This road, divided into six lanes, *carries/carry* most of the north-bound traffic.
(d) An outbreak of fowl pest, involving five hundred birds, *have/has* been reported.
(e) The new president, like his brothers, *is/are* well known for *their/his* skill at polo.
(f) The uninjured passengers, including Sir John Craig, *were/was* able to continue *their/his* journey.
(g) Drier weather, with some showers, *are/is* expected to spread to all areas.
(h) The choir, of two hundred voices, *were/was* formed five years ago.

8. **I and me.** It is correct to say *Father gave it to me*, therefore it is correct to say, *Father gave it to you and me*.

It is correct to say *I have been swimming*, therefore it is correct to say *You and I have been swimming*.

There is a mistaken idea that it is always right to say *You and I*, but the correct word to use is often *me*. To decide which is right, leave out the other person and imagine yourself alone in the sentence.

An article on page 66 of *A First English Companion* tells you more about this.

In the following sentences put **I** or **me** in place of each dash.

(a) Put it in the oven for baby and ——
(b) Can Elizabeth and —— sit here?
(c) You and —— are the only ones without raincoats.
(d) The coach drove off and left Gwen and —— behind.
(e) Carl and Joan are playing against Robert and ——
(f) Kathleen and —— decorated the room; the cakes were made by Mildred and ——.
(g) Brian, Alan, Gerald, and —— were all born in June.

43

(*h*) This snowman was made by Eric and ——;
Frank and —— are going to make another one.

(*i*) In front of my father and —— sat the president
and his wife.

(*j*) It was to Howard and —— that these rabbits
were given.

See also the Exercises on *Choosing the Right Pronoun*
(pages 30 and 31).

9. Either, or; neither, nor. *Either* is followed by *or*;
neither is followed by *nor*:

> *Either hot or cold*
> *Neither wet nor dry*

Complete the following sentences by putting *or* or
nor in place of each dash.

(*a*) Either dogs —— foxes could have done this.

(*b*) Neither the hat —— the coat belongs to me.

(*c*) He can neither bat —— bowl.

(*d*) You may do the picture either in water-colour
—— in pencil.

(*e*) She neither saw —— heard anyone.

(*f*) This might be either silk —— rayon; it is definitely neither cotton —— linen.

(*g*) Her holiday is either in May —— in June.

(*h*) I shall neither buy him a new satchel —— pay
for the repair of the old one.

(*i*) This cannot possibly be either mahogany ——
teak.

(*j*) I shall not lend him either my bat —— my pads.

★ REVISION

1. Each dash in these phrases stands for the comparative
or the superlative of the adjective given in brackets.
Complete the sentences correctly.

(*a*) The —— of three ways   (*quick*)

(*b*) The —— of two trains   (*slow*)

(*c*) The —— of ten people   (*foolish*)

(*d*) The —— of five boys   (*courteous*)

(*e*) The —— of two leaders   (*experienced*)

(*f*) The —— of two occasions   (*memorable*)

2. In the following sentences choose the correct words
from those given as alternatives.

(*a*) You must not go swimming either in the pool
or/nor in the river.

(*b*) Each of the bedrooms *have their has its* own
separate bathroom.

(*c*) Tom, with his sisters, *are/is* coming later.

21. RELATIVE PRONOUNS

1. Complete each of these sentences by inserting a
relative pronoun from the following list:

> *who   whom   whose   which   that   what*

(*a*) Here is a child —— knee is bleeding.

(*b*) Morphia, —— is a dangerous drug, cannot be
obtained without a prescription.

(*c*) Is there anyone from —— I can borrow a
pencil?

(*d*) I do not know —— they have decided to do.

(*e*) Ask the teacher —— takes you for English.

(*f*) Make a list of all the things —— you have
bought.

2. **Which, who, whose (i).** Each of these pairs of
sentences can be joined into one sentence by the use
of a relative pronoun. Replace the word in italics
by *which*, *who*, or *whose*, and put a comma instead of
the first full stop.

> EXAMPLE: We saw the world's first gramophone.
> *It* was invented by Edison.
> ANSWER: We saw the world's first gramophone,
> which was invented by Edison.

(*a*) The French were led by Joan of Arc.   *She* was
only a young girl.

(*b*) This picture shows the Sandwich Islands.   *They*
were discovered by Captain Cook.

(*c*) St. Paul's Cathedral was built by Wren.   *His*
tomb can be seen in the crypt.

(*d*) The Roman invaders were defeated by Boadicea.
She was queen of the Iceni tribe.

(*e*) Columbus encountered the Sargasso Sea.   *It* is
a mass of floating seaweed.

(*f*) Another early aviator was Blériot.   *He* was the
first to fly across the English Channel.

(*g*) George VI was followed by Elizabeth II.   *Her*
coronation took place in 1953.

(*h*) Napoleon was defeated at Waterloo.   *Waterloo*
is near Brussels.

(*i*) The finest tenor at that time was Caruso.   *His*
fame was world-wide.

3. **Which, who, whose (ii).** Each of these pairs of
sentences can be joined by inserting the second one
into the first one at the point marked by a caret (∧).
The word in italics must be replaced by *which*, *who*,

or *whose*, and the part inserted must be marked off by commas.

EXAMPLE: The miller and his son∧ slung the donkey on a pole and carried him into town. *They* did not realize how foolish they looked.

ANSWER: The miller and his son, who did not realize how foolish they looked, slung the donkey on a pole and carried him into the town.

(a) The purple grapes∧ were a great temptation to the fox. *They* hung just out of his reach.

(b) The hare∧ was amazed to find that the tortoise had reached the winning-post before him. *He* had been asleep all day.

(c) When the peasant picked up the egg∧ he saw that it was made of pure gold. *It* shone in the morning sunlight.

(d) The mouse∧ was able to free the lion by gnawing through the ropes that held him. *His* life had once been spared by the lion.

(e) The jar∧ was too deep for the fox to reach any of the frog stew. *The jar* had a long neck.

(f) The young mouse∧ had not thought of how the bell was to be tied round the cat's neck. *His* suggestion had been received with delight.

(g) The shepherds∧ took no notice when they again heard the cry of 'Wolf!' *They* had already been hoaxed twice by the foolish boy.

4. **What does it stand for?** A relative pronoun should be put as near as possible to the noun to which it refers. For example:

1. The Sherpas, *who* are hardy people, live in Nepal.
2. The Sherpas live in Nepal, *which* is on the slopes of the Himalayas.

In the first sentence, *who* refers to the Sherpas.
In the second sentence, *which* refers to Nepal.

———————————

In the sentences below, the relative pronouns are printed in italics. Say which noun each one refers to.

(a) Dennis, *who* is ten years old, is taller than Robert.
(b) Philip is friendly with Eric, *who* lives on a farm.
(c) Chester, *which* is a city I know well, still has its Roman walls.
(d) This is the cat *that* killed the rat.
(e) I have a box with a lid *that* is painted red.

(f) Golf would suit him better than tennis, *which* is a strenuous game.
(g) Is this the little boy for *whom* those people are looking?
(h) Give this letter to the girl *whose* father came to see me.

5. **Sense and nonsense.** You have seen in Exercise 4 that a relative pronoun should be put as near as possible to the noun to which it refers. If this is not done, the results can be both ridiculous and humorous, as in the sentences below. Say what these sentences actually mean in their present form, and say also what they are intended to mean.

(a) I have a parrot in a cage that can talk.
(b) We saw an old man with a little boy whose beard was white and bushy.
(c) Father bought me a watch for my birthday, which winds itself automatically.
(d) Children in charge of parents who are under five years of age are admitted free.
(e) We have a cupboard for storing bread that was made a hundred years ago.
(f) Fill in the form, giving the required information about your house, which should then be sent to the surveyor.
(g) Visitors with dogs who wish to come into the park must keep them under control.
(h) The queen rode out on a fine black horse, to whom all the people bowed low.

6. Here are some more sentences in which relative pronouns (together with the parts of the sentences they introduce) are misplaced. The consequence is that the sentences mean something quite different from what is obviously intended. Re-arrange them correctly, and insert commas wherever necessary.

EXAMPLE: Nelson was greatly feared by the French, in whose honour Trafalgar Day is still celebrated.

ANSWER: Nelson, in whose honour Trafalgar Day is celebrated, was greatly feared by the French.

(a) The gorilla lives in the African forest which climbs trees in search of food.
(b) Queen Mary married Philip of Spain who was one of the daughters of Henry VIII.
(c) Jason set out in search of the Golden Fleece whose companions were known as the Argonauts.

45

(d) Marconi showed his instrument to the king with which he had sent messages across the Atlantic.

(e) Any bee is killed or driven out of the hive that strays in from another colony.

(f) Norfolk still has many quiet and unfrequented villages to which thousands of visitors go each year.

7. **Which, who, whose (iii).** In Exercises 2 and 3 you have used two methods of joining pairs of sentences into single sentences, using the relative pronouns *which*, *who*, and *whose*. In this exercise both methods are used.

For each main sentence you are given two others (numbered 1 and 2) to be joined to it in different ways; one of these can be made to follow the main sentence (as in Exercise 2), but the other must be inserted at the point marked by the caret (as in Exercise 3). There will therefore be two separate answers for each set of sentences.

The two methods to be used do not always occur in the same order.

(a) Bob Cratchit ∧ tried to warm himself at the candle.
   1. *It* was brighter than the fire.
   2. *He* shivered in his dismal little cell.

(b) Bob ∧ wore a long comforter.
   1. *It* hung down before him.
   2. *His* threadbare clothes were darned and brushed.

(c) The pudding ∧ was carried in proudly by Mrs. Cratchit.
   1. *It* was like a speckled cannon-ball.
   2. *Her* face was flushed and smiling.

(d) The smaller Cratchits ∧ had smelt the goose.
   1. *It* was being cooked at the baker's.
   2. *They* had stood outside the baker's shop.

(e) The active little crutch ∧ was that of Tiny Tim.
   1. *It* was heard at that moment upon the floor.
   2. *His* limbs were supported by an iron frame.

✔ MARK THESE YOURSELF

The answers are on page 144

Say where you would look for these topics in the encyclopedia illustrated on page 41.

(a) glycerine   (d) Mars   (g) source of Nile
(b) judo   (e) Mt. Everest (h) rules of polo
(c) Bunyan   (f) St. Paul   (i) G. Stephenson

8. **WHICH with a preposition.** In this and the next three exercises you will construct sentences in which a preposition comes before the relative pronoun *which*.

Pairs of sentences, (a), (b), (c) and so on, are given, and you are to join each pair into one sentence. This is the way to do it:
   1. Replace the first full stop by a comma.
   2. Follow on with the second sentence, using a small letter for the preposition with which it begins.
   3. Replace the word or words in italics by the relative pronoun *which*.

   EXAMPLE: We found an overhanging ledge.
             Beneath *this ledge* we sheltered.
   ANSWER: We found an overhanging ledge, beneath which we sheltered.

(a) They saw a blackbird's nest.
    In *the nest* were four eggs.

(b) At the end of the room was a fire-place.
    Above *the fire-place* hung a large mirror.

(c) At the top of the cylinder is a valve.
    Through *the valve* oxygen is introduced.

(d) Firing-practice is indicated by a red flag.
    Beyond *the flag* we are not allowed to go.

(e) Outside stood a new fire-engine.
    Round *it* a crowd had already gathered.

(f) From beneath his cloak he drew a flute.
    On *it* he began to play a slow sad tune.

9. This exercise is similar to the previous one, but with one exception: the preposition that you must use immediately after the comma will be found near the *end* of the second sentence, before the italics.

   EXAMPLE: Around the prison was a great wall.
             No-one had ever climbed over *it*.
   ANSWER: Around the prison was a great wall, over which no-one had ever climbed.

(a) His favourite pastime was archery.
    He was highly skilled at *it*.

(b) The garden was alive with caterpillars.
    There seemed to be millions of *them*.

(c) At the back of the car is a coupling.
    A caravan can be attached to *this coupling*.

(d) They are now drilling through a layer of shale.
    They expect to find petroleum beneath *the shale*.

(e) The water swirled me against a slimy post.
    I flung my arms around *it* desperately.

46

(f) The entrance to the cave was a narrow slit.
We wriggled through *it* with difficulty.

10. The pairs of sentences given below can be joined satisfactorily in the same way as Exercise 9, but the result is improved by moving the verb in the second sentence and putting it immediately after the word *which*.   In the example, this verb is picked out in bold type.

> EXAMPLE: The sea is held back by a great dike.
> A wide road **runs** along *the dike*.
>
> ANSWER: The sea is held back by a great dike, along which **runs** a wide road.

Use the above method to join the following sentences.

(a) Concealed behind the curtain he found a small cupboard.
A rusty key hung inside *this cupboard*.

(b) In the middle of the hall was a round table.
The king and his knights sat round *it*.

(c) His attention was attracted by an oak chest.
A cross-bow leaned against *the chest*.

(d) At the west end is a statue of Bishop Gray.
An ancient font stands beside *the statue*.

(e) A few palm-trees mark the edge of the oasis.
Empty, barren desert lies beyond *the palm-trees*.

(f) Between the mountains is a broad plain.
A sluggish river meanders across *this plain*.

11. In Exercises 8–10 you have joined pairs of sentences by adding the second one to the end of the first—after making certain changes.   This has been possible because the word *which* has referred to something mentioned at the *end* of the first sentence. (Look back over those exercises and see that this is so.)

In the sentences given below it is necessary to insert the second sentence at the point marked by the caret, so that the word *which* is as close as possible to the word to which it refers.

> EXAMPLE: The snow⌄ is a protection from the icy winds.
> Beneath *the snow* the spring flowers are already in bud.
>
> ANSWER: The snow, beneath which the spring flowers are already in bud, is a protection from the icy winds.

(a) A bottle⌄ was found at the water's edge.
Inside *the bottle* a letter could be seen.

(b) The tunnel⌄ is five kilometres long.
Through *the tunnel* hundreds of cars pass daily.

(c) The wall⌄ is in danger of falling.
Across *the wall* is a wide crack.

(d) This hotel⌄ is said to be the last hotel in Spain.
Beyond *the hotel* there is nothing but sand and sea.

(e) Castle Hill⌄ is the highest point in the district.
From *Castle Hill* can be seen nine counties.

(f) The town⌄ became famous for its pottery.
Near *the town* there were abundant supplies of coal and clay.

12. **WHOM with a preposition.** Look at these two sentences:

> *There is the racing motorist.   I told you about him.*

Notice that the second sentence ends with a pronoun (*him*), and that the previous word is a preposition (*about*). By changing the position of these two words, and at the same time altering *him* to *whom*, we can make the two sentences into one:

> *There is the racing motorist about whom I told you.*

Join the following pairs of sentences in the same way. If your answers are given in writing, underline each pair of words in which a preposition is followed by *whom*.

(a) Stella is a good-natured girl.   I have a great admiration for her.

(b) Mr. Quinn was an old man.   The children bought puppets from him.

(c) Andrew Dahl was a botanist.   The dahlia was named after him.

(d) Monsieur and Madame Curie were scientists. Few people had ever heard of them.

(e) Huddled against the wall was a woman.   A small child lay beside her.

(f) Did you notice the very tall lady?   I was sitting behind her.

(g) Gerald is an easy-going boy.   Nothing comes as a surprise to him.

(h) Handel was a composer.   Some of the world's greatest music was written by him.

(i) Captain Jones was the commander.   My brother served under him.

(j) Socrates was a great philosopher.   Many people studied with him.

13. Whom (i). Each of these pairs of sentences can be joined into one sentence in the following way:

1. Change the first full stop to a comma.
2. Follow the comma with the word *whom*.
3. In the second sentence omit the italicized word, which is not needed now that you have replaced it by the word *whom*.

> EXAMPLE: We are sorry to say good-bye to Mr. Wyles. We have known *him* for many years.
>
> ANSWER: We are sorry to say good-bye to Mr. Wyles, whom we have known for many years.

(*a*) The king gave the golden bell to his youngest daughter. He loved *her* dearly.

(*b*) The governor of Egypt was Joseph. None of the brothers recognized *him*.

(*c*) All eyes turned upon Gustav. Rupert had thrust *him* to the doorway.

(*d*) At a table in the corner sat a young man. The rest of the travellers avoided *him*.

(*e*) Alarm was spreading among the villagers. Julian had told *them* of the rebellion.

(*f*) The two rogues turned with whips upon the helpless merchant. They had tied *him* to the wheel of his own cart.

(*g*) So they took sticks and went in search of Kriska. Everyone called *her* a witch.

(*h*) Rob handed the letter to Dick. Rob regarded *Dick* as a trustworthy messenger.

14. Whom (ii). Each of the following pairs of sentences can be joined by inserting the second one into the first one at the point marked by a caret. Two changes must be made in the second sentence: introduce it with the word *whom*, and omit the word printed in italics. Insert commas at the right places.

> EXAMPLE: Rogers ∧ has not been chosen for the next Test Match. Many people regarded *him* as a certainty.
>
> ANSWER: Rogers, whom many people regarded as a certainty, has not been chosen for the next Test Match.

(*a*) Two bystanders ∧ are known to have witnessed the accident. The police are anxious to trace *them*.

(*b*) Mrs. Parker ∧ is thus within sight of winning two championships. No-one has yet beaten *her*.

(*c*) A young woman ∧ was found lying on the ledge. The rescue party was unable to identify *her*.

(*d*) Mr. Faulkner ∧ is a retired civil servant. The bandits are holding *him* to ransom.

(*e*) The Chancellor ∧ will make a statement in the Commons today. The Prime Minister saw *him* last night.

(*f*) Mr. Scott ∧ is an architect by profession. The society has chosen *him* as its first president.

(*g*) Several young actors ∧ will make their début in this play. The producers have recently discovered *them*.

(*h*) Two doctors ∧ immediately offered their services. Passers-by had told *them* of the explosion.

15. Who or Whom? (i) The words *who* and *whom* are often wrongly used. Look at these two sentences, which are both correct:

1. This is the boy *who* caught the thief.
2. This is the thief *whom* the boy caught.

In the first sentence the word *who* refers to the SUBJECT of the verb *caught*. That is, it refers to the boy who did the catching.

In the second sentence the word *whom* refers to the OBJECT of the verb *caught*. That is, it refers to the thief who was caught by the boy.

The rule, then, is:

> Use *who* as the subject of the verb.
> Use *whom* as the object of the verb.

———————————

Complete these sentences correctly by inserting either *who* or *whom*.

(*a*) These bees belong to the lady —— lives next door.

(*b*) The man —— we suspected has been arrested.

(*c*) These are the people —— we admire.

(*d*) The architect —— designed this church died yesterday.

(*e*) She is the only person —— I can recommend.

(*f*) The children —— she had taught were there to say good-bye.

(*g*) I am unable to say —— the culprit is.

(*h*) Is he the juggler —— we saw on television?

16. Who or Whom? (ii) Many people find it hard to decide whether to use *who* or *whom* in sentences such as those below. Here is an easy way of choosing the correct word:

Omit the words in italics, and put *who* in place of the dash. If the sentence makes sense in this form, *who* is the correct word. If not, the word should be *whom*.

> EXAMPLE: Edward is a boy —— *we hope* will do well.

According to the above rule this becomes
> *Edward is a boy who will do well.*

This is a correct and sensible sentence, so *who* is the right word. The complete sentence is therefore
> *Edward is a boy who we hope will do well.*

(a) Choose four boys —— *you know* are reliable.
(b) Choose four boys —— *you know* to be reliable.
(c) The progress prize goes to Yvonne, —— *I believe* to be the most deserving girl in the class.
(d) The progress prize goes to Yvonne, —— *I feel sure* has earned it.
(e) Give the job to a man —— *you can trust* to do it well.
(f) Give the job to a man —— *you are sure* will do it well.
(g) The captain will be Alec, —— *we consider* is well worthy of the position.
(h) The captain will be Alec, —— *we consider* well worthy of the position.

22. VOICE

If the subject of a sentence is the *doer* of the action, the verb is said to be in the *active* voice:

> The Romans *invaded* Britain.

If the subject is the *victim* or the *receiver* of the action, the verb is said to be in the *passive* voice:

> Britain *was invaded* by the Romans.

By choosing carefully which of these two forms we use, we can emphasize certain words or contrast one statement with another. We can even use both forms in one sentence:

> Blake *played* well, but the finest performance *was given* by Collins.

In general, the active voice is more direct and forceful than the passive.

---

1. **Active to passive.** The following sentences are in the active voice. Re-arrange them in the passive voice.

(a) Payton handled the ball.
(b) A passer-by rescued the drowning boy.
(c) Meteorologists study the weather.
(d) The customers will spend more money.
(e) Molly will write an apology.
(f) Landslides can cause serious accidents.

2. The following sentences are in the active voice. Re-arrange them in the passive voice, beginning each sentence with the adverbial phrase or clause that is printed in italics.

> EXAMPLE: Mr. Edwards gave a film show *after tea.*
> ANSWER: After tea a film show was given by Mr. Edwards.

(a) Parsons invented the turbine *in 1884.*
(b) The Prime Minister will unveil the memorial *tomorrow morning.*
(c) The police prosecuted the driver *because he had no licence.*
(d) The audience cheered the professor *at the end of the lecture.*
(e) Mosquitoes torment me *at night.*
(f) His parents will maintain him *until he is eighteen.*

3. **Passive to active.** Change these sentences from the passive voice to the active voice.

> EXAMPLE: The safe was broken open by thieves.
> ANSWER: Thieves broke open the safe.

(a) These trout were caught by Clive's uncle.
(b) Several buildings were damaged by rioters.
(c) Outer space can be reached by rockets.
(d) The wedding photographs will be taken by Mr. Parsons.
(e) The money should be banked immediately by the treasurer.
(f) Gifts are sometimes brought by the natives.

4. **You must.....** A notice saying *You must keep this door closed* would annoy many people because they would feel that they were being given a personal order. One way of avoiding this is to use the passive voice and say *This door must be kept closed.* Although this means *This door must be kept closed by you* we omit the last two words.

Re-arrange the following notices in the passive voice.

(a) You must print these particulars in block capitals.
(b) You must not use this lift without written authority.

(c) You should complete this form and return it to the office.

(d) You may not bring dogs into the store.

(e) You must show your tickets to the inspector on request.

(f) You should leave your umbrella in the cloak-room.

5. They say . . . . . People who complain about public affairs and local government often refer vaguely to the persons in authority as *they*:

They charge us too much for electricity.
They should sweep the streets more often.

It is usually better (unless one says clearly who *they* are) to re-arrange such sentences so that the verbs are used passively:

We are charged too much for electricity.
The streets should be swept more often.

Re-arrange the following sentences in the same way.

(a) They should reduce the price of coal.

(b) They should improve the fire station.

(c) They told us that we should have a new school.

(d) They promised us lower taxation.

(e) They gave us no say in the matter.

(f) When will they build swimming-baths for the children?

📖 LOOK THESE UP

See page 29 for instructions

1. A streamlet is a small stream, and a hillock is a small hill. What name is given to words such as *streamlet* and *hillock*?

What other suffixes are used in this way, besides *-let* and *-ock*? 87 Ex. 11

2. Give the comparative of *crazy* and the superlative of *precious*. 36 **18**

3. Rewrite these sentences, omitting the phrases in parenthesis so as to show that complete sentences still remain.

(a) My father, who is an active man, thinks nothing of walking fifty kilometres.

(b) Send your reply on a postcard (not by letter) to reach us not later than Monday.

(c) I spent the whole of yesterday—not because I liked it—weeding the garden. 72 **36**

23. PHRASES AND CLAUSES

Look at these two sentences:

1. *Walking homewards*, he was caught in a storm.
2. *As he walked homewards* he was caught in a storm.

The words in italics in the first sentence are a *phrase*, and do not make a complete statement.

The words in italics in the second sentence have a subject and a predicate; they contain a short statement that is part of the whole sentence. A group of words of this kind is called a *clause*.

---

1. Say whether the italicized parts of the following sentences are phrases or clauses.

(a) *Not long afterwards*, the messenger returned.

(b) *Throughout the afternoon* the snow fell steadily.

(c) He cannot ride a bicycle, *although he is a good athlete.*

(d) *While she was reading the letter* there was a knock at the door.

(e) The rescue party, *because of the fall of rock*, could go no farther.

(f) We went for a walk *when the rain had stopped.*

(g) *If I can find the tin-opener* we will have these peaches for tea.

(h) *Not to be beaten*, she tried again.

(i) *Before lighting the lamp* you should clean the wick.

(j) This is the lady *who let me use her telephone.*

2. **Noun clause as object.** Look at these two sentences:

1. I know Geoffrey.
2. I know that you will forgive me.

The object of the first sentence is a single word—*Geoffrey.*

The object of the second sentence is a group of words—*that you will forgive me.* Because this group of words is a clause, and because it serves as a noun, it is called a noun clause.

In each of the following sentences the object is a noun clause; pick it out. (You may find it helpful to refer to the rule given on page 26.)

(a) I should like to know why you are angry.

(b) We were told that the train was late.

(c) Paul imagined that he was a cowboy.

(d) I have forgotten what you told me.

(e) Tell me how I can loosen this screw.

3. **Noun clause as subject.** In Exercise 2 you saw that a noun clause can be the object of a sentence. A noun clause can also be the subject:

What is sauce for the goose is sauce for the gander.

Pick out the noun clauses that are the subjects of the sentences below. (You may find it helpful to refer to the rule given on page 8.)

(*a*) What he saw made him tremble with fright.

(*b*) How the accident happened has not yet been discovered.

(*c*) Whatever I suggest meets with disapproval.

(*d*) Why he blushed is best not mentioned.

(*e*) That he will recover completely is very doubtful.

4. **Subject or object?** In each of these sentences pick out the noun clause and say whether it is the subject or the object of the sentence.

(*a*) I wish that I could swim.

(*b*) What she did was very brave.

(*c*) I suddenly remembered what I had been asked to do.

(*d*) Derek wanted to know how he could mend his air-gun.

(*e*) How the lion escaped is not known.

(*f*) Why he said such a stupid thing is a mystery.

5. **Adjectival clauses and phrases.** Look at this pair of sentences:

1. We met a farmer *who had two sheep-dogs*.
2. We met a farmer *with two sheep-dogs*.

In both sentences the groups of words in italics serve as adjectives, telling us more about the farmer. The group of words in the first sentence is an adjectival *clause*. (Think of *who* as *he*.) In the second sentence we have an adjectival *phrase*.

In the following sentences convert the adjectival clauses (in italics) into adjectival phrases that have the same meaning, as in the example above.

(*a*) A boy *who was not wearing shoes* was standing outside the door.

(*b*) I prefer a coat *that has a belt on it*.

(*c*) The guardsman, *who was unbelievably tall*, stooped at the low doorway.

(*d*) The coupons, *which are given free in every packet*, can be exchanged for valuable presents.

(*e*) In the top drawer you will find a tool *with which it is possible to open bottles*.

(*f*) This wine is made from grapes *that have been grown in Germany*.

6. A *pendulum* may be described as *a hanging weight*, but a more helpful description is *a hanging weight that is free to swing*.

Here is the pattern of this kind of definition:

A/An	Adjective	Class or group	Adjectival phrase or clause

Define the following words according to the pattern shown above, and underline any adjectival phrase or clause.

EXAMPLE: **toadstool.** A poisonous fungus shaped like a mushroom.

(*a*) mistletoe

(*b*) porcupine

(*c*) tartan

(*d*) planet

(*e*) orange

(*f*) privet

(*g*) mildew

(*h*) mammoth

7. **Adverbial clauses and phrases.** You have seen how clauses and phrases can serve as adjectives; they can also serve as adverbs:

The ring, *because it is very valuable*, is kept in a safe.

The group of words in italics in the above sentence is an adverbial clause. We could convert it into an adverbial phrase like this:

The ring, *because of its value*, is kept in a safe.

OR The ring, *being valuable*, is kept in a safe.

Do the same thing with the adverbial clauses in the sentences below.

(*a*) He can climb a rope *as a monkey does*.

(*b*) *After we have had lunch* we are going to the circus.

(*c*) We were awake *before the sun had risen*.

(*d*) Meet me *where the two roads cross each other*.

(*e*) No spectators are allowed *while a rehearsal is in progress*.

(*f*) I punished Rover *because he clawed the arm chair*.

8. **Simple, compound, or complex?**

A *simple* sentence has only one subject and one predicate:

My name is Stephen.
I was born in York.

A *compound* sentence consists of two or more simple and independent sentences joined by a conjunction or separated by a punctuation mark:

My name is Stephen, *and* I was born in York.
My name is Stephen; I was born in York.

A *complex* sentence contains one main clause and one or more subordinate clauses:

The boy, *whose name is Stephen*, was born in York.

Say whether the following sentences are simple, compound, or complex.

(a) The shark is a fish, but the whale is a mammal.
(b) Queen Elizabeth II, who came to the throne in 1952, was crowned in the following year.
(c) On the hilltop stood a ruined tower, which was silhouetted against the sky.
(d) Lawrence has gone rock-climbing, and Raymond is touring in Spain.
(e) She rode to Banbury Cross, with rings on her fingers and bells on her toes.
(f) They live in a cottage that stands on the edge of the sand-dunes.
(g) Below us lay the Pacific; we had reached our goal.
(h) Have they gone by car, or did they catch a train?
(i) Kyle, with a pulled muscle, could not hope to win the race.
(j) He kept on baling out the water until the boat was empty.

24. PARTICIPLES

1. The present participle: verb or adjective? Look at these two sentences:

1. The fire was *roaring* fiercely.
2. We sat in front of a *roaring* fire.

The word *roaring* is the present participle of the verb *to roar*, and in the above sentences it has been used in two different ways:

1. As a verb, helped by the auxiliary verb *was*.
2. As an adjective, describing the fire.

Pick out the present participles in the following sentences, and say whether they are used as verbs or as adjectives.

(a) We heard a whistling kettle.
(b) Mother was darning socks.
(c) A dripping tap annoys me.
(d) Dancing children followed the piper.
(e) She is swimming strongly.
(f) Galloping horses came into sight.
(g) Was he flying a kite?
(h) Walking home I met Molly.

2. The present participle is not limited in use to the present tense; it can be used in any of the three tenses. In this exercise you will introduce it into sentences that are in the past tense.

Re-arrange each sentence so that it begins with the present participle of the first verb.

EXAMPLE: He shouted for help as he ran downstairs.
ANSWER: Shouting for help he ran downstairs.

(a) They collected their belongings and went back home.
(b) We looked northwards and saw strange lights in the sky.
(c) He held the child shoulder-high and waded into the flood.
(d) He said that he would be away for some time, and stumbled out of the tent.
(e) He thought he had won, so he stopped running.
(f) I saw that there was no hope of escape, so I gave myself up.

3. Each pair of sentences below can be joined to make a single sentence. Use this method:

1. Put a comma instead of the first full stop.
2. Omit the pronoun (*He*, *She*, etc.) from the beginning of the second sentence.
3. Instead of the past tense (the word in italics) use the present participle.

EXAMPLE: "Drat the things," said Mrs. Squeers. She *opened* the cupboard.
ANSWER: "Drat the things," said Mrs. Squeers, opening the cupboard.

(a) "This is our shop, Nickleby," said Squeers. He *stepped* into the school.
(b) Mrs. Squeers stood at one of the desks. She *presided* over an immense basin of brimstone and treacle.
(c) "I was driven to do it," said Smike faintly. He *cast* another imploring look about him.
(d) "Stop!" cried Nicholas. He *started* up and *stepped* forward.
(e) Squeers fell violently. He *struck* his head against a form in his descent.

4. Each of the following pairs of sentences can be joined to make one sentence. Instead of the past

tense (the word in italics) use the present participle, and make this the first word of the sentence.

EXAMPLE: Oliver *rose* from the table.
He picked up his basin and spoon.
ANSWER: Rising from the table, Oliver picked up his basin and spoon.

Notice that in this example the name *Oliver* is moved to the second half of the sentence in place of the pronoun *he*.

(a) Mr. Bumble *rushed* into the room in great excitement.
He cried, "Oliver Twist has asked for more!"
(b) Oliver *decided* that he would stand it no longer.
He slipped out of the shop and ran away.
(c) Fagin *gave* Oliver a shilling.
He said, "You're a clever boy, my dear."
(d) The Dodger *plunged* his hand into the gentleman's pocket.
He drew out a handkerchief.
(e) Sikes *pointed* to the door with his pistol.
He told Oliver that if he faltered he would shoot him.

5. **The past participle: verb or adjective?** The past participle of a verb may end in **ed** (jumped), **d** (heard), **t** (spoilt), **en** (broken), or **n** (grown). Like the present participle, it may be used either as a verb (helped by an auxiliary verb) or as an adjective:

1. You have *grown* very tall. (*Verb*)
2. He is a *grown* man. (*Adjective*)

———————————————

Pick out the past participles in the following sentences, and say whether they are used as verbs or as adjectives.
(a) Thieves have stolen the money.
(b) Pictures were drawn with charcoal.
(c) Do you like my knitted scarf?
(d) The verandah is full of driven snow.
(e) He has batted well.
(f) She is the only known survivor.
(g) He catches fish with a bent pin.
(h) Fewer eggs have been laid this week.

6. **Auxiliary verbs.** * In each of the following sentences there is an auxiliary verb that is closely associated with a past participle. In some sentences the two

* Pages 172–3 of *A First English Companion* will help you with Exercises 6 and 7.

words are next to each other, but in some they are separated by other words. Pick out the pair of words (auxiliary verb and past participle) in each sentence.

EXAMPLES:
1. These oranges were grown in Spain.
2. Was all the food eaten?

ANSWERS:
1. were grown.
2. was eaten.

(a) We have begun to move.
(b) We are chosen to play for the school.
(c) The Channel was swum twice last week.
(d) I am well known in this district.
(e) Has anyone rung the bell?
(f) Had you forgotten the date?
(g) Were any of your clothes stolen?
(h) Is the lock broken?
(i) Having wakened us, he ran for help.

7. Each of these pairs of sentences can be joined to make one sentence. First of all you must decide on a word to put in place of the dash; you will find that this is the past participle of the clue given in brackets. Use this word as the first word of the combined sentence. Insert commas wherever necessary.

EXAMPLE: Several trees obstructed the road.
They had been —— down by the wind. (*blow*)
ANSWER: Blown down by the wind, several trees obstructed the road.

(a) Chimneys tottered and fell.
They were —— by the earthquake. (*shake*)
(b) The old man trudged on alone.
He had been —— by the tribe. (*forsake*)
(c) The brooch had passed unnoticed for weeks.
It had been —— into the soft turf. (*tread*)
(d) The *Titanic* carried nearly 1500 people to their deaths.
She was —— in a collision with an iceberg. (*sink*)
(e) These shirts will retain their shape.
They have been —— by a special process. (*shrink*)
(f) The lorry was found on Monday in Norwich.
It had been —— from the factory yard on Saturday. (*take*)

(*g*) These tunes are as popular today as ever they were.

They have been —— by generations of children. (*sing*)

See also the exercise on *Past Tense or Past Participle?* on page 108.

8. The unattached participle. Consider this sentence:

Turning the corner, the town hall came into sight.

This actually means that the town hall was turning the corner. To avoid such a ridiculous statement we must say clearly *who* was turning the corner. When a participle is used in this uncertain way it is said to be *unattached, disconnected, unrelated, loose, hanging,* or *dangling.*

———

Say why the following sentences are incorrect, and rewrite them correctly. You are given some help with the first two.

(*a*) Following the instructions, the puzzle was easy.
(Say *who* was following the instructions.)
(*b*) Hobbling on blistered feet, the road seemed endless.
(Say *who* was hobbling.)
(*c*) Bleeding from wounds in their arms, the duel was brought to an end.
(*d*) Climbing up the hillside, the view became more and more extensive.
(*e*) Wrapped in warm clothes, the journey was thoroughly enjoyable.
(*f*) Discouraged by many difficulties, the task appeared hopeless.
(*g*) Hoping for a big prize, the competition gives me a thrill.
(*h*) Requesting you to pay this account immediately, the matter will be put in the hands of our solicitor if there is further delay.

9. The gerund. Most words ending in **ing** are present participles; but some are gerunds, and it is important to know which is which.

A gerund is a noun that is formed by adding **ing** to a verb; it must be treated according to the rules of grammar as a noun:

Did you hear **me** *singing*? (*Present participle*)
I was complimented on **my** *singing*. (*Gerund*)

In the same way, it is correct to say

Excuse **my** interrupting you.
(NOT Excuse **me** interrupting you.)

Choose the correct pronouns in the sentences below.

(*a*) Was there any danger of *his/him* being killed?
(Think of the phrase *being killed* as meaning *death*.)
(*b*) The water leaked away without *us/our* noticing it.
(Think of the phrase *noticing it* as meaning *knowledge*.)
(*c*) Did they give any reason for *their/them* leaving?
(*Leaving=departure*.)
(*d*) Do you mind *my/me* smoking?
(*e*) I am thankful for *you/your* helping me.
(*f*) I cannot understand *them/their* forgetting us.

10. In this exercise some of the words ending in **ing** are gerunds, but others are participles. Choose the correct pronoun for each. Remember to treat gerunds as nouns, and participles as verbs.

(*a*) Father caught *my/me* climbing the apple tree.
(*b*) There is no hope of *us/our* being chosen.
(*c*) I saw *him/his* being helped to his feet.
(*d*) The picture fell without *my/me* touching it.
(*e*) I cannot agree to *you/your* breaking the rules.
(*f*) They watched *our/us* launching the boat.

———

📖 LOOK THESE UP

See page 29 for instructions

1. In the quotations given below there is an example of *euphemism* (129 **111**), an example of a *pun* (129 **112**), and an example of *ambiguity* (109 **81**). Say which is which.

(*a*) Teacher, to boy who has spelt *weather* as *wever*:
"*That's the worst spell of weather we've had for some time.*"
(*b*) Comment in a school report:
His work leaves much to be desired.
(*c*) Extract from a magazine story:
He went to the kitchen and made a beef sandwich. Returning to the lounge he slumped into an arm-chair, threw a leg casually over the arm, and began to munch it.

2. Form abstract nouns from the following words by adding suitable suffixes:

member   kind   man   critic
short   just   vandal   partner

24 **13** and 87 Ex. 9

54

25. THE PARTS OF SPEECH

In previous exercises you have been studying the various parts of speech, one by one. It will be helpful if we now bring them all together and have some practice in recognizing and identifying them.

There are eight parts of speech:

noun. We went by *train* to *London*.
pronoun. *They* gave *it* to *me*.
adjective. There are *dirty* marks on *this* book.
verb. *Tell* me if he *is coming*.
adverb. Salute *smartly*, and walk out.
preposition. Is it *in* the drawer or *on* the table?
conjunction. I hurt my foot *so* I sent for the doctor *and* went to bed.
interjection. *Fire! Help!*

Here is a rhyme that may help you to remember these eight parts of speech.

> Every name is called a NOUN,
> As *field* and *fountain*, *street* and *town*;
>
> In place of noun the PRONOUN stands,
> As *he* and *she* can clap their hands;
>
> The ADJECTIVE describes a thing,
> As *magic* wand or *bridal* ring;
>
> The VERB means action, something done—
> To *read* and *write*, to *jump* and *run*;
>
> How things are done the ADVERBS tell,
> As *quickly*, *slowly*, *badly*, *well*;
>
> The PREPOSITION shows relation,
> As *in* the street or *at* the station;
>
> CONJUNCTIONS join, in many ways,
> Sentences, words, *or* phrase *and* phrase;
>
> The INTERJECTION cries out, "*Hark!*
> I need an exclamation mark."

If necessary, use the index at the end of this book, and refresh your memory from exercises that you have done previously.

NOTE. Some words can be used as more than one part of speech. For instance, *beat* can be a noun as well as a verb, and *then* can be either an adverb or a conjunction. You will find many other examples on page 59.

1. **Homonyms.** Look at these two sentences:

> This is a *grave* matter.
> They laid him in the *grave*.

The words in italics are really two different words. The first one is an adjective, meaning *serious or important*; the second one is a noun, meaning *a burial-place*. The only thing they have in common is that they happen to be spelt and pronounced in the same way. Words of this kind are called *homonyms*. You must be careful, when looking up such words in the dictionary, not to confuse the different meanings.

In the following sentences give the meanings of the words in italics, and say whether each one is an adjective, a noun, or a verb.

EXAMPLE: The Eskimoes belong to a hardy *race*.
ANSWER: A people of one kind and colour (*noun*).

(a) The knights decided to *found* a hospital.
(b) Sire, he lives a good *league* hence.
(c) He was the *sole* survivor.
(d) The native women use poles to *pound* the grain.
(e) The ship was wrecked in Melville *Sound*.
(f) The cabin boy took a *spell* at the wheel.
(g) The noise of the *fray* was heard by the sentry.
(h) A wife should *cleave* to her husband.
(i) An aircraft shows a red light on its *port* side.
(j) The captain decided to *scuttle* the ship.

2. Make a copy of the table below, and fill in all the blank spaces. Use your dictionary, and be sure that each word agrees with the heading at the top, thus: Mr. X is *bold*. He behaves *boldly*. He is noted for his *boldness*.

ADJECTIVE Mr. X is....	ADVERB He behaves....	NOUN He is noted for his...
bold	boldly	boldness
honest	honestly	honesty
modest		
mean		
violent		
wicked		
brave		
stupid		
		anger
		pluck
		efficiency
		wisdom
		prudence
		humility

3. Say what parts of speech these words are, and check your answers by trying the words in the headings of the table in Exercise 2.

1. courage	4. respectfully	7. insolence
2. contentedly	5. sullen	8. cheerfully
3. vulgarity	6. humorous	9. skilful

4. Make a copy of the table below, and fill in all the blank spaces. Use your dictionary, and to be sure that you are using the right parts of speech try each word according to the following guide:

VERBS: *He may* ———.
ADJECTIVES: *This is very* ———.
ADVERBS: *It was done* ———.
NOUNS: *I noticed his (or its)* ———.

VERB	ADJECTIVE	ADVERB	NOUN
economize	economical	economically	economy
agree			
boast			
differ			
amaze			
excite			
	playful		
	pitiful		
	irritable		
	reliable		
	preferable		
		enjoyably	
		satisfactorily	
		admirably	
			hurry
			obedience
			deceit
			doubtfulness
			defiance

☑ MARK THESE YOURSELF

The answers are on page 144

Rewrite these sentences correctly.

(a) He says my left eye is the weakest.
(b) Clive told us a far fetched story.
(c) Pasteur benefitted the whole of mankind.
(d) Gwen is a brunette, but Eric is blonde.
(e) The most hardiest of the crew was Bowers.
(f) Neither of the propellors were damaged.

5. Find a suitable synonym for each of the words in italics in the sentences of (a)–(i) below. Arrange your answers as shown in the example, and say whether the words are nouns, adjectives, or adverbs. Make sure that each synonym can be used in place of the given word in the corresponding sentence.

EXAMPLES: 1. We were received *courteously*.
2. He is a most *courteous* man.
3. He is well known for his *courtesy*.

SUGGESTED 1. courteously = politely (*adverb*)
ANSWERS: 2. courteous = polite (*adjective*)
3. courtesy = politeness (*noun*)

If you are using *A First English Companion*, you will find pages 174–82 helpful.

(a) 1. It was a *magnificent* occasion.
2. We were astonished by its *magnificence*.
3. The ceremony was arranged *magnificently*.

(b) 1. They resisted the enemy *stubbornly*.
2. Their *stubbornness* delayed the enemy.
3. They were *stubborn* in their resistance.

(c) 1. This rod must be measured with great *exactness*.
2. Measure this *exactly*.
3. This measurement must be *exact*.

(d) 1. There is no excuse for his *indolence*.
2. He has been *indolent*.
3. He has spent his time *indolently*.

(e) 1. His *awkwardness* annoys me.
2. Trust him to do it *awkwardly*!
3. He was born *awkward*.

(f) 1. She is old and *feeble*.
2. Her *feebleness* is due to her age.
3. In her old age she walks very *feebly*.

(g) 1. You have behaved very *foolishly*.
2. I am surprised at your *foolishness*.
3. You have been very *foolish*.

(h) 1. Be *careful* with this chisel.
2. Use this chisel *carefully*.
3. Use this chisel with *care*.

(i) 1. Alan was in *danger*.
2. Alan had a *dangerous* adventure.
3. Alan was *dangerously* near death.

6. The passage at the head of the next column is taken from *The Children of the New Forest*. From it, pick out the following parts of speech.

1. Two common nouns in line 16
2. Three verbs in line 17
3. A common noun in line 17
4. Two proper nouns in lines 13–18
5. An adjective in line 4
6. Three verbs in lines 7 and 8
7. An adjective in line 13
8. A collective noun in lines 16–18
9. Two common nouns in line 3
10. A conjunction in lines 7–8
11. Two personal pronouns in line 5
12. A relative pronoun in line 9
13. An adjective in line 18
14. An interjection in lines 1–2
15. Two auxiliary verbs in lines 11 and 12
16. An abstract noun in lines 14–15
17. A personal pronoun in line 15
18. Two common nouns in line 13
19. Four verbs in lines 2 and 3
20. A relative pronoun in line 3
21. Two prepositions in line 8
22. An adverb in line 14
23. A conjunction in lines 10–13
24. A personal pronoun in line 2
25. Two verbs in lines 13 and 14
26. A preposition in line 4
27. Two common nouns in lines 7–8
28. A verb in line 9
29. A relative pronoun in line 11
30. An adverb in line 7
31. Two auxiliary verbs in line 4
32. A conjunction in line 15
33. A personal pronoun in lines 12–13
34. An adjective in line 2
35. Two prepositions in line 13
36. An adverb in line 17
37. An adjective in line 12
38. An adverb in line 11
39. An adverb in line 10
40. A preposition in line 15
41. Two personal pronouns in lines 19 and 20
42. A compound noun in lines 22–26
43. A compound adjective in lines 22–26
44. Two adverbs in lines 25 and 26
45. The present participle of a verb in lines 19–22
46. The past participle of a verb in lines 19–22

"Ah! Humphrey; you have just come in time: I have some provision for Alice's larder. I took my gun and came out on the path which I knew you would return on, and I have killed a young buck. He is good meat, and we are scarce of provisions." (2) (4) (6)

Humphrey gladly helped Edward to put the venison in the cart, and they returned to the cottage, which was not more than three miles off. Humphrey told Edward the result of the journey that he had made, and then proposed that Edward should stop at home for a few days and help him with the new inclosure. To this Edward consented cheerfully and with eagerness, so as soon as they arrived at the cottage and Humphrey had had his breakfast they took their axes and went out to fell trees in a cluster of small spruce about a mile off. (8) (10) (12) (14) (16) (18)

"Now, Humphrey, what do you propose to do?"

"This," replied Humphrey: "I have marked out very nearly three acres of the land running behind the garden. There are no trees on it, and it is good feeding-ground. What I intend to do is to enclose it with the spruce-fir posts and rails that we are now going to cut down." (20) (22) (24)

The following words can be used as more than one part of speech. Say how they are used in the passage above.

47. The word *result* in line 10
48. The word *stop* in line 12
49. The word *time* in line 1
50. The word *good* in line 5
51. The word *journey* in line 11
52. The word *return* in line 4
53. The word *buck* in line 5
54. The word *provision* in line 2
55. The word *spruce* in line 18
56. The word *in* in line 18
57. The word *off* in line 18
58. The word *this* in line 14
59. The word *in* in line 1
60. The word *just* in line 1

7. The dictionary will tell you. You will see that the opposite page is made up of extracts from a dictionary in which it is possible to find the meanings of words when they are used as different parts of speech. A key to the abbreviations is given at the foot of the page.

In each of the seventy-six sentences that are set out below, one word is printed in italics. Refer to this word on the opposite page, and—bearing in mind how the word is used in the given sentence—say which part of speech it is.

If the word in italics is marked by an asterisk, choose from the dictionary definitions a word or phrase that could be substituted for that word.

EXAMPLE: He failed to *calm** the mob.
ANSWER: verb (transitive); pacify

1. Graham has a painful *burn* on his leg.
2. In a *calm* sea, every man is a pilot.
3. Did you *iron* my collars?
4. The pot hung from an *iron* hook.
5. The plains are covered with *dwarf* shrubs.
6. Tall gate-posts would *dwarf* our bungalow.
7. This billiard table must be checked with a *level*.
8. The studio is a large, *light* room.
9. Sheila bought me a *fancy* waistcoat.
10. She bought whatever appealed to her *fancy**.
11. You will not be allowed in without a *pass**.
12. *Pass* the salt, please.
13. Did you *salt* the potatoes?
14. He maketh the *deep** to boil like a pot.
15. *Begone*, dull Care!
16. The boat capsized, but we were able to *right* it.
17. This *foul* deed must not go unpunished.
18. The machine is worked *by* electricity.
19. When the snow lay round about,
    Deep and crisp and even.
20. We *level* the scales by adjusting these screws.
21. Thank you for having me. *Good-bye!*
22. *Hard** words break no bones.
23. Many hybrid flowers have little *smell**
24. You can trust them to give you a *square** deal.
25. She fell backwards in a dead *faint**.
26. *Square* the board before you make the joint.
27. She bade him an affectionate *good-bye*.
28. *All* eyes were on the clock.
29. After a storm comes a *calm**.
30. Is the billiard table *level**?
31. *Faint* not nor fear.
32. Did they give you a *welcome**?
33. I had a mouthful of *salt* water.
34. Have you qualified for the second *round**?
35. Onions make my eyes *water**.
36. Can you *smell* gas?
37. We sat *near* the fire.

38. This lotion should give you *ease*.
39. We were delayed by a traffic-*jam*.
40. It looks like a *kind* of plastic.
41. They are building an *upper* storey.
42. The *vault* was full of sherry-casks.
43. I ran a splint into the *quick*.*
44. The soles are worn, but the *uppers* are sound.
45. Give John a *taste** of your ginger wine.
46. *Vault* over the fence if you can.
47. A little oil should *ease** this nut.
48. Are we *nearing** the coast yet?
49. The brake is *jammed*.*
50. Mother sends her *kind** wishes.
51. Come *quick*!
52. She dresses with excellent *taste*.*
53. We shall take a *fast* train to Brighton.
54. All they could do was to watch the house *burn*.
55. Ought I to *water* these cacti?
56. Did they *welcome* you?
57. The oil-well blazed up a month ago, and the fire is burning *yet**.
58. We had better make a *move* before long.
59. If you try *hard** you can do it.
60. *Some* said that the earth was flat.
61. Here you are at last; *welcome*!
62. He annoys me, *yet* I like him.
63. *All* is lost.
64. What should *one* do if a child's clothes catch fire?
65. You must not *move** while the photograph is being taken.
66. *Some* people prefer brown bread.
67. Does the milk *smell* sour?
68. We could not get the fire to *light*.
69. A rescue team is standing *by*.
70. No-one could *pass* in either direction.
71. I sheltered *while** it was raining.
72. The boat was stuck *fast**.
73. If I remember *right**, his name is Quayle.
74. We looked around the shops for a *while**.
75. Wait until he turns *round*.
76. Make sure that your mooring-rope does not *foul* the propeller.

all, *a.* the whole amount of; every one of. *n.* everyone; the whole. *adv.* wholly; entirely.

begone, *int.* away with you!

burn, *v.i.* to be consumed by fire. *v.t.* to consume or scorch something by heat. *n.* a sore or mark made by burning.

by, *adv.* near; at hand. *prep.* near to; beside; through the action of.

calm, *a.* still; quiet; windless. *v.i.* to become still and quiet. *v.t.* to pacify. *n.* stillness; quietness.

deep, *a.* going far down from the top. *n.* the sea. *adv.* far down or far in.

dwarf, *n.* a person or thing much smaller than is usual. *a.* undersized; stunted. *v.t.* to make something look small by comparison.

ease, *n.* freedom from pain or difficulty; rest. *v.t.* to relieve someone of pain; to slacken something. *v.i.* to become less painful or difficult.

faint, *a.* weak; dim; pale. *v.i.* to swoon and become unconscious. *n.* a swoon.

fancy, *n.* imagination. *a.* ornamental. *v.t.* to imagine; to desire.

fast, *a.* firmly fixed; moving quickly. *adv.* firmly; quickly.

foul, *a.* dirty; filthy; loathsome. *n.* an unfair action in a game. *v.i.* to become entangled. *v.t.* to block, soil, or collide with something.

good-bye, *int. & n.* farewell.

hard, *a.* firm and solid; difficult; harsh. *adv.* strenuously; with difficulty.

iron, *n.* a strong, hard metal. *a.* made of iron. *v.t.* to smooth with an iron.

jam, *v.t.* to squeeze things together. *v.i.* to become wedged. *n.* fruit boiled with sugar; a crowded mass.

kind, *n.* a sort or class. *a.* gentle and friendly.

level, *n.* a flat and even surface; an instrument to show whether something is horizontal; height. *a.* horizontal. *v.t.* to make something even or horizontal.

light, *n.* the brightness from the sun or from a lamp. *a.* having plenty of light; pale-coloured. *v.t.* to set burning. *v.i.* to begin to burn.

move, *v.t.* to change the position of something. *v.i.* to pass from one place to another; to change position. *n.* a change in place or position; an action.

near, *adv.* within easy reach. *prep.* close to. *a.* close; closely related. *v.t.* to approach something.

one, *a.* single; only. *n.* the number or figure 1. *pron.* some person who is not specified or named.

pass, *v.t.* to hand something on. *v.i.* to move onward; to proceed. *n.* a narrow passage through the mountains; a ticket of admission.

quick, *a.* rapid; lively. *n.* sensitive flesh below the nails or skin. *adv.* quickly.

right, *a.* correct; true; on the side opposite to the heart. *v.t.* to restore to the proper position. *n.* something to which one is entitled. *adv.* correctly.

round, *a.* shaped like a ball or ring. *n.* a kind of part-song; one cartridge, etc. for a gun; one stage in a competition. *adv.* with circular motion. *prep.* so as to encircle or enclose. *v.t.* to give a round shape to. *v.i.* to make a turn.

salt, *n.* a white mineral used for seasoning food, etc. *a.* containing or tasting of salt. *v.t.* to preserve or season with salt.

smell, *n.* a perfume or odour that can be detected by the nose. *v.i.* to give off an odour. *v.t.* to detect an odour with the nose.

some, *a.* a certain amount or number of. *pron.* some people.

square, *a.* having four equal sides and four right angles; right and honest. *n.* a square figure or space. *adv.* squarely. *v.t.* to give rectangular edges to something.

taste, *v.t.* to experience the flavour of something. *v.i.* to have a flavour. *n.* the sense that distinguishes flavours; a small portion; a good judgement of style and beauty.

upper, *a.* higher. *n.* the upper part of a boot or shoe.

vault, *n.* an arched roof; a cellar. *v.i.* to spring over an obstacle with one's hands resting on it.

water, *n.* the liquid that forms rain, rivers, etc. *v.t.* to give water to something. *v.i.* to run with water.

welcome, *int.* your arrival gives pleasure. *a.* gladly received. *n.* a glad reception. *v.t.* to greet someone with pleasure.

while, *n.* a space of time. *v.t.* to pass the time away. *conj.* during the time that; at the same time as.

yet, *adv.* still; even now. *conj.* but at the same time.

KEY TO THE ABBREVIATIONS USED IN THE ABOVE DICTIONARY DEFINITIONS

a. adjective. *adv.* adverb. *conj.* conjunction. *int.* interjection. *n.* noun.
prep. preposition. *pron.* pronoun. *v.i.* verb (intransitive). *v.t.* verb (transitive).

★ REVISION

1. Complete this invitation in the third person:

   Mr. John Holt thanks Miss K. Shaw for inviting —— to —— birthday party, but regrets that owing to the serious illness of —— parents —— will be unable to be present.

2. Rewrite these notices in the passive voice:
   (a) You must write these particulars in ink.
   (b) You may not park your car here.
   (c) You should leave this column blank.

3. In each of these sentences, make the verb agree with the subject.
   (a) Each of them *were/was* interviewed.
   (b) Beneath these waters *lies/lie* a galleon.
   (c) Neither Tom nor Pat *are/is* related to me.
   (d) Either of these needles *is/are* suitable.
   (e) Joy, as well as Sally, *is/are* coming.

4. Correct these sentences:
   (a) Enjoying the fine weather, Brighton was crowded with visitors.
   (b) Flying at a height of ten thousand metres, the sky was blue and cloudless.

5. Insert *who* or *whom* in these sentences:
   (a) Pick someone —— you know to be honest.
   (b) This year we have a team of athletes —— we hope will break many records.

6. The remaining questions refer to the extract from *Travels with a Donkey* on page 14.
   (a) Find one adverb in line 35 and another in line 2.
   (b) In lines 28–33, find three compound words used as a noun, an adjective, and an adverb respectively.
   (c) Find one preposition in each of the following lines:
       (i) line 24   (ii) line 1   (iii) line 6
   (d) In lines 13–15, Stevenson (for a good reason) uses a plural verb with a singular noun. Pick out this pair of words, in the order in which they appear.
   (e) *A pronoun stands instead of a noun.*
       Illustrate this definition by reference to lines 1–2.

✅ MARK THESE YOURSELF: Errors in Composition
The answers are on page 144

IMAGINE that this is part of a composition written by a boy or girl sitting near you and that you have been asked to look through it and point out any mistakes.

   Make a list of all the errors you can find, indicating the lines on which they occur.   Do not mark this book in any way.

1 We loved Fritzi and Popov, the clowns. Popov was the funniest he kept
2 us all laughing with his humourous antics. After the Arizonas had given an
3 equestrian display on horseback we saw a sea lion that balanced a ball
4 skillfully on it's nose, and a chimpanzee on a trapeze that clapped after every
5 trick. We were alarmed when the chimpanzee came towards us. But only for a
6 moment. It was really a man, and neither of us were afraid when he shook hands
7 with us. He did'nt seem to mind me giving him a playful slap on the head with

26. BEGINNING AND ENDING A SENTENCE

1. *In your ordinary handwriting*, write out the following passage in four separate sentences, beginning each one with a capital letter and ending each one with a full stop.

GORILLAS LIVE IN THE TROPICAL FORESTS THEY CLIMB TREES IN SEARCH OF FOOD WHEN THEY ARE ANGRY THEY BEAT THEIR BREASTS A SINGLE BLOW FROM A GORILLA'S PAW CAN KILL A MAN

2. In this exercise do as you did in Exercise 1. There are five separate sentences.

THE JACKDAW IS VERY LIKE THE ROOK IT IS SOMETIMES KEPT AS A PET WITH PATIENCE IT CAN BE TAUGHT TO SPEAK JACKDAWS ARE MISCHIEVOUS BIRDS THEY CARRY OFF AND HIDE ANY SMALL GLITTERING OBJECT

3. This exercise is similar to the two previous ones. A Finnish peasant, who writes English very simply and in short sentences, is telling his life story.

I WAS BORN IN A LAND OF ICE AND SNOW I HAD SIX BROTHERS AND TWO SISTERS MY FATHER WORKED IN THE FOREST I DO NOT REMEMBER MY MOTHER WE WERE VERY POOR THE WINTERS WERE ALWAYS BITTERLY COLD SOMETIMES WE HAD NOTHING TO EAT THEN THE LITTLE ONES CRIED WE CROUCHED TOGETHER FOR WARMTH OUTSIDE THE WOLVES WERE HOWLING IT WAS A HARD AND SAD CHILDHOOD

27. CAPITAL LETTERS FOR PROPER NOUNS*

1. Rewrite these sentences in your ordinary handwriting, using capital letters for proper nouns and wherever else they are necessary.

(*a*) THE LARGEST COUNTY IN ENGLAND IS YORKSHIRE.
(*b*) YESTERDAY WE MET JOYCE WEBB'S UNCLE IN BRIGHTON.
(*c*) LAST TUESDAY I WENT TO WINDSOR.
(*d*) MY FRIEND ALEC LIVES IN MILL STREET.
(*e*) I SPENT EASTER IN EXETER WITH MY BROTHER JOHN AND HIS WIFE.
(*f*) THE POPE SENT A MESSAGE TO ROMAN CATHOLICS THROUGHOUT THE WORLD.

* For other work on proper nouns see pages 4–5.

(g) IF WOLVERHAMPTON WANDERERS BEAT MANCHESTER UNITED THEY WILL MEET WEST BROMWICH ALBION AT WEMBLEY.

(h) THE BIGGEST SCHOOL IN THE TOWN IS QUEEN MARY'S SCHOOL.

2. Write out these titles and names in your ordinary handwriting, using capital letters in the proper places.

(a) GREATER LONDON COUNCIL
(b) CHURCH OF ENGLAND
(c) LORD MAYOR OF LONDON
(d) EDWARD THE CONFESSOR
(e) UNITED STATES OF AMERICA
(f) VICTORIA CROSS
(g) VICTORIA AND ALBERT MUSEUM
(h) JUSTICE OF THE PEACE
(i) HER ROYAL HIGHNESS THE DUCHESS OF KENT
(j) THE ROYAL SOCIETY FOR THE PREVENTION OF CRUELTY TO ANIMALS

3. Write out these book titles in your ordinary handwriting, putting in the right capital letters.

(a) ALICE'S ADVENTURES IN WONDERLAND
(b) THE ADVENTURES OF DON QUIXOTE
(c) UNDER THE GREENWOOD TREE
(d) A TALE OF TWO CITIES
(e) THE CLOISTER AND THE HEARTH
(f) THREE MEN IN A BOAT
(g) ROUND THE WORLD IN EIGHTY DAYS

4. Write out this passage in your ordinary handwriting, inserting capital letters where necessary.

MR. THIRLBY'S HOME IS NOW IN AMERICA, AND HE HAS BROUGHT HIS FAMILY OVER TO SEE BRITAIN. AFTER A WEEK IN LONDON THEY WENT TO OXFORD TO VISIT MR. THIRLBY'S OLD COLLEGE (CHRIST CHURCH); THEY THEN MADE FOR STRATFORD-ON-AVON, WHERE ADRIAN HEALEY AND FRANCES HARMAN ARE APPEARING IN "ROMEO AND JULIET." FROM STRATFORD THEY MOVED ON TO NORTH WALES (MR. THIRLBY HAS A BROTHER AT CAERNARVON), AND THEY SPENT A FEW DAYS IN SNOWDONIA. SINCE THURSDAY THEY HAVE BEEN IN THE LAKE DISTRICT, AND I UNDERSTAND THAT DURING THE LAST WEEK OF AUGUST THEY INTEND TO VISIT THE EDINBURGH FESTIVAL.

28. CAPITAL LETTERS IN POETRY

In your ordinary handwriting, arrange each of the following exercises as a rhymed verse of four lines. Use capital letters wherever necessary.

---

1. IT WAS THE TIME WHEN LILIES BLOW, AND CLOUDS ARE HIGHEST UP IN AIR, LORD RONALD BROUGHT A LILY-WHITE DOE TO GIVE HIS COUSIN, LADY CLARE.

2. IT WAS UPON AN APRIL MORN, WHILE YET THE FROST LAY HOAR, WE HEARD LORD JAMES'S BUGLE-HORN SOUND BY THE ROCKY SHORE.

3. TO YOU IN DAVID'S TOWN THIS DAY IS BORN OF DAVID'S LINE A SAVIOUR, WHO IS CHRIST THE LORD; AND THIS SHALL BE THE SIGN.

See also Exercise 6 on page 135.

29. ABBREVIATIONS*

In these exercises remember that whenever a word is shortened to an abbreviation, that abbreviation must be followed by a full stop.

---

1. What do these abbreviations mean?

A.A.	P.T.O.	R.N.	F.H.
R.A.C.	B.A.	C.I.D.	G.M.T.
Q.C.	Y.M.C.A.		

2. Arrange these abbreviations in five columns (headed *Ranks, Medals, Sport, Councils, Countries*) according to whether they are concerned with military ranks, medals awarded for bravery, sport, councils, or countries, etc.

G.M.	G.C.	Gen.	F.A.	N.C.O.
G.L.C.	N.Z.	M.C.C.	V.C.	D.S.C.
Col.	U.K.	c. & b.	U.D.C.	M.C.
R.D.C.	N.S.W.	Lieut.	l.b.w.	Maj.

* Helpful lists of abbreviations may be found in various reference books. The list in *A First Dictionary* is on pages 187–8.

3. Find the correct abbreviations for the following:

Headquarters	Bachelor of Science
anonymous	Honorary Secretary
Commander	centimetre
per hundred	manuscript
Doctor of Medicine	Monsieur

4. Say what abbreviations you would use when addressing letters to towns in the following counties:

Somersetshire	Cambridgeshire
Northamptonshire	Bedfordshire
Oxfordshire	Hampshire
Shropshire	Monmouthshire
Glamorganshire	Hertfordshire

Page 186 of *A First English Companion* will help.

5. These abbreviations are sometimes used by men who sign their names in a hurry. Can you say what their names are in full?

Thos.   Chas.   Geo.   Wm.   Hy.
Fdk.   Jas.   Jos.   Jno.

6. Give the abbreviations for the following titles. It is unlikely that you will be able to find all of them in any book that you have in your desk, but they follow the usual rules.

Amateur Athletic Association
British Summer Time
Blessed Virgin Mary
Very Important Person
Master of Fox Hounds
Navy, Army, and Air Force Institutes
Fellow of the Royal Institute of British Architects
Member of the Royal College of Veterinary Surgeons
National Society for the Prevention of Cruelty to Children

7. Copy this list of names, with an equals-sign after each one:

The Rev. B. Matthews =
Edward Hollis, D.F.C. =
W. A. Dennis (Hon. Treas.) =
Nigel Watson, M.D. =
Bradbury of the C.I.D. =
Mlle Temple =
James Ross Snr. =
Maj. D. C. Rogers =
L. Thornton, M.A.(Cantab.) =
Sir Charles Roberts, Q.C. =

Now read the list below, in which the persons whose names you have copied are described—but in a different order. Decide how they should be paired off, and letter your list accordingly. The answer to the first one is

The Rev. B. Matthews = D

A is an Army officer.
B is in charge of money.
C attends to your aches and pains.
D is a clergyman.
E is unmarried and lives in France.
F is a barrister.
G has a son of the same name.
H is a detective.
I has been decorated for gallantry in the air.
J obtained an Arts degree at Cambridge.

8. These are much-used abbreviations of certain Latin and French words. Say what they mean *in English*.

A.D.	Messrs.	N.B.
a.m.	p.m.	v.
i.e.	e.g.	R.S.V.P.

9. Say which books of the Bible are indicated by these abbreviations. The introductory pages of a Bible should help you.

(*a*) Cor.	(*g*) Matt.
(*b*) Eph.	(*h*) Phil.
(*c*) Exod.	(*i*) Prov.
(*d*) Gal.	(*j*) Ps.
(*e*) Gen.	(*k*) Rev.
(*f*) Isa.	(*l*) Rom.

30. QUESTION-MARKS

1. Answer these questions by re-arranging the words so as to form statements.

EXAMPLE: Is Sicily an island?
ANSWER: Sicily is an island.

(*a*) Must vehicles stop at a *Give Way* sign?
(*b*) Can ostriches run quickly?
(*c*) Was Victoria a famous queen?
(*d*) Were the Vikings great sailors?
(*e*) Have many expeditions been to the Antarctic?

2. Re-arrange these statements so that they become questions.

> EXAMPLE: Salmon are able to leap over waterfalls.
> ANSWER: Are salmon able to leap over waterfalls?

(a) The middle of the earth is still molten.
(b) A chameleon can change colour.
(c) The mammoth was a long-tusked elephant.
(d) These coral reefs were made by tiny animals.
(e) Fossils of shell-fish are found in rock.

There are extra alterations to make in the next two sentences.

(f) The worker bees kill the drones at the end of the summer.
(g) Great tree-ferns grew in the swamps.

3. Say whether question-marks are needed or not after these sentences. Answer *Yes* or *No* for each one.

(a) Why did you leave early.
(b) Tell me how you did this.
(c) I wonder what Mother will say.
(d) Would you like to stay to tea.
(e) How did you break your arm.
(f) She asked me where the exhibition was.
(g) Guess who arrived last night.
(h) Whatever is the matter.

4. Write out these sentences, inserting question-marks or full stops as required.

(a) When do we break up
(b) I wonder how that trick is done
(c) Where is the salt
(d) Can Olive swim
(e) Tell me if this is wrong
(f) I want to know whose catapult this is
(g) Would you mind making less noise
(h) Say why you asked that question

5. Each of these unpunctuated sentences is in the form of either a direct question or an indirect question; say which, answering *Direct* or *Indirect* for each one.

(a) Will you help me with this arithmetic
(b) Please tell me how you made these cakes
(c) I want to know why your coat is torn
(d) Would Father be annoyed if I woke him

(e) Say how many metres there are in a kilometre
(f) To which school do you go
(g) I am asking all of you if you will subscribe a pound each
(h) Telephone me when you know what is the reason for the delay

31. COMMAS

1. Each of the following statements is either a single sentence containing a comma, or two short sentences separated by a full stop. The caret ($\wedge$) tells you where the comma or full stop should be. Decide whether a comma or a full stop is the right punctuation, and write out the sentences in your ordinary handwriting.

(a) THE ELM IS ONE OF OUR TALLEST TREES$\wedge$ IT HAS A THICK AND RUGGED TRUNK.
(b) POPLARS GROW VERY QUICKLY$\wedge$ THEIR WOOD IS NEITHER STRONG NOR DURABLE.
(c) YOU CAN EASILY RECOGNIZE THE BEECH$\wedge$ FOR ITS BARK IS LIKE SMOOTH OLIVE-GREY METAL.
(d) BECAUSE WALNUT TAKES A FINE POLISH AND DOES NOT SPLIT$\wedge$ HIGH-CLASS FURNITURE IS MADE FROM IT.
(e) OAK TREES ARE SLOW IN GROWTH$\wedge$ THEY LIVE TO A VERY GREAT AGE.
(f) THE YEW WAS ONCE A VERY IMPORTANT TREE$\wedge$ ITS WOOD BEING USED FOR MAKING LONG-BOWS.
(g) NOT EASILY HARMED BY SMOKE AND FUMES$\wedge$ THE PLANE TREE THRIVES IN LARGE CITIES.

2. Each of these sentences contains a list or series. Use commas to mark off the separate items.

(a) In my garden I have marigolds candytuft larkspur and cornflowers.
(b) The five largest cities in Britain are London Birmingham Glasgow Liverpool and Manchester.
(c) Tennis cricket and swimming are my main pastimes in the summer.
(d) In his pocket he had three marbles a piece of string a French coin a broken penknife two boiled sweets and a conker.
(e) Five gold rings four calling birds three French hens two turtle doves and a partridge in a pear tree.
(f) We had fish and chips bread and butter and a pot of tea.

"*You have not left enough space between Coach and and and and and Horses.*"

3. Punctuate the inn-keeper's complaint to the sign-writer so that it makes sense.

4. Punctuate these instructions by putting in commas where you think they are needed.

(*a*) Melt the butter in a saucepan stir in the flour add the fish stock and stir until it thickens.

(*b*) Check the settings of the camera make sure that your subject is correctly arranged in the view-finder hold your breath and gently press the shutter-release.

(*c*) Wash cut-glass vases in warm soapy water rinse well dry with an old linen cloth and polish with soft tissue-paper.

(*d*) Add the hot water to the dye bring it to boiling-point plunge the wet curtain into the dye-bath and stir continually with a wooden rod.

(*e*) Fill the cracks with plaster of Paris rub down with fine sandpaper apply a coat of thin size allow to dry rub down again and then apply the first coat of paint.

5. Each of these sentences contains a phrase that needs to be marked off with commas. Follow the pattern of the example.

EXAMPLE: Rome the capital of Italy is a beautiful city.

ANSWER: Rome, the capital of Italy, is a beautiful city.

If you wish to know more about this particular construction, look up **apposition** in *A First English Companion*.

(*a*) Sir Humphry Davy the inventor of the safety-lamp died in 1829.

(*b*) Schubert one of Germany's finest composers wrote many beautiful melodies.

(*c*) John Bunyan a travelling tinker wrote *Pilgrim's Progress* in prison.

(*d*) The South Pole a featureless spot in a wilderness of ice and snow was first reached by Amundsen.

(*e*) The first English printer William Caxton was not actually the inventor of printing.

6. Each of these sentences begins with an introductory word or phrase that needs to be marked off with a comma. Follow the pattern of the example.

EXAMPLE: Nevertheless the regatta was completed with only one cancellation.

ANSWER: Nevertheless, the regatta was completed with only one cancellation.

(*a*) However at long last we reached the top of the hill.

(*b*) Indeed there was enough food left for another good meal.

(*c*) In fact I was too warm.

(*d*) For instance we could do a charade.

(*e*) By the way Rebel is my new pony.

(*f*) On the other hand it may be that the letter never reached him.

7. The example given in Exercise 6 could have been re-arranged like this, with the word *nevertheless* between two commas.

The regatta, nevertheless, was completed with only one cancellation.

Re-arrange the other sentences in Exercise 6 in the same way.

8. You will see that each of the following sentences begins with a form of address, followed by a comma (e.g., *Ladies and gentlemen, . . .*). Re-arrange each sentence in two ways: (i) with the form of address in the middle, between two commas; (ii) with the form of address at the end, after a comma.

> EXAMPLE: Betty, come in and have your supper.
> ANSWERS: (i) Come in, Betty, and have your supper.
> (ii) Come in and have your supper, Betty.

(a) Peter, wash your hands and do your homework.
(b) Sir, I assure you that I am telling the truth.
(c) Mother, I have been wondering if you would like a brooch for Christmas.
(d) Ladies and gentlemen, I intend to be as brief as I can.
(e) My dear boy, if you really want to play the piano you must practise.

9. Here are five pairs of sentences. In each pair both sentences have the same words, but the punctuation is different. Answer the question in italics about each of the pairs.

(a) (i) Girls who are fond of knitting will enjoy making this jumper.
 (ii) Girls, who are fond of knitting, will enjoy making this jumper.

Which of the above sentences means that all girls like knitting? What does the other mean?

(b) (i) Men who like the open air often take up golf.
 (ii) Men, who like the open air, often take up golf.

Which of the above sentences means that golf is suitable for those men who like the open air? What does the other mean?

(c) (i) Donald thinks Paul is stupid.
 (ii) Donald, thinks Paul, is stupid.

Who is it, in each of the above sentences, that is thought to be stupid?

(d) (i) The man with a walking-stick showed us the way to go.
 (ii) The man, with a walking-stick, showed us the way to go.

Which sentence means that the man used his stick as a pointer? What does the other mean?

(e) (i) I have just had my first flight in a glider.
 (ii) I have just had my first flight, in a glider.

Which sentence means that I had never flown at all before I had this flight in a glider? What does the other mean?

The use of commas is also dealt with in the exercises on Direct Speech (page 69), Relative Pronouns (page 44), and Parenthesis (page 72).

32. THE APOSTROPHE

1. The following words, all of which make use of the apostrophe, are known as contractions. Say what they mean in full.

hasn't	we've	we'll	can't
o'clock	tho'	o'er	e'er
ne'er	e'en	'tis	'twas
Hallowe'en	didn't		

2. Making use of apostrophes, write these pairs of words as contractions.

I am	I have	I would	I shall
could not	you have	he will	you are
there is	it is	who is	who has
	where is	were not	

3. In *Tom Brown's Schooldays* we meet the guard of a stage coach. He uses expressions such as those given below. Say in full what he means.

(a) Lor' bless you.
(b) All 'long the road.
(c) Reg'lar roughs.
(d) Just as 'twas gettin' serious.
(e) What do they do wi' 'em?
(f) You'd ha' laughed to see 'em.
(g) He's a 'mazin' fine runner.

4. Re-arrange these phrases, using in each one an apostrophe to show possession.*

* To decide where to put the apostrophe, ask yourself *Who is the owner?* or *Who are the owners?* When you have found the answer, put the apostrophe immediately after it.

> EXAMPLE: The saw belonging to the carpenter.
> ANSWER: The carpenter's saw.

(a) The shop belonging to the grocer.
(b) The shops belonging to the grocers.
(c) The fields belonging to the farmer.

(d) The fields belonging to the farmers.
(e) The tail belonging to the pony.
(f) The tails belonging to the ponies.
(g) The broom belonging to the witch.
(h) The brooms belonging to the witches.

5. If we write about *the cook's apron* we are referring to *the apron belonging to the cook*, or *the apron of the cook*. Explain in the same way the meanings of the following phrases.

(a) The doctor's surgery
(b) The miners' lamps
(c) The flies' wings
(d) The pygmy's weapons
(e) The princess's parents
(f) The princesses' father
(g) The wasps' nest.
(h) The ladies' committee.

6. Show how you would express each of the following if you had to print a title of only *two words* to be displayed on a door or notice-board.

EXAMPLE: The office belonging to the manager.
ANSWER: MANAGER'S OFFICE

(a) A library for children.
(b) A school for boys.
(c) A parlour provided for the Mayor.
(d) A hospital ward reserved for women.
(e) An outfitter who stocks clothes for men.
(f) A hairdresser for ladies.
(g) An entrance for girls.
(h) Stores kept by a tradesman named Jones.
(i) A corner for pets.
(j) A canteen provided for employees.

7. These names have been taken from the index of a London guide-book, but the apostrophes have been omitted. Write them correctly.

Cleopatras Needle
Queen Annes Gate
Poets Corner
St. Martins in the Fields
Boy Scouts Headquarters
Peoples Palace
All Souls Church
St. Jamess Palace

8. Print these newspaper headlines in capital letters, inserting apostrophes wherever necessary. At least one of the headlines needs no apostrophe at all.

LORRYS BRAKES FAIL ON HILL
TODAYS SOCCER RESULTS
FIRE DESTROYS NURSES HOSTEL
NEWS FROM ALL QUARTERS
SHIPS CREW ADRIFT IN BOATS
CABINET MINISTERS AT ST. PAULS
NEW ROUTES FOR LONDON BUSES
PENSIONS FOR SOLDIERS WIDOWS
TWO MONTHS RAIN IN THREE WEEKS
ART GALLERIES FINANCIAL DIFFICULTIES

✓ MARK THESE YOURSELF

The answers are on pages 144–5

1. Write out the names of these radio programmes, inserting apostrophes wherever necessary.

(a) Womans Hour
(b) Sports Report
(c) You and Yours
(d) Whats On?
(e) Gardeners Question Time
(f) The Weeks Good Cause
(g) Songs from the Shows
(h) Bachs Organ Works

2. Some of the following could not possibly be correct. Pick out those that could.

(a) ladys' hats
(b) babies' prams
(c) fairie's wing
(d) mices' tails
(e) gentlemen's outfitter
(f) housewive's meeting
(g) heroe's memorial
(h) buses' radiators

3. Correct the punctuation of these sentences:
(a) Mr. Hughes the Director of Education spoke to us.
(b) Breakfast finished mother washed up.
(c) Stephen replied, "That he would be as quick as possible."
(d) "If you look in the drawer," he said, "You will find a pair of scissors.
(e) I asked him why he would'nt let me in?
(f) He took his B.S.c. at Birmingham.

4. Put *to, too* or *two* in place of each dash:
These —— apples are —— small —— bake and —— sour —— eat.

5. Re-arrange the letters of a four-letter word meaning *a slight suggestion or sign* so as to form a word meaning *not thick or fat*.

33. QUOTATION-MARKS

1. Write out these sentences in your usual handwriting; insert quotation-marks, punctuation, and capital letters in the proper places.

In all these sentences the spoken words occur at the end.

(*a*) SHE LOOKED AT HIM AND SAID YOU BROKE MY WINDOW

(*b*) FATHER OFTEN SAYS MAKE HAY WHILE THE SUN SHINES

(*c*) SHE PAUSED FOR A FEW MOMENTS AND THEN ADDED PLEASE FORGIVE ME

(*d*) I ASKED HIM IF HE WAS ANGRY AND HE ANSWERED NOT REALLY.

(*e*) LESLIE REPLIED I THINK YOUVE MADE A MISTAKE

(*f*) I SAID IS THERE A THEATRE IN THIS TOWN

2. Follow the instructions given in Exercise 1.

In all these sentences the spoken words occur at the beginning.

(*a*) TODAY IS MY BIRTHDAY SHE SAID

(*b*) I BOUGHT THIS IN VENICE SAID KEITH

(*c*) THIS WAY PLEASE SAID ONE OF THE NURSES

(*d*) THIS IS A NEW TYPE OF ENGINE HE TOLD ME

(*e*) ARE YOU BEING ATTENDED TO ASKED THE ASSISTANT

(*f*) PERHAPS MOTHER SAID WHEN I ASKED HER IF WE WERE GOING TO THE SEASIDE

3. Follow the instructions given in Exercise 1.

In all these sentences the spoken words are interrupted.

(*a*) MY LADS SAID CAPTAIN SMOLLETT IVE A WORD TO SAY TO YOU

(*b*) WELL SQUIRE SAID DR LIVESEY I DONT PUT MUCH FAITH IN YOUR DISCOVERIES

(*c*) TOSS OUT THE FIRE SAID THE CAPTAIN FOR WE MUSTNT HAVE SMOKE IN OUR EYES

(*d*) IF I SEE ANYONE SAID JOYCE AM I TO FIRE

(*e*) ONE MORE STEP MR HANDS SAID I AND ILL BLOW YOUR BRAINS OUT.

(*f*) JOHN SILVER HE SAID YOURE A PRODIGIOUS VILLAIN AND IMPOSTOR

4. In your ordinary handwriting write out each of the following in *three* sentences. Insert quotation-marks, punctuation, and capital letters wherever necessary.

EXAMPLE: USE A BRADAWL SUGGESTED MY FATHER THE NAILS ARE TOO BIG YOU WILL SPLIT THE WOOD

ANSWER: "Use a bradawl," suggested my father. "The nails are too big. You will split the wood."

(*a*) THIS IS MY HOME SAID THE PEASANT I LIVE HERE ALONE YOU MUST NOT EXPECT TO FIND MUCH COMFORT

(*b*) I WAS NOT ASLEEP REPLIED THE CHILD THE THUNDER HAS KEPT ME AWAKE PLEASE COME AND TALK TO ME

(*c*) YOU SURPRISE ME HE ANSWERED I WAS TALKING TO HIM ONLY YESTERDAY IS HE BADLY HURT

(*d*) ARE YOU ANGRY SHE ASKED HAVE I OFFENDED YOU I DID NOT MEAN TO HURT YOUR FEELINGS

5. Insert quotation-marks in the following sentences wherever they are needed to indicate quotations, nicknames, slang, titles of books, etc.

(*a*) The Invisible Man was written by H. G. Wells.

(*b*) Curly Stevens is a most amusing person.

(*c*) I am never sure of how to spell immediately.

(*d*) He said that the cops were looking for him.

(*e*) Corrections is all you need write at the top of the page.

(*f*) John Fearn recited John Gilpin.

(*g*) The description used on the application form is disabled persons.

(*h*) The word before going should be and.

6. In each of these sentences we are told that something was said. What words were actually spoken?

EXAMPLE: Father told me that it was time I was in bed.

SUGGESTED ANSWER: "It's time you were in bed."

(*a*) Helen asked me how old I was.

(*b*) She said that if I broke anything I should have to pay for it.

(*c*) Jim wanted to know if I felt hungry.

(*d*) Frank looked at his map and said he thought he knew where we were.

(*e*) The girl at the cash desk told Mother that she must pay full price for me.

7. *Direct speech* means the words that were actually spoken. *Indirect speech* is what we are told when someone is reporting or talking about what was said.

The following sentences give the words that were actually spoken—that is, the direct speech. Rewrite each of them in indirect speech.

EXAMPLE: John said, "I am hungry."
ANSWER: John said that he was hungry.

(a) Molly said, "I have finished my examinations."
(b) Trevor said, "The fire has gone out."

Begin the next sentence (c) with the words *The policeman told my uncle that* . . .

(c) The policeman said to my uncle, "You are not allowed to park your car here."
(d) Uncle John said to me, "When I was your age I had a pony of my own."
(e) I said to the conductor, "Does this bus go to Piccadilly?"
(f) The answer Mr. Ward gave her was, "I think you are being very selfish."

8. Express these sentences in indirect speech. Begin each one with the name of the speaker.

EXAMPLE: "It can't be helped," said the Rat.
ANSWER: The Rat said that it could not be helped.

(a) "It's all very well to talk," said the Mole.
(b) "It's time we were all in bed," said the Badger.
(c) "The master's gone into his study," replied the Hedgehog.
(d) "I quite understand," said the Rat soothingly.

In the next two sentences use *told* instead of *said*.

(e) "I feel strangely tired, Rat," said the Mole.
(f) "Do be quiet a minute, Toad," said the girl.

9. Imagine that the following sentences represent a conversation between yourself and a railway porter. Give an account of it in indirect speech, beginning with *The porter told me that* . . .

(a) The porter said, "The Bedford train has just gone."
(b) "What time is the next one?" I asked.
(c) "There's a slow train at 10.15," he replied, "but you won't get a fast train until 1.45."
(d) "Is there a refreshment room here?" I enquired.
(e) "Yes, sir," he answered; "you'll find it on platform 3."

10. These sentences are extracts from a newspaper report of a speech at a prize-giving. Rewrite them in direct speech, as actually spoken, beginning *I feel honoured* . . .

You will need to make alterations (chiefly of tense and person) wherever words are printed in italics.

(a) *He felt* honoured that *he had* been asked to distribute the prizes on *that* important occasion.
(b) *They were* all glad that the weather *had* been so kind.
(c) It *was* inevitable that some competitors *were* disappointed.
(d) However, many records *had* been broken.
(e) *He congratulated* those who *had* been successful.
(f) *They would* all look forward, *he was* sure, to meeting *there* again next year.

11. The following sentences are extracts from a lady's speech at a village meeting. Rewrite them in indirect speech, as they would be reported in a newspaper, beginning *She was delighted* . . .

You will need to make alterations (chiefly of tense and person) wherever words are printed in italics.

(a) "*I am* delighted to be *here*."
(b) "The people of Manbury *have* always made *me* welcome."
(c) "There *is* no lovelier place in *this* county."
(d) "The village green where *we are* gathered *has* been like *this* for centuries."
(e) "*We* must be on *our* guard against those who *wish* to destroy it."

12. The following sentences are extracts from a speech at a council meeting. Rewrite them in indirect speech, as they would be reported in a newspaper.

This exercise is similar to Exercise 11, except that you will have to decide for yourself which words must be altered.

(a) "I have been mayor of this town for three years."
(b) "Many improvements have been carried out during my term of office."
(c) "We can pride ourselves on being progressive and enterprising."
(d) "I hope that we shall continue to develop in this way."
(e) "There is still much that has to be done."
(f) "I am sure that my successor can count upon your full support."

34. EXCLAMATION-MARKS

1. Rewrite these statements in the form of exclamations, beginning with *How* or *What*. Use exactly the same words as those given, but re-arrange them as shown in the examples.

> EXAMPLES: (i) This is a lifelike portrait.
> (ii) The sea is cold today.
> ANSWERS: (i) What a lifelike portrait this is!
> (ii) How cold the sea is today!

(a) Your father is a tall man.
(b) You are stupid.
(c) The lake is calm.
(d) It is a nuisance.
(e) The bridesmaids look pretty.
(f) It is a pity that I missed you.

2. Reduce the following sentences to exclamations consisting of *not more than three words*. Some can be shortened to a single word.

(a) Will you please let me go at once?
(b) I want you to be quick.
(c) I need your help urgently and immediately.
(d) Your life will be in danger unless you are very careful.
(e) Our team has just scored a goal.
(f) You must hold tight if you wish to avoid being thrown off.
(g) The curtains are ablaze, and I am afraid that the house may be burned down.

3. Change these exclamations into statements without altering the meaning.

> EXAMPLE: How amused I was!
> SUGGESTED ANSWER: I was highly amused.

(a) What a lot of nonsense he talks!
(b) How well you look!
(c) How cold it is!
(d) What a gale we had last night!
(e) What a pity it is!
(f) How he ran!

4. If you are feeling despondent because you cannot swim you may exclaim *If only I could swim!* Make up similar exclamations (each one beginning *If only . . .*) in which you express keen regret that

(a) your tooth will not stop aching;
(b) Alan will not lend you his racket;
(c) the sun is not shining;
(d) you cannot remember Jim's address;
(e) you have not worked hard enough;
(f) you are not a little taller;
(g) you are not old enough to drive a car.

5. Look at these two sentences:

That will fetch a fine price.
A fine price that will fetch!

Although the same words are used in both, the second sentence is opposite in meaning to the first; it is an ironical or sarcastic way of saying *That will not fetch a fine price.*

In the same way, arrange the following in the form of ironical exclamations.

(a) You are a fine cook.
(b) It looked a pretty sight.
(c) That is a great help.
(d) That will do us much good.
(e) You'll buy a lot of furniture for ten pounds.
(f) It was a peaceful spot, with dogs barking all night.

6. The proprietor of a circus had this notice printed on a board near the entrance:

WHAT DO YOU THINK
WE MAKE NO CHARGE FOR ADMISSION

When people asked to be let in free they were told they were not reading the notice correctly. Punctuate the notice so that it means what the proprietor intended it to mean.

35. HYPHENS

1. Sometimes it is necessary to divide a word so that part is on one line and part on the next. When this happens, a *hyphen* is put at the end of the first part. Look up the rules for dividing words (for instance, on p. 65 of *A First English Companion*), and then divide the following words so that neither part has less than three letters in it.

   You will find it instructive to refer to *A First Dictionary* to see how the printer has divided these words.

(a) scrapped, dragged, stunning, trotting, budding, shamming.
(b) appearance, avoidable, regretful, systematic, peculiarity, knowingly.

(c) changing, gliding, lounging, combining, procuring, increasingly.

(d) craziness, godliness, thriftiest, thirstiest, melodiously, reliability.

2. A rail that is ten metres long is called *a ten-metre rail*—not *a ten-metres rail*. In the same way, say what the following things are called; if you write the answers, use a hyphen in each one.

(a) A race over a distance of ten kilometres.
(b) A bill for one hundred pounds.
(c) A clock that runs for eight days.
(d) A kettle that holds two litres.
(e) A field of ten hectares.
(f) A weight of half a kilogramme.
(g) A programme of eight pages.
(h) A saloon car with four doors.
(i) A junction where five ways meet.
(j) An electric fire rated at three kilowatts.
(k) A golf-course that has eighteen holes.
(l) An interval that lasts for five minutes.

3. Compound adjectives (see pages 19–20) are formed by joining two or more words with hyphens. E.g., a person who is blind to colour is *colour-blind*. Use compound adjectives to express the following phrases more concisely.

> EXAMPLE: An animal with keen eyes.
> ANSWER: A keen-eyed animal.

(a) A vase that is heavy at the top.
(b) A poker so hot that it is red.
(c) A tin that has been made tight against air.
(d) A shelter that is proof against bombs.
(e) An orange with thin skin.
(f) A dog with rough hair.
(g) A liquid with an evil smell.
(h) A man who works hard.
(i) A person with flat feet.
(j) A building like a prison.

In the remaining phrases, only *one* of the required words is suggested to you.

(k) Meat that has not been done long enough in the oven.
(l) A house that is said to be worth more than its true value.
(m) A youth whose boisterous spirits often lead him into trouble.
(n) A person who habitually has evil thoughts.

4. From each of the following pairs of phrases choose the one that should contain a hyphen, as shown in this example.

> EXAMPLE: A sleeping baby; a sleeping tablet.
> ANSWER: A sleeping-tablet.

A sleeping-tablet does not sleep as a baby does; it only *causes* sleep. Similarly a walking-stick does not walk, but is *used* for walking.

(a) Dancing slippers; dancing children.
(b) A running tap; a running track.
(c) A working man; a working jacket.
(d) A skipping rope; a skipping lamb.
(e) A jumping frog; a jumping pit.
(f) A rocking boat; a rocking horse.
(g) A smoking chimney; a smoking concert.
(h) A skating rink; a skating couple.
(i) A burning glass; a burning house.
(j) Laughing hyenas; laughing gas.

When you have finished, read through your answers aloud, and say which word is accented in each one.

5. We say that a person shows *common sense*, but if we put these two words together to make a compound adjective we join them with a hyphen like this:

He made a *common-sense* suggestion.

In the pairs of sentences given below, say which of the words in italics should be hyphenated.

(a)
- This catalogue has been *out of date* for a long time.
- This is an *out of date* catalogue, and cannot be trusted.

(b)
- We saw a beggar who was *down and out*.
- Asleep on the seat was a *down and out* beggar.

(c)
- Brian Mills gives an *on the spot* report in our next week's issue.
- Our reporter *on the spot* gives the latest news.

(d)
- The *first night* audience gave the play a good reception.
- On the *first night* the audience was enthusiastic.

(e)
- During a friendship of *long standing* I have come to know him well.
- Ours has been a *long standing* friendship.

(f)
- It was a *never to be forgotten* race.
- It was a race *never to be forgotten*.

6. A book is *re-bound*, but a ball is caught on the *rebound*. Here are some other pairs of words in which one word has a hyphen and the other has not:

re-sign, resign	re-cover, recover
re-mark, remark	re-count, recount
re-strain, restrain	re-dress, redress

Say which of these words you would use in connection with each of the following circumstances:

(*a*) To fit a new cover on an armchair.
(*b*) To get well after an illness.
(*c*) To put your clothes on again.
(*d*) To give up a job.
(*e*) To make a comment.
(*f*) To write your signature again.
(*g*) To pass lemon-juice through a sieve for a second time.
(*h*) To tell a story.

36. PARENTHESIS

A parenthesis is an explanation or a piece of additional information which is inserted into a sentence. The parenthesis is kept separate from the main sentence by being put between commas, brackets, or dashes.

If the parenthesis is left out completely, the main sentence will still make sense.

1. **Commas.** Each of these sentences contains a phrase that is in parenthesis. Put that phrase between commas.

> EXAMPLE: Ten persons three of them women are still missing.
> ANSWER: Ten persons, three of them women, are still missing.

(*a*) Several boys none of whom I knew walked over to us.
(*b*) Now and then as though dreaming she smiled in her sleep.
(*c*) I asked him thinking that he was a policeman which was the way to the library.
(*d*) I have decided having considered the situation very carefully to postpone the event until next week.

(*e*) This book though not the one I asked for will do.
(*f*) Albert however he tried never managed to win a game.

See also the exercises on *Relative Pronouns* (3, 6, 7, 11, and 14 on pages 44–48).

2. **Brackets.** Each of these sentences contains a phrase that is in parenthesis. Put brackets round each parenthesis.

> EXAMPLE: I shall need a kit-bag a big one to hold my personal belongings.
> ANSWER: I shall need a kit-bag (a big one) to hold my personal belongings.

(*a*) We rode on to the next village Gamston to see my aunt.
(*b*) On the following day Easter Monday we went to Torquay.
(*c*) Kenneth told Lionel that he Lionel had won a prize.
(*d*) I took ten pence all I had from my purse and gave it to him.
(*e*) A man was giving samples of chocolate very small ones to a queue of children.
(*f*) My presents included a book, a pen, a torch just the kind I wanted and a pair of gloves.

3. **Dashes.** Each of these sentences contains a phrase that is in parenthesis. Put dashes before and after each of these phrases.

> EXAMPLE: George says I hope he is right that these catalogues are free.
> ANSWER: George says—I hope he is right—that these catalogues are free.

(*a*) Complete the coupon in ink pencil will not do and send it to the Editor.
(*b*) I suggest that you go to Mr. Richards remember to take your school report and ask if he has a vacancy.
(*c*) He searched the drawers all the cupboards were locked and found several photographs.
(*d*) The great floods of 1953 nothing like them had been experienced for many years caused widespread destruction.
(*e*) Gloves woollen ones are the best should be grey or dark blue.
(*f*) Of the three names that have been suggested for my baby brother Roger, Gordon, and Gerald I prefer Roger.

37. SEMI-COLONS

1. In these sentences insert either a comma or a semi-colon at each of the places indicated by a caret, according to which of these two punctuation-marks is correct in the circumstances.

   (a) Football is a game for young men ∧ many older men prefer golf.

   (b) Robins can sometimes be persuaded to come indoors ∧ though this is not usual.

   (c) Cotton is a vegetable fibre ∧ asbestos is a mineral.

   (d) Whereas linen is a natural fibre ∧ nylon is artificial.

   (e) The inhabitants do not belong to the Christian faith ∧ they are chiefly Hindus and Mohammedans.

   (f) Wise men learn by other men's mistakes ∧ fools learn by their own.

   (g) As you make your bed ∧ so you must lie on it.

2. In the following sentences insert commas and semi-colons wherever you think they are needed.

   (a) Cumulus clouds are heaped-up clouds they look like piles of cotton wool.

   (b) These birds fly great distances a journey of two hundred kilometres is nothing to them.

   (c) A mountain is made of harder rocks than its surroundings and its shaping has been done mostly by running water.

   (d) The sun sets night falls suddenly and after the great heat of the day the desert becomes suddenly cold this causes rocks to split and crumble.

   (e) The layers of tree-trunks and moss become more covered over with sand and mud more compressed by the weight above them.

   (f) Like alligators crocodiles lay eggs snakes also reproduce themselves in this way.

✓ MARK THESE YOURSELF
The answers are on page 145

1. When does a professional sportsman agree to play for his club for another season—when he *re-signs* or when he *resigns*?

2. Give the full names, correctly spelt, of the English counties for which these abbreviations stand:

   Glos. Hants. Northants. Oxon. Salop

★ REVISION

1. In this exercise follow the instructions given in Exercise 8 on page 67.

   (a) BRITAINS LEAD IN EXPORTS

   (b) APPEAL TO DOCKERS UNION

   (c) TWO MINISTERS SHARE FOREIGN AFFAIRS

   (d) PRINCE MEETS CRASH SURVIVORS

   (e) WOLVES CHAMPIONSHIP HOPES

   (f) PRINCESSS JEWELS STOLEN

2. In these Shakespearian quotations the apostrophes show that words have been contracted or shortened. Give the full meanings of the shortened words.

   (a) *All's Well that Ends Well*

   (b) *Like a worm i' the bud*

   (c) *And some have greatness thrust upon 'em.*

   (d) *O, what a noble mind is here o'erthrown!*

   (e) *Thou know'st 'tis common.*

   (f) *I 'gin to be aweary of the sun.*

   (g) *When my heart hath 'scaped this sorrow*

   (h) *Home art gone, and ta'en thy wages.*

   (i) *His purse is empty already; all's golden words are spent.*

3. Using capital letters where necessary, copy these sentences in your ordinary handwriting.

   (a) JOAN OF ARC INSPIRED THE FRENCH TO DRIVE THE ENGLISH OUT OF ORLEANS.

   (b) WHEN NAPOLEON HAD BEEN DEFEATED AT WATERLOO HE WAS EXILED TO ST. HELENA.

   (c) MARY QUEEN OF SCOTS WAS EXECUTED AT FOTHERINGHAY.

   (d) SIR FRANCIS DRAKE, ONE OF QUEEN ELIZABETH'S ADMIRALS, WAS LARGELY RESPONSIBLE FOR THE DESTRUCTION OF THE SPANISH ARMADA.

   (e) IT WAS SIR CHRISTOPHER WREN WHO RECONSTRUCTED ST. PAUL'S CATHEDRAL AFTER THE GREAT FIRE OF LONDON.

4. Each of these sentences should end with a full stop, a question mark, or an exclamation mark. Write them out and insert the correct pronunciation.

   (a) What is the name of this village

   (b) What a fine view this is

   (c) I wonder where he went

   (d) How sharp is your pencil

   (e) How sharp your pencil is

   (f) Tell me how far it is to York

   (g) Can you tell me how far it is to York

   (h) Say how many people there are in the room

★ REVISION

1. Read these phrases, and then answer the questions that follow them.

> Five-year-old children
> Five year-old children
> Two litre paint tins
> Two-litre paint tins
> Forty-odd people
> Forty odd people

(a) Which phrase refers to five children?
(b) Which phrase refers to two paint tins?
(c) Which phrase refers to exactly forty people?

2. Which of these sentences suggests that the only gipsies not often seen nowadays are those who live in caravans?

(a) Gipsies, who live in caravans, are not often seen nowadays.
(b) Gipsies who live in caravans are not often seen nowadays.

3. Punctuate this sentence correctly.

> SALLY IS AS TALL AS IF NOT TALLER THAN PAMELA

What information does the sentence give us if the phrase in parenthesis is omitted?

4. This unpunctuated passage is from Tolstoy's *What Men Live By*. Copy it in your ordinary handwriting, correctly punctuated.

> AFTER THEY HAD FINISHED THEIR SUPPER THE WOMAN CLEARED OFF THE THINGS AND BEGAN TO QUESTION THE STRANGER
> WHERE ARE YOU FROM
> I DO NOT BELONG HEREABOUTS
> HOW DID YOU HAPPEN TO GET INTO THIS ROAD
> I CANNOT TELL YOU
> WHO MALTREATED YOU
> GOD PUNISHED ME
> AND YOU WERE LYING THERE STRIPPED
> YES THERE I WAS LYING ALL NAKED FREEZING TO DEATH WHEN SIMON SAW ME HAD COMPASSION ON ME TOOK OFF HIS COAT PUT IT ON ME AND BADE ME COME HOME WITH HIM YOU HAVE FED ME GIVEN ME SOMETHING TO EAT AND TO DRINK AND HAVE TAKEN PITY ON ME MAY THE LORD REQUITE YOU

✔ MARK THESE YOURSELF

The answers are on page 145

1. These abbreviations are taken from a telephone directory; what do they mean?

> tbcnsts mkt gdnr chrpdst
> hrdrsr   smlhldr   sgnwtr
> mtl mchts

2. The following contracted words are in common use. See if you can say what they mean in full.

mike	prep	soccer	fridge
vet	maths	jeep	op
mack	hi fi	cinema	piano
rep	loco	amps	fan

3. If you were to be operated on for appendicitis, whom would you prefer to perform the operation—an F.R.C.S. or an F.R.C.O.?

4. What does REV. mean

(a) in a clergyman's name;
(b) in an index to the Bible;
(c) in the term *one rev. per second*?

5. Boys' names are often shortened in popular use. Write out these shortened names in full:

Alf	Bert	Chris	Dan	Don
Fred	Geoff	Joe	Ken	Len
Les	Mike	Pat	Phil	Ray
Reg	Ron	Sam	Sid	Stan
Steve	Tom	Tony	Wilf	

6. Say where you would look for these topics in the encyclopedia illustrated on page 41.

(a) margarine   (c) smuggling   (e) the river Missouri
(b) Dover   (d) Charles Dickens

7. If we refer to *Bob the farmer's dog*, who is Bob—the farmer or the dog? How would you punctuate the same phrase so as to alter the meaning?

8. Punctuate this sentence so that it means that Jill is good at hockey:

> *Jill says Jane is good at hockey.*

9. Punctuate this sentence correctly, using quotation-marks and *two* question-marks:

> *Did you say how old is she.*

74

THERE are several ways in which you can improve your spelling. You can refer to a dictionary whenever you are in doubt. You can learn to recognize the commonest prefixes and suffixes, and so avoid many stupid mistakes. Etymology will help you, as explained on page 88. And a few simple rules will enable you to spell large groups of words correctly.

Some spelling-rules are so complicated or have so many exceptions that they confuse more than they help. But you should know (for example) why the **e** is kept in *amazement* but not in *amazing*, and why there is a double **t** in *fitted* but not in *benefited*. The following exercises will explain such things and will give you practice in rules that you can understand. They will also introduce you to some interesting groups of words to think about and remember. Harder rules—and some exceptions—have been omitted, for there are many words in the English language that are best learned by looking at them carefully and using them often.

38. FIFTY TRICKY WORDS

Here are fifty unfinished words that cause many people to stumble in their spelling. Using your dictionary, complete them correctly.

reco·nize	maint·nance	mis·letoe
sep·rate	cat··pill·r	mant··piece
lib·ary	her·tic	par··lel
prof··sor	sat··lite	asp·rin
campai·n	manœ·vre	laburn·m
liter·ry	vac·um	par··fin
shep··rd	ras·berry	rhod·dendron
parl··ment	rhinocer·s	vet··inary
lunch·on	propel··r	rest····nt
choc·late	dip·theria	sacr·l·gious
uncon·cious	auxil·ary	Feb·uary
substan·ial	lab·rinth	Portug·ese
contempor··y	diaphra·m	mis····aneous
cu·board	terrest·ial	ex·aust
second·ry	pomegran·te	ex·ibition
min·ature	mack·rel	b·oyant
cemet·ry	hyg·enic	

75

39. -ABLE AND -IBLE

From the word *prevent* we get *preventable*, spelt with an **a**, but *convert* gives us *convertible,* with an **i**. There is no easy rule for deciding whether to use **-able** or **-ible** when making adjectives of this kind; your best plan is to learn each word as you meet it, and to use a dictionary whenever you are not sure.

Complete the following:

(*a*) What makes him so irrit·ble?
(*b*) This is a sens·ble suggestion.
(*c*) He would make an admir·ble prefect.
(*d*) Is the disease cur·ble?
(*e*) Smoking is not permiss·ble in this hall.
(*f*) Do you think it advis·ble for us to go without coats?
(*g*) The frost did a neglig·ble amount of damage.
(*h*) Her stockings are almost invis·ble.
(*i*) Strong boots are indispens·ble for rock climbing.
(*j*) She is a very excit·ble girl.
(*k*) I hold you respons·ble for the safe keeping of this book.
(*l*) His insulting manner was contempt·ble.
(*m*) They told us an almost incred·ble story of hardship and danger.
(*n*) The village is not approach·ble from the north.
(*o*) The village is easily access·ble from the west.
(*p*) Is it practic·ble for man to reach Mars?

40. DISAPPEARING LETTERS

The feminine form of the word *waiter* is *waitress* (not *waiteress*), and a person who is full of *vigour* is *vigorous* (not *vigourous*). You will see that the **e** is dropped from the word *waiter*, and the **u** from the word *vigour*.

To each of the following words add the suffix shown in brackets, omitting one letter from the given word as you do so. Use a dictionary to check your answers.

(*a*) tiger (-ess)
(*b*) humour (-ous)
(*c*) remember (-ance)
(*d*) wonder (-ous)
(*e*) winter (-y)
(*f*) proprietor (-ess)
(*g*) encumber (-ance)
(*h*) disaster (-ous)
(*i*) enter (-ance)
(*j*) humour (-ist)
(*k*) hinder (-ance)
(*l*) administer (-ation)
(*m*) monster (-ous)
(*n*) enchanter (-ess)

(*o*) labour (-ious)
(*p*) vapour (-ize)
(*q*) carpenter (-y)
(*r*) generous (-ity)
(*s*) curious (-ity)
(*t*) glamour (-ous)
(*u*) exclaim (-ation)
(*v*) register (-ar)
(*w*) repeat (-ition)
(*x*) impetuous (-ity)

The last two are slightly different:

(*y*) pronounce (-ation)
(*z*) (de-) odour (-ant)

41. SOME USEFUL ASSOCIATIONS

If you think of a *battalion* as a body of soldiers ready for *battle* you will not have to wonder whether you should use double **t** or double **l**. Other associations and connections that you might usefully remember are given below. Using the words in italics as clues (and as the words to be kept in mind), complete the unfinished words. Many people spell them wrongly, so check your answers by reference to a dictionary.

(*a*) The function of the ——ment is to *govern*.
(*b*) A ——ic explosion fills one with *terror*.
(*c*) A ——ary may have to deal with *secret* documents.
(*d*) ——ine should be taken only on *medical* advice.
(*e*) A ——ette is a small *cigar*.
(*f*) Inflammation of the ——al tubes is called *bronchitis*.
(*g*) A ——oon is shaped like a large *ball*.
(*h*) ——mas is the festival of the birth of *Christ*.
(*i*) A birth ——cate *certifies* the date of one's birth.
(*j*) We com—— an event by keeping it in our *memory*.

✓ MARK THESE YOURSELF
The answers are on page 145

1. What do you notice about the vowels in the word *facetious*?

2. In this limerick replace the dashes by *to*, *too*, or *two*.

> *A fussy old lady from Crewe*
> *Was running to catch the 2.2;*
> * Said the porter, "Don't hurry,*
> * Don't scurry, don't flurry;*
> *It's a minute or —— —— —— ——."*

42. -FUL, -FULLY

Each dash in the following phrases is to be replaced by a word formed from the word given in brackets; it must end either with **-ful** or with **-fully**.

If the given word ends in **y** with a consonant before it, change the **y** to **i**, like this:

mercy—merciful—mercifully

EXAMPLES: (1) A —— reply (*truth*)
(2) Waiting —— (*hope*)
ANSWERS: (1) A truthful reply
(2) Waiting hopefully

(*a*) A —— puppy (*play*)
(*b*) A —— supply (*plenty*)
(*c*) Sleeping —— (*peace*)
(*d*) A —— occasion (*joy*)
(*e*) Yours —— (*respect*)
(*f*) A —— story (*fancy*)
(*g*) —— embroidered (*beauty*)
(*h*) A —— sprain (*pain*)
(*i*) A —— answer (*scorn*)
(*j*) Treated —— (*shame*)
(*k*) —— ill (*pity*)
(*l*) A lady —— (*bounty*)

43. I BEFORE E

Write out the following words underneath each other, either in a single column or in two widely-spaced columns. Then carry out the instructions given beneath.

brief	height	rein	shield
priest	deceive	veil	receipt
thief	believe	ceiling	pier
leisure	piece	weight	conceit

1. Put a tick by each word in which the **ie** or the **ei** rhymes with *bee*.

2. Looking through the words you have ticked, underline any of them containing **ei**.

3. Say what you notice about all the words you have underlined.

4. Say what you notice about all the words you have not ticked.

5. Discuss the rule for "i before e" and try to understand what you have done in this exercise.

44. WORDS ENDING IN Y

1. **Plurals.** The rules for forming the plurals of words ending in y are as follows:

If the letter before **y** is a consonant, change the **y** to **i** and add **es**:

dictionary, dictionaries

If the letter before **y** is a vowel, add **s**:

highway, highways

———

Obeying the above rules, give the plurals of the following words:

factory	supply	railway	butterfly
abbey	jockey	dummy	industry
colliery	journey	ceremony	lorry
trolley	volley	colony	ferry
turkey	policy	ally	alley
alloy	beauty	kidney	pygmy
melody	medley	laundry	story
storey	balcony	decoy	

2. **Adding suffixes.** The rules for adding suffixes to words ending in y are as follows:

If the letter before the **y** is a consonant, change the **y** to **i** when adding the suffix—except when the suffix is **-ing**:

tidy—tidier, tidiest, tidily, BUT *tidying*

If the letter before the **y** is a vowel, keep the **y** when adding a suffix:

play—player, played, playing

———

Obeying the above rules,* supply the missing words in the following sentences, using the words in brackets as clues.

* A few words such as *dryness* and *shyness* are exceptions.

(*a*) Have you —— yourselves? (*enjoy*)
(*b*) We were —— by fog. (*delay*)
(*c*) The story has been shortened and —— (*simplify*)
(*d*) I am —— to solve this puzzle. (*try*)
(*e*) And there I —— a fair pretty maid. (*espy*)
(*f*) Three shops were —— by fire. (*destroy*)
(*g*) He was disqualified for not —— the rules. (*obey*)
(*h*) She is now —— biology. (*study*)

(*i*) The factory gives —— to many people. (*employ*)

(*j*) They turned and —— to the queen. (*curtsy*)

(*k*) The notices were prominently ——. (*display*)

(*l*) Is my dog —— you? (*annoy*)

(*m*) The land has not yet been ——. (*survey*)

(*n*) They stood firm, —— all attempts to move them. (*defy*)

(*o*) He bolted the door and —— us admission. (*deny*)

45. DROPPING THE E

If a word ends in a silent **e**, drop the **e** when adding a vowel-suffix*: *replace, replacing*.

The **e** is not dropped when a consonant-suffix is added: *replace, replacement*.

* Exercise 2 explains the exception to this rule.

---

1. Observing the above rule, combine the following words with the suffixes given in brackets. Use a dictionary if necessary.

excite	(-ment)	sense	(-less)
amaze	(-ing)	grope	(-ing)
fame	(-ous)	white	(-ish)
assure	(-ance)	idle	(-ness)
lone	(-ly)	amaze	(-ment)
spite	(-ful)	separate	(-ly)
love	(-ing)	separate	(-ing)
excite	(-able)	postpone	(-ment)

2. An exception to the above rule is that words ending in **ce** and **ge** keep the **e** when adding **-able** or **-ous**: *replace, replaceable; courage, courageous*.

Bearing this in mind, continue with the following combinations of words and suffixes:

overtake	(-ing)	trace	(-able)
elope	(-ment)	dine	(-ing)
change	(-able)	white	(-ness)
outrage	(-ous)	peace	(-able)
desire	(-able)	nightmare	(-ish)
desire	(-ous)	advantage	(-ous)
late	(-ly)	observe	(-ant)
late	(-ish)	true	(-ly)
manage	(-able)	notice	(-able)

46. HARD AND SOFT C AND G

The letters **c** and **g** are usually *hard* when they come before the vowels **a, o,** and **u**:

musi**c**al,   apri**c**ot,   **cu**shion,
re**g**ard,   **go**spel,   fi**g**ure.

They are usually *soft* when they come before **i,*** **e,** and **y**:

rejoi**c**ing,   re**c**eive,   en**c**yclopedia,
re**g**iment,   dun**g**eon,   **gy**mnasium.

* Except for some words beginning with *gi*.

Supply the missing letter in each of the following words, and say whether it keeps the letter that comes before it hard or soft.

(*a*) courag ·ous	(*n*) chang ·able
(*b*) catalog ·e	(*o*) frolic ·ed
(*c*) notic ·able	(*p*) serg ·ant
(*d*) gorg ·ous	(*q*) dialog ·e
(*e*) picnic ·ed	(*r*) panic ·ed
(*f*) pig ·on	(*s*) servic ·able
(*g*) grac ·ous	(*t*) surg ·on
(*h*) peac ·able	(*u*) outrag ·ous
(*i*) plag ·e	(*v*) vag ·e
(*j*) manag ·able	(*w*) pag ·ant
(*k*) fatig ·e	(*x*) pronounc ·able
(*l*) veng ·ance	(*y*) mimic ·ing
(*m*) spac ·ous	(*z*) intrig ·e

47. DOUBLING THE LAST LETTER

This exercise is about adding vowel-suffixes (*-ed, -ing*, etc.) and concerns only words of *one* syllable that do not end in **w, x,** or **y**.

The rule is: when you are adding a vowel-suffix, double the last letter if it follows immediately after a *single* vowel.

EXAMPLES: stop, stopped; wet, wetting
BUT leap, leaped; wet, wetness

Make two (or three) words from each of the following words, using the suffixes shown in brackets.

Do not use your dictionary until you have finished; then check your answers and *correct any mistakes.*

step	(-ed, -ing)	read	(-able, -er)
drop	(-ed, -ing)	rob	(-ed, -er)
thin	(-er, -est)	sharp	(-en, -est, -ly)
hot	(-er, -est)	sin	(-er, -ing, -ful)
sad	(-er, -est, -ness)	big	(-er, -est)
red	(-est, -ish, -ness)	hop	(-ed, -ing)
brim	(-ing, -ful)	fit	(-ed, -ness, -ment)
hat	(-ed, -less)	flat	(-en, -er)
greet	(-ed, -ing)	dread	(-ed, -ing, -ful)
break	(-able, -ing)	great	(-er, -est, -ly)

48. DOUBLE L

Mistakes are often made when **-ed** and **-ing** are added to verbs ending with the letter l. Here are the rules:

Double the l if it is preceded by a single vowel:

propel, propelled
control, controlling

Do not double the l if it is preceded by a pair of vowels:

fail, failed
deal, dealing

Obeying the above rules, combine the following words with the suffixes given in brackets.

label	(-ed)	quarrel	(-ing)
conceal	(-ed)	total	(-ed)
prevail	(-ing)	pencil	(-ed)
pedal	(-ing)	appeal	(-ing)
toil	(-ed)	expel	(-ed)
travel	(-ing)	feel	(-ing)
patrol	(-ing)	marvel	(-ed)
cool	(-ed)	uncoil	(-ed)
wheel	(-ed)	curtail	(-ed)
unveil	(-ing)	stencil	(-ing)
signal	(-ed)	foul	(-ed)
reveal	(-ed)	fulfil	(-ed)
panel	(-ed)	jewel	(-ed)
retail	(-ed)	unseal	(-ing)
assail	(-ing)	shovel	(-ing)
marshal	(-ing)	initial	(-ed)

49. DOUBLE T

1. This exercise concerns adding **-ed** or **-ing** to verbs of *one syllable* that end with t.

Double the t if it is preceded by a single vowel (a short vowel-sound): *jot, jotted.*

Do not double the t if it is preceded by a double vowel or by a long vowel-sound: *seat, seated; dart, darting.*

Obeying the above rules, combine the following words with the suffixes given in brackets.

bat	(-ing)	root	(-ed)
pet	(-ed)	pot	(-ed)
greet	(-ing)	net	(-ed)
fit	(-ing)	flirt	(-ing)
rot	(-ed)	chat	(-ing)
start	(-ed)	snort	(-ed)
meet	(-ing)	fret	(-ing)
wait	(-ed)	jut	(-ing)
strut	(-ing)	pout	(-ed)
knit	(-ing)	spurt	(-ing)
cheat	(-ed)	quit	(-ed)
suit	(-ed)	float	(-ing)

2. When we come to words of more than one syllable we have to ask ourselves where the accent falls. For example, *packet* is accented on the first syllable, but *admit* is accented on the second syllable.*

First of all, arrange the following words in two columns—on the left, those accented at the beginning; on the right, those accented at the end:

fidget	omit	regret	profit
defeat	pivot	trumpet	await
commit	acquit	fillet	pilot
submit	rivet	transmit	ferret
ballot	recruit	pocket	outwit
retort	budget	permit	benefit

The rules are:

If the accent is on the first syllable, do not double the t: *ballot, balloted.*

If the accent is on the end syllable, follow the rule for words of one syllable (see Exercise 1 above):

admit, admitted; repeat, repeating.

Now go back to the words that you have arranged in two columns, and add either **-ed** or **-ing** to each one of them, doubling the t whenever necessary.

* See Exercise 5 on page 84

50. DOUBLE R

I. This exercise concerns adding **-ed** or **-ing** to verbs of *one syllable* that end with **r**.

Double the **r** if it is preceded by a single vowel:

> *jar, jarred*

Do not double the **r** if it is preceded by a double vowel:

> *bear, bearing*

Obeying the above rule, combine the following words with the suffixes given in brackets.

bar	(-ed)	moor	(-ed)
fear	(-ing)	pair	(-ed)
cheer	(-ed)	stir	(-ing)
blur	(-ed)	air	(-ed)
whir	(-ing)	tear	(-ing)
tar	(-ed)	slur	(-ed)
wear	(-ing)	soar	(-ed)
roar	(-ed)	spur	(-ing)
swear	(-ing)	spar	(-ing)
star	(-ed)	chair	(-ed)

2. Words of two syllables must be treated according to whether they are accented on the first syllable or on the second syllable. We have already seen in Set 49 how a similar procedure is adopted with words that end in **t**.

Arrange the following words in two columns—on the left, those accented on the first syllable; on the right, those accented on the second syllable.

offer	refer	suffer	order
occur	repair	forbear	hinder
conquer	prefer	render	alter
enter	inter	pilfer	debar
motor	defer	differ	recur
incur	deter	bestir	labour

Now add either **-ed** or **-ing** to each of the words, obeying the following rules:

If the accent is on the first syllable, do not double the **r**:

> *filter, filtered*

If the accent is on the end syllable, follow the rule for words of one syllable. (See Exercise 1 above):

> *confer, conferred; despair, despairing*

51. DOUBLING BY PAIRING

I. See what happens when the prefix **un-** is added to the words *certain* and *noticed*:

> *un + certain = uncertain*
> *un + noticed = unnoticed*

The double **n** in *unnoticed* is really a *pair* of **n**'s that is caused by the bringing together of the last letter of the prefix and the first letter of the word, but there is no such pair in *uncertain*. In a similar way, *dis + service* gives *disservice*, but there is no double **s** in *disapprove*.

From the following list make up as many words as you can in which a double letter occurs at the point where the prefix and the given word are joined.

dis- appear, satisfied, organize, similar, obey.
un- necessary, invited, natural, named, intelligent, occupied, numbered, eventful, inhabited.
under- wear, current, rate, ground, run, go.
over- reach, rule, look, turn, run, ride.
im- probable, mortal, mature, patient, perfect, measurable, possible, moral, movable, modest.

2. We do not double the last letter of a word when adding consonant-suffixes such as **-ness** and **-less**, but if the last letter of the word happens to be the same as the first letter of the suffix the result is a pair:

> *stubborn + ness = stubbornness*

To each of the following words add either **-ness** or **-less**:

green	soul	wheel
keen	thin	tail
drunken	soil	sudden
plain	oil	veil
goal		

Other spelling problems are dealt with on pages 103–107.

✔ MARK THESE YOURSELF

The answers are on page 145

Find six words beginning with

(a) *ch* pronounced as *k*;
(b) *ch* pronounced as *sh*;
(c) a silent *w* followed by *r*;
(d) a silent *k* followed by *n*;
(e) a silent *g* followed by *n*.

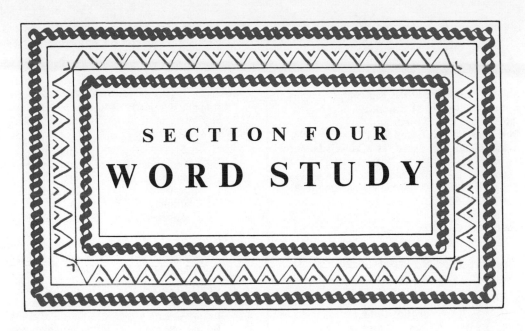

SECTION FOUR
WORD STUDY

52. VOWELS AND CONSONANTS

1. The following names of subjects on a school time-table have been abbreviated by omitting the vowels; write them out in full:

    mthmtcs   cmpstn   ndlwrk   wdwrk
    gmtry   hstry   typwrtng scrptr

Now write out the names of these games and pastimes in the same kind of shorthand:

    football   hockey   badminton billiards
    rounders skating squash

2. In each of these words there is at least one consonant that is not sounded. Copy the words and underline the silent consonants.

    knife   comb   gnat   honest
    wrinkle   listen   island   solemn
    salmon   psalm   reign   weight

3. In the word *salt* the vowel sound is **aw**; in *rude* it is **oo**, and in *piece* it is **ee**. Now look through the words that follow and answer questions (*a*), (*b*), (*c*), and (*d*). Write your answers and underline the vowels referred to.

board	fall	fate	feast	fought
fruit	gaol	great	maul	pain
rude	rue	seize	shoe	soon
veil	wheel	yield	you	fête

(*a*) Which four words in the above list have the vowel sound of **aw**?

(*b*) Which six words have the vowel sound of **oo** as in *food*?

(*c*) Which four words have the vowel sound of **ee**?

(*d*) Which six words have the vowel sound of **ay**?

4.

aisle	any	blood	bury	choir
find	float	friend	head	height
hoe	hunt	leisure	leopard	lie
mend	rough	said	sold	son

(*a*) Which three words in the above list have the vowel sound of **oh**?

(*b*) Which five words have the vowel sound of **i** as in *child*?

(*c*) Which eight words have the vowel sound of **e** as in *pet*?

(*d*) Which four words have the vowel sound of **u** as in *cup*?

5.

lamb	football	ragged
banana	knit	searchlight
gaiety	try	freedom

Say which of the above words

(*a*) has a silent consonant at the beginning;
(*b*) has a silent consonant at the end;
(*c*) has three consecutive vowels;
(*d*) has four consecutive consonants;
(*e*) has a consonant that serves as a vowel, but no other vowel;
(*f*) has alternate consonants and vowels;
(*g*) has double vowels and double consonants (both pairs in one word);
(*h*) has double vowels;
(*i*) has double consonants.

6. If you read the following words aloud you will realize that vowels can be either short or long.

pan	(short **a**);	cake	(long **a**)
wet	(short **e**);	demon	(long **e**)
grin	(short **i**);	sign	(long **i**)
mop	(short **o**);	soldier	(long **o**)
rush	(short **u**);	tune	(long **u**)

Using the above words as a guide, say whether the vowels underlined in the words below are long or short.

(*a*)	baby	(*i*)	stupid
(*b*)	baboon	(*j*)	stumble
(*c*)	finger	(*k*)	angle
(*d*)	final	(*l*)	angel
(*e*)	feminine	(*m*)	empty
(*f*)	female	(*n*)	item
(*g*)	robe	(*o*)	open
(*h*)	robin	(*p*)	ugly

7. a and **an** (i). Putting *a* before every word that begins with a consonant that is sounded, and *an* before every word beginning with a vowel or a silent *h*, see how quickly you can read the following list correctly.

earwig	hour	donkey	picnic	infirmary
hero	oath	escalator	honour	lily
anchor	question	island	operation	hyacinth
oar	village	guitar	house	message
circus	aircraft	footstep	husband	yacht
hospital	index	aviary	emerald	heirloom

8. a and **an** (ii). You may not have noticed that in Exercise 7 there were no words beginning with *u*. In deciding whether to put *a* or *an* before a word that begins with the letter *u* we must ask ourselves whether the *u* is long (as in *unit*) or short (as in *ulcer*). It is how the word is pronounced, not how it is spelt, that leads us to the correct choice.

Say whether *a* or *an* should be used before the following words.

uncle	uniform
umbrella	undergraduate
unicorn	utensil
umpire	university
ukulele	union
upheaval	ultimatum

9. a and **an** (iii). Bearing in mind what you have done in Exercises 7 and 8, say whether the following phrases should be preceded by *a* or *an*.

daring escape	unique occasion
idle scamp	unexpected event
hard-working boy	antique chest
hourly service	horrible expression
unusual shape	diesel engine
usual custom	ugly house
remote ancestor	open door
icy wind	large orchard
handsome man	unison song
useful tool	endless belt
obvious mistake	triumphal arch
unwise remark	accurate timekeeper
tall iris	uphill climb
even keel	unanimous decision
honourable agreement	honorary secretary

See Exercise 24 on page 89.

✅ MARK THESE YOURSELF

The answers are on page 145

Replace each word in italics with *one* other word of the same meaning. Use a dictionary.

(*a*) Please *tender* the correct change.
(*b*) Rice is their *staple* food.
(*c*) In the face of danger he did not *quail*.
(*d*) The nail made a long and jagged *rent*.
(*e*) Tribesmen had come to *rifle* the tomb.
(*f*) Sandbags were brought to *stem* the flood.
(*g*) Bilberries are not as *tart* as cranberries.
(*h*) A thousand skeletons were found in a *barrow*.

53. SYLLABLES

1. Divide these words into their separate syllables, using hyphens to mark the breaks.

EXAMPLE: trans-par-ent

subtract	energetic
condemn	compartment
magnetic	discontentment
publishing	telegraph
relentless	rotation

2. Read the following words aloud to yourself, slowly and deliberately, and say how many syllables each one has. If you give your answers in writing, give the number of syllables as a figure in brackets after each word.

EXAMPLE: entertainment (4)

tomato	modern	locomotive
invent	jamboree	misunderstanding
encyclopedia	film	complimentary
explorer	straight	unintelligently
revolution	fortunate	discontentedly
octave	war	systematically
impatiently	umbrella	intercommunication

3. Find words of one syllable that mean the same or almost the same as the following words.

The list of "One Thousand Adjectives" in *A First English Companion* will help you.

EXAMPLE: brilliant
SUGGESTED ANSWER: bright

(a) ancient	(h) cheerful
(b) rapid	(i) lofty
(c) tiny	(j) feeble
(d) enormous	(k) wicked
(e) gallant	(l) incorrect
(f) gloomy	(m) melancholy
(g) difficult	(n) rugged

4. Write a short account (about five or six lines) of a morning spent on the beach, using words of one syllable only. Make a rough draft first, as you will probably have to make a number of alterations. (Instead of *We were playing at cricket and rounders*, for instance, you might say *We played games with bat and ball*.)

5. Some of the finest English is written in the simplest and shortest words. In the whole of Psalm 148 there are only six words of more than two syllables; what are they?

6. For each of the words given below, find a word which has the same meaning (or almost the same meaning) and which has the number of syllables indicated by the figure in brackets.

EXAMPLE: affectionate (2)
SUGGESTED ANSWER: loving

The list of "One Thousand Adjectives" in *A First English Companion* will help you.

(a) brave (2)	(g) tiny (4)
(b) astonished (2)	(h) unskilful (4)
(c) shy (2)	(i) polluted (5)
(d) bright (3)	(j) angry (5)
(e) strange (3)	(k) unpleasant (5)
(f) scared (3)	(l) disgraceful (5)

54. PRONUNCIATION *

1. Every word in this list has two syllables. Some of them are accented on the first syllable and the others on the second. Arrange them in two columns headed *First* and *Second*.

daughter	forget	silence	deceive
repose	dreaming	broken	mountains
divide	woven	farewell	withdrawn
asleep	midnight	awake	obey
bushes	garland	complete	lightning
slumber	unfurled	proclaim	morning

2. Every word in this list has three syllables. Arrange them in three columns according to whether they are accented on the first, second, or third syllable. Head the columns accordingly.

innocent,	eternal,	disappear,
melody	understand,	weariness,
reflection,	triumphant,	overhead,
discontent,	galloping,	devotion,
violin,	interrupt,	forgetful,
universe,	remembrance,	mutineer,
nightingale,	reluctant,	reunite,
immortal,	sorrowful,	festival.

*See also Exercises 3–6 in Set 52.

83

3. Say how many syllables each of these words has, and on which syllable the accent falls when the word is spoken.

EXAMPLE: rejoicing
ANSWER: Three; 2nd.

(a) magic
(b) beware
(c) remember
(d) maiden
(e) daffodil
(f) exclaim
(g) commanding
(h) highlands
(i) fellowship
(j) disciple
(k) hyacinth
(l) hawthorn
(m) canoe
(n) creator
(o) electrical
(p) crusade
(q) contemplate
(r) consecrated
(s) eclipse
(t) particularly

4. Divide these words into syllables by means of hyphens, and in each one underline the syllable on which the accent is placed; for example,

mul-ti-ply

(a) earwig
(b) explain
(c) employment
(d) faultlessly
(e) doctor
(f) discontinue
(g) gymnastic
(h) disgust
(i) hippopotamus
(j) photograph
(k) photography
(l) photographic

5. In *A First Dictionary* the accented syllable of a word is shown by means of bold type, like this:

mer-maid   pre-**pare**

More advanced dictionaries show the accent by means of a small stroke immediately *after* the accented syllable, like this:

mer′maid   prepare′

Here are three more examples, taken from the previous exercise (No. 4); you will notice that the hyphens are omitted.

ear′wig   explain′   employ′ment

Using the same method, show how the following words are accented:

(a) midland
(b) establishment
(c) enjoy
(d) locomotive
(e) frankincense
(f) eventful
(g) repeat
(h) personality
(i) perform
(j) acorn
(k) overcoat
(l) overflowing

6. Look at these two sentences:

That is an insult.
That would insult him.

In the first sentence the word *insult* is a noun, and the accent falls on the first syllable (in′sult). In the second sentence the word *insult* is a verb, and the accent falls on the second syllable (insult′). There are other words that follow this pattern, as you will now see.

In each of the following phrases and sentences say whether the word in italics is a noun or a verb. Write the word, and show where the accent falls. Use a dictionary.

EXAMPLE: Oil is one of our *imports*.
ANSWER: Noun; im′ports.

(a) A gramophone *record*.
(b) They do not *suspect* anything.
(c) How will they *transport* this machine?
(d) A prize for good *conduct*.
(e) The sale of dairy *produce*.
(f) *Transfer* these books to the top shelf.
(g) A bin full of *refuse*.
(h) Did the jury *convict* him?

7. These words are sometimes mispronounced by being wrongly accented; e.g., some people say *prefer′able* instead of *pref′erable*. Look them up in the dictionary, and then—using the method explained in Exercise 5—show how they should be pronounced.

impotent,   flamingo,   catastrophe,
formidable,   lamentable,   superfluous,
inventory,   infamous,   incomparable,
reputable,   gondola,   vehement.

8. Arrange these words in two columns according to whether they contain a hard **c** or a soft **c**:

local	city	correct	calico
cellar	recipe	script	façade
hyacinth	concrete	incense	piccolo

9. Arrange these words in three columns according to whether they contain a hard **g**, a soft **g**, or a silent **g**:

grind	general	gnat	magic
dagger	pilgrim	sergeant	gnash
reign	golliwog	giggle	pageant
gnaw	disgusting	longitude	gnarled
gesticulate	poignant	orgy	gesture

See also *Hard and Soft C and G* on page 78.

84

10. Write out these words and underline every aspirate.

EXAMPLES: <u>h</u>undred, child<u>h</u>ood

overhang	hollyhock	headlight
cloth	thigh	wholesome
honesty	haphazard	hourly
when	shorthand	withhold

11. Say which consonants in these words are silent and appear to play no part in the pronunciation.

(*a*) heir
(*b*) corps
(*c*) subtle
(*d*) feign
(*e*) sabot
(*f*) debtor
(*g*) debris
(*h*) gnarled
(*i*) pneumatic
(*j*) thyme
(*k*) gunwale
(*l*) poignant

12. You have seen in Exercise 6 on page 82 that vowels can be either short or long. A common method of showing which is which is to use the signs shown below:

Short		Long	
păn	**a**	cāke	
wĕt	**e**	dēmon	
grĭn	**i**	sīgn	
mŏp	**o**	sōldier	
rŭsh	**u**	tūne	

Using this system, write out the following words and show whether the vowels underlined are long or short.

timber	social	penny	diver
apricot	monarch	bugle	battery
bungalow	prehistoric		

13. The following words are sometimes wrongly pronounced. Look them up in your dictionary, and then set them out in the same way as you did those in the previous question, so as to show whether the vowels underlined are long or short.

bade	hover	pageant	vineyard
glacier	crochet	lichen	tornado
puny	zebra	topaz	gratis
cobra	babel	dinosaur	recuperate
vacuum	depot		

14. Using a dictionary, and referring to the *Key to Pronunciation* given below, answer the following questions.

EXAMPLE: What is the sound of the *ch* in *chasm*?
ANSWER: **k**

WHAT IS THE SOUND OF...

(*a*) the *au* in *mauve*?
(*b*) the *er* in *clerk*?
(*c*) the *o* in *cobalt*?
(*d*) the *ch* in *orchid*?
(*e*) the *et* in *crochet*?
(*f*) the *æ* in *phœnix*?
(*g*) the *is* in *viscount*?
(*h*) the *ai* in *plait*?
(*i*) the *er* in *sergeant*?
(*j*) the *eau* in *plateau*?
(*k*) the *i* in *fatigue*?
(*l*) the *ot* in *depot*?
(*m*) the *ch* in *chateau*?
(*n*) the *a* in *scallop*?
(*o*) the *ê* in *fête*?
(*p*) the *i* in *physique*?
(*q*) the *ui* in *sluice*?
(*r*) the *g* in *orgy*?
(*s*) the *g* in *longitude*?
(*t*) the *ch* in *architect*?
(*u*) the middle letter of *suede*?

KEY TO PRONUNCIATION

ă (as in *cat*)	oo (as in *moon*)
ā (as in *bake*)	ar (as in *park*)
ĕ (as in *pen*)	er (as in *jerk*)
ē (as in *equal*)	g (as in *get*)
ĭ (as in *pit*)	j (as in *job*)
ī (as in *kind*)	k (as in *key*)
ŏ (as in *pot*)	sh (as in *shed*)
ō (as in *home*)	

15. Using the methods you have already learned for indicating long vowels, short vowels, and accent, write these words so as to show how they are pronounced. You should be familiar with them, so do not use a dictionary, but work them out yourself for practice. Only the vowels underlined need be marked.

EXAMPLES: explanation, inhale
ANSWERS: ĕxplanā'tion, ĭnhāle'

(*a*) acrobat
(*b*) inhabit
(*c*) ridiculous
(*d*) commence
(*e*) identical
(*f*) latitude
(*g*) population
(*h*) insulate
(*i*) human
(*j*) humane
(*k*) rhododendron
(*l*) commotion

55. PREFIXES AND SUFFIXES

1. Each of the following words is made up of three parts—a central word with a prefix on its left and a suffix on its right. Break up each word into these three parts, which should be arranged as shown in the example.

EXAMPLE: unenjoyable
ANSWER: un-enjoy-able

(a) unemployment
(b) unpleasantness
(c) imprisonment
(d) disappearance
(e) uncertainty
(f) reappearing
(g) indefinitely
(h) reconstruction
(i) misunderstanding
(j) irregularly
(k) informally
(l) inaccurately
(m) dishonourable
(n) disrespectful

2. Some people make the mistake of spelling *disappear*, *disappoint*, *disapprove*, and *disagree* with a double s. Look at the last two words in the previous exercise, and then see if you can suggest a sensible way of remembering the right way to spell the above four words.

Why is there a double s in *dissatisfied*?

See also *Doubling by Pairing* on page 80.

3. The word *impatient* means *not patient*, because the prefix **im-** means *not*. Other prefixes that mean *not* are **il-**, **in-**, **ir-**, and **un-**. Using these prefixes in place of the dots, complete the following sentences. Check your answers by reference to a dictionary.

(a) I am ··certain about the date.
(b) Destroy any copies that are ··perfect.
(c) His attendance is ··regular.
(d) These are ··expensive handbags.
(e) Be careful not to do anything that is ··legal.
(f) That sounds an ··probable story.
(g) Have I called at an ··convenient time?
(h) Good team-work calls for ··selfish co-operation.
(i) The stone slab was ··movable.
(j) My future plans are ··decided.
(k) This tape-measure is ··accurate.
(l) The vicar reproved them for their ··reverent behaviour.

4. Each of the following words begins with a prefix, which is printed in italics. Find the meanings of the prefixes,* and use them to explain the meanings of the

* Page 170 of *A First English Companion* will help.

words. Do not copy definitions from the dictionary unless they happen to fit in with this pattern.

EXAMPLE: *non*sense
ANSWER: not sense

(a) *im*possible
(b) *arch*bishop
(c) *im*mortal
(d) *hemi*sphere
(e) *fore*head
(f) *in*curable
(g) *vice*-president
(h) *auto*mobile
(i) *un*natural
(j) *trans*atlantic
(k) *ir*responsible
(l) *semi*-circle
(m) *anti*-septic
(n) *il*legible

5. In this exercise follow the instructions given in Exercise 4, with one exception: the meaning of the prefix is best put at the *end* of your definition.

EXAMPLE: to *mis*lead
ANSWER: to lead wrongly

(a) to *mis*use
(b) to *re*join
(c) to *fore*tell
(d) a *sub*way
(e) to *re*capture
(f) *fore*going
(g) *inter*woven
(h) to *pre*judge

6. The following definitions are such as might be found in a dictionary. Each one defines a word that ends with the suffix **-ary**, **-ery**, or **-ory**. Look these words up, and write them out. (Use the words in italics as clues.)

EXAMPLE: Concerning *discipline*.
ANSWER: disciplinary

(a) Coming *second*.
(b) Existing in the *imagination*.
(c) A place for the *observation* of the stars, etc.
(d) *Embroidered* work.
(e) Goods sold by a *stationer*.
(f) Concerned with *preparation*.
(g) A place for *infirm* people.
(h) Concerning a *legend*.
(i) Disagreeable work such as a *drudge* would do.
(j) A place where medicine is *dispensed*.
(k) In the habit of *migrating*.
(l) A *monastic* establishment.

7. Each word defined here ends with the suffix **-ant** or **-ent**. Following the same procedure as in the previous exercise, say what the words are.

(a) A person who *assists* others.
(b) A person who *resides* in a place.
(c) Able to float like a *buoy*.

(d) Watchful, like someone keeping a *vigil*.

(e) So good that it *excels* its rivals.

(f) Having no knowledge, like someone who *ignores* learning.

In the next two answers, omit the bracketed letters.

(g) Willing to *obe(y)*.

(h) Able to *ab(o)und* in great quantities.

8. Each word defined here ends with the suffix **-ance** or **-ence**. Following the same procedure as in the previous two exercises, say what the words are.

(a) The act of *appearing*.

(b) Deep respect shown by a person who *reveres*.

(c) Sympathy offered by a person who *condoles*.

(d) The state of *existing*.

(e) A statement by someone who *assures* others.

(f) The act of *abst(a)ining* from certain pleasures, etc.

9. The abstract noun *friendship* is formed by adding the suffix **-ship** to the word *friend*. In a similar way, form an abstract noun from each of the words below by adding one of the following suffixes:

-ship	-hood	-ness
-age	-ice	-ism

(a) dark   (g) bond

(b) owner   (h) knight

(c) child   (i) patriot

(d) coward   (j) shrink

(e) hero   *(k) weary

(f) fellow   *(l) serve

* A slight change in spelling is necessary here.

10. The adjective *childish* is formed by adding the suffix **-ish** to the noun *child*. In the same way (with a slight adjustment of the spelling), by adding **-ous** to *industry* we get *industrious*. Form at least one adjective (more if possible) from each of the words below by using any of the following suffixes:

-ish	-ful	-ly	-ous	-ic
-less	-like	-y	-en	

(a) fever   (g) dust

(b) danger   (h) war

(c) sin   (i) hat

(d) hero   (j) magnet

(e) fear   (k) saint

(f) wood   (l) flax

(m) king   (q) plenty

(n) god   (r) stone

(o) glory   (s) style

(p) sun   (t) volcano

See also Exercises 13 and 14 on page 18.

11. By adding the suffix **-let** to the word *stream* we get *streamlet*. This means *a small stream*, and is therefore a **diminutive** of the word *stream*.

Here are some more suffixes that can be used in the formation of diminutives:

-ling	-ock	-ette
-let	-et	-ule

Keeping the above suffixes in mind, give the correct diminutives for the following:

(a) a tiny book;

(b) a small kitchen;

(c) a little hill;

(d) a small lance (as used by doctors);

(e) a small statue;

(f) a young duck;

(g) a small *maison* (house).

In your answers to the next three examples, omit the bracketed letters.

(h) a small *gra(i)n*;

(i) a small *glob(e)*—e.g., a drop of water;

(j) a young *go(o)s(e)*.

☑ MARK THESE YOURSELF

The answers are on page 145

1. How many syllables are there in each of these words?

(a) café   (c) unique   (e) ague

(b) recipe   (d) fatigue   (f) catastrophe

2. Where does the accent fall in the word *gondola*?

3. In the word *courtesy* does the first syllable rhyme with *fort* or with *hurt*?

4. What is the sound of the *x* in *xylophone*?

5. Here is an old word in a new shape; what is it?

KGHUITIB

Pronounce it like this:

The *k* as in *knob*; the *gh* as in *rough*; the *ui* as in *build*; the *ti* as in *nation*; the *b* as in *lamb*.

THE ORIGINS OF WORDS

IN the remaining exercises in this section on *Word Study* you will learn something of the way in which the English language has developed through the centuries. By finding the answers to these questions you will see how we have borrowed and adapted words from many foreign languages; you will come to understand the meanings of the words more clearly; and you will begin to find good reasons for spellings that may have puzzled or annoyed you in the past.

You will of course need a dictionary. For Sets 56–62, almost any dictionary will do, but from Set 63 onwards an etymological dictionary is essential.

To whet your appetite for these exercises, and to show that the study of words can be a fascinating pastime, we begin with interesting facts and stories about well-known words.

---

56. STORIES ABOUT WORDS

1. When wandering bands of dark-skinned people appeared in England several centuries ago they were thought to be Egyptians. Omit the first syllable of the word *Egyptians* and you have a clue to the present-day name of these people; what is it? Give two alternative spellings.

2. The Strand in London is now separated from the Thames by many buildings, but its name is a reminder that it used to be within sight of the river. What does the word *strand* mean in this connection?

3. A certain kind of iris is called the *gladiolus* because it has sword-shaped leaves and the Latin word for *sword* is *gladius*. Can you suggest why a certain kind of man was called a *gladiator*?

4. Roman soldiers used to be paid an allowance for the purchase of salt. The Latin word for *salt* is *sal*, and this is a clue to an English word meaning *wages paid by the month or by the year*. What is the word?

5. Canals used to be called *navigations*, and the labourers who dug them in the 18th century were called *navigators*. The word *navigator* became abbreviated, and is used to this day in its shortened form as a name for a labourer on roads, etc. What is it?

6. The French word for *day* is *jour*. A well-known English word beginning with *jour* used to mean *a day's travel*, and another one means *a daily newspaper or record of events*. What are these two words?

7. (a) How would you *don* a garment?
   (b) How would you *doff* it?
   (c) The word *don* is a shortened form of the words *do on*; what do you think was the original form of the word *doff*?
   (d) In the 16th century, people spoke of *douting* a fire; Shakespeare used the word, and in some dialects the word is still used. What do you think it means?

8. Pilgrims going to Canterbury used to ride at an easy gallop that was called a *Canterbury gallop*. In modern English this phrase has been shortened to a word of six letters. What is it?

9. During the night we fast, or go without food. What name is given to the meal that breaks or puts an end to this fast?

10. The Hospital of St. Mary of Bethlehem, in London, was founded in 1547 as an asylum for the insane. The name was shortened to Bethlem and then to Bedlam. What does the word *bedlam* mean nowadays?

11. (a) A certain kind of flatfish was called a *holy fish* because it was eaten on holy days. The Old English word for *holy* was *halig*, and another name for a flatfish is *butt*; find the modern name for this fish.
    (b) On holy days people did no work. What are holy days called now?

12. In the Middle Ages there was a sport in which an umpire decided how much forfeit-money each player should put into a cap. The game was called *hand in the cap*, and this is a clue to a word still used by sportsmen to describe a system of giving some competitors a start over others; what is this word?

13. (a) What is a *grotto*?

(b) Things that are queer and fantastic in shape, like the decorations in grottoes, can be described by an adjective that begins with the first few letters of the word *grotto*; what is this word?

14. In olden times a well-known measure of land was the length of the furrow in the common field. The first half of the word *furrow* is a clue to this measure, which is still in use. What is it called?

15. From the name of a river in Asia Minor—the Mæander, or Meander—we have an English word that reminds us of how this river made its way to the sea. What was of particular interest about it?

16. What do we call a man who deals in *iron* goods? Now can you say what name we give to a man who sells fruit in the street? (It reminds us that street traders used to sell apples called *costards*.)

17. A method of protecting a person from smallpox is to inoculate him with a preparation obtained from a cow. The Latin word for *cow* is *vacca*, and this is a clue to the English word now used for this treatment. What is the word?

18. We are told in the Old Testament that in a Jewish ritual the chief priest used to allow a goat to escape into the wilderness after he had laid the sins of the people upon it. Drop the first letter of the word *escape*, and you have a clue to a modern word that reminds us of this ancient ritual. What is it, and what does it mean?

19. Pan, the horned god of flocks and shepherds, used to appear suddenly before travellers in the forest and fill them with terror. A great fright of this kind used to be referred to as · · · · · fear. Can you supply the missing word? The clue to it is the name *Pan*.

20. The Spartans of ancient Greece were people of simple habits and few words. They lived in Laconia, and it is from this name that we get a word meaning *said in a few words*. What is it?

21. (a) It was once the custom in some countries to spend the week before Lent in revelry and riotous amusements. The people then "put away flesh" (that is, went without meat) until Easter. The name for this time of merrymaking comes partly from the Latin word for *flesh*, which is *carnis*; what is it?

(b) Find two other words from the same root; one is the name of a flesh-coloured garden-flower, and the other is used to describe a flesh-eating animal.

(c) What does the word *incarnate* mean?

22. A well-known word describes goods of the kind that used to be sold at the fair of St. Audrey in the Isle of Ely. The word is made by dropping the initial letter of the name *St. Audrey*, and making a slight change of spelling that does not affect the pronunciation. Say what the word is and what it means.

23. Some people (e.g., missionaries) feel that God has called them to do a special work in life, so they refer to their occupation as a *calling*. Another word with the same meaning comes from the Latin word *vocare* (to call); what is it?

24. (a) Hundreds of years ago a housewife would wear *a napron*, and boys knew how to kill *a naddre* or catch *an ewt*. What do we call these things nowadays? Look at the words in italics and read them aloud; then see if you can explain exactly what changes have taken place.

(b) The word *eke* used to mean *an addition*. Sometimes a person was given an additional name called an *eke-name*; what word has this become?

25. See if you can suggest why it is that the word *nausea* is derived from the same Latin root as the word *nautical*. The dictionary should tell you all you need to know.

26. A writer in the year 1583 said, "Galaxia is a white way or milky Circle in the heavens." What is the modern word for *Galaxia*? What does it mean when it is used metaphorically?

27. The Latin word *calculus* means *small stone*. Using this as a clue, find words that mean:

(a) a substance that forms the basis of limestone;
(b) to count or reckon, using pebbles as counters.

The German word for *lime* is *kalk*; can you think of an English word, very similar to the German one, that means the same thing?

28. The Latin name for the eyebrow is *supercilium*, and this has given us an English word that describes a person who raises his eyebrows in a haughty and contemptuous way. What is this word?

57. WORDS FROM OLD ENGLISH

Thousands of our most-used words have their roots in Old English, but some of them have undergone so many changes that it is difficult to see the connection between the modern word and the Old English root. Here are a few that you should be able to recognize. They are given like definitions in a dictionary, but the words defined have been omitted. Supply the missing words.

> EXAMPLE: A passage between rows of seats.
> [O.E. *gangan*, to go]
> ANSWER: gangway

(a) A container for carrying water, etc. [O.E. *buc*, a pitcher]

(b) A small village. [O.E. *ham*, home]

(c) The master of the house. [O.E. *hus*, house]

(d) Not often. [O.E. *seld*, rare]

(e) To leave lonely by death. [O.E. *bereafian*, to rob]

(f) To go with the wind or tide. [O.E. *drifan*, to drive]

(g) To be consumed and tormented by worry. [O.E. *fretan*, to eat]

(h) Sour, sharp, or painful. [O.E. *bitan*, to bite]

(i) A bench with a high back and arms. [O.E. *setl*, seat]

(j) Firm, constant, and unchanging. [O.E. *stede*, place]

58. NEAR RELATIONS

Each of the French words given below has a near relation in the English language—a word with at least the first three letters exactly the same. The meanings of most of the English words are not quite the same as the meanings of the French words, but the connection is very close and very easy to recognize; e.g., the answer to No. 1 could be *dignity*, or *dignified*. Find at least one near relation for each French word. Study the meanings of the words you write out, and be prepared to answer questions about them.

(1) **digne,** worthy
(2) **appeler,** to call
(3) **chambre,** room
(4) **mort,** dead
(5) **coucher,** to lie down
(6) **facile,** easy
(7) **comprendre,** to understand

(8) **chanson,** song
(9) **temps,** time
(10) **langue,** tongue
(11) **utile,** useful
(12) **coffre,** chest or trunk
(13) **céleste,** heavenly
(14) **terminer,** to finish
(15) **rougir,** to blush
(16) **porte,** door
(17) **tard,** late
(18) **malade,** ill
(19) **pendre,** to hang
(20) **dormir,** to sleep
(21) **pensée,** thought
(22) **chandelle,** candle
(23) **brun,** brown
(24) **cygne,** swan
(25) **escalier,** staircase
(26) **année,** year
(27) **orner,** to decorate
(28) **avion,** aircraft
(29) **libre,** free
(30) **femme,** woman
(31) **soleil,** sun
(32) **lune,** moon
(33) **terre,** earth
(34) **lumière,** light
(35) **petit,** small
(36) **donner,** to give
(37) **vérité,** truth
(38) **vin,** wine
(39) **arbre,** tree
(40) **laver,** to wash
(41) **jaune,** yellow
(42) **vendre,** to sell
(43) **nom,** name
(44) **matin,** morning
(45) **ami,** friend
(46) **blanc,** white
(47) **pont,** bridge
(48) **mur,** wall
(49) **parler,** to speak
(50) **fil,** thread

59. WORDS FROM THE LATIN

1. The list below contains a number of Latin roots, with their meanings. By looking up the first three (or more) letters of each one in your dictionary you can find an English word derived from it. The definitions given in your dictionary are not exactly the same as the meanings of the roots, but the connection is very close and very easy to recognize; e.g., the answer to (a) could be *aviary* or *aviation*. Find at least one word derived from each root. Study the meanings of the words you write out, and be prepared to answer questions about them.

(a) **avis,** bird
(b) **gradus,** a step or degree
(c) **gratus,** pleasing; thankful
(d) **vestis,** garment
(e) **linum,** flax
(f) **tremo,** shake; quiver
(g) **fames,** hunger
(h) **barba,** beard
(i) **locus,** place
(j) **alter,** the other of two
(k) **rota,** a wheel
(l) **vagor,** wander
(m) **frater,** brother
(n) **sanctus,** sacred; holy
(o) **filum,** thread
(p) **verus,** true
(q) **augeo,** make larger; increase

(r) **festum,** a holiday or feast (u) **erro,** wander; stray

(s) **durus,** hard (v) **canis,** dog

(t) **granum,** seed (w) **feles,** cat

  (x) flos, **floris,** flower

2. Do these as you did those in the previous exercise, but with the following addition. In brackets you are given one or more prefixes. Each prefix is a clue to another word derived from the same root. E.g., in (a) this could be *incredible*—which is made up of the prefix **in-** and part of the root **credo.**

(a) **credo,** believe (*in-*)

(b) **fides,** faith (*in-*)

(c) **folium,** leaf (*port-*)

(d) opus, **operis,** work (*co-*)

(e) **frigus,** cold (*re-*)

(f) **tribuo,** give (*con-*) (*dis-*)

(g) **numerus,** number (*e-*) (*in-*)

(h) **anima,** breath, life (*in-*)

(i) rumpo, **ruptum,** break (*e-*) (*inter-*)

(j) **radix,** root (*e-*)

(k) **migro,** remove; depart to another place (*e-*) (*im-*)

(l) **rodo,** gnaw (*cor-*)

📖 LOOK THESE UP

See page 29 for instructions

1. Pick out any examples of *anachronism* in these sentences: 110 **83**

(a) Cæsar ordered his officers to attack the city when the clock struck six.

(b) In the reign of Charles II, gentlemen wore silks and nylons, and looked more like women than men.

2. Why is it wrong to use the expression *a constellation of stars*? 12 **8** Ex 3 and 108 **78**

3. In which *person* is each of these sentences written?

(a) I shall come if I can.

(b) He will come if he can.

(c) They will come if they can.

(d) We shall come if we can.

(e) She will come if she can.

31 Ex. 8

4. Which of these words are *onomatopœic*? 131 **116**

fall, tinkle, clatter, pour, quack

5. What is it that can be described as a *compressed simile*? 125 **108**

Revision. The words represented by these pictures have all occurred in the exercises of Set 56 on pages 88–89. Each word is illustrated in black. The red picture reminds you of the word's history.

Identify the words, and say briefly what you remember about how they came into being.

ROOTS AS WE SEE THEM

alone	mon(o)	marriage	gam
	sol	measure	meter
angle	gon	men	See man
back	re-	mind	anim
bad	mal-	new	nov
between	inter-	one	uni
body	corp	peace	pac
call	voca	pig	por(c)
carry	port	point	punct
cross	cruc	rock	petr
	crus	round	peri
cut	sect	say	dict
doll	pup	sea	mari
draw	tract	see	scope
earth	geo		vis
	terr	seed	See grain
eight	oct	self	auto-
end	fin	ship	nav
far	tele	shout	clam
father	pater	side	later
feet	See foot	single	mon(o)
first	prim	small	micro
flow	flu	solid	stereo
fold	plic	sound	phone
foot	ped		son
	pod	star	aster
	pus		astr
four	quad	stone	lith
grain	gran	strong	fort
great	magn	teeth	See tooth
	mega	ten	dec
hand	man	three	tri-
haul	See draw	time	chron
head	cap		temp
hear	audi	tooth	dent
hold	ten	two	bi-
hollow	cav		dou
horn	corn		du
hundred	cent	voice	phone
ill	mal-		voc
join	junct	walk	ambul
law	nom	water	aqua
life	bio		aque
	vita	weight	bar
light	phos	well	bene
	phot	wish	vol
look	spec	word	log
love	am	write	graph
lover of	phil		scrib
make	fact		script
man	anthrop		
many	multi	year	ann
	poly		enn

This list shows how a number of the commonest roots sometimes appear in modern words; that is to say, it gives fragments of the old roots in their present-day spelling. To remind you that they are neither whole words nor the original roots they are printed in italics; but a few unchanged roots (and some prefixes) are shown in ordinary type.

60. FIND THE ROOT

The definitions given below are taken from a dictionary. What you have to do is to find the words to which they refer—that is, *one word* that corresponds with each definition. Work like this:

(a) Notice which word is printed in italics.

(b) Look up this word in the list on the left, and find out how a root with this meaning can be recognized in modern words.

(c) The root will give you a clue to the first few letters of the word you want to find, so turn to a dictionary and find a word which begins in this way *and which has the right meaning*.

EXAMPLE: In No. 1 the main word is *hundred*; in the list of roots, opposite the word **hundred**, you find *cent*; turning now to the dictionary you find *centenarian*, *centenary*, *centigrade*, *centurion*, and other words beginning with *cent*; but the only one of these words that means *a Roman officer commanding a hundred men* is *centurion*, so this is the answer.

(1) A Roman officer commanding a *hundred* men.
(2) A lever moved by the *foot*.
(3) To tell a person what to write, *say*, or do.
(4) A loud, confused *shouting*.
(5) Something *new* or strange.
(6) Concerning *teeth*.
(7) A *water*-tank for live fish, etc.
(8) A *sea*-creature with *eight* arms.
(9) To make *peace*ful and quiet; to calm; to soothe.
(10) *Ill* will; spiteful feelings.
(11) The *father* and ruler of a family or tribe.
(12) Coming last; definitely the *end*; conclusive.
(13) The science of plant and animal *life*.
(14) To turn into stone or *rock*.
(15) A united *body* of persons.
(16) A *body* of troops; a division of an army.

In each of the remaining questions use the same procedure as for those above, but give as your answer a word that can be substituted for the contents of the brackets. The answer to the example is *corporation*.

EXAMPLE: Broadcasting is controlled by a [*body* of persons] responsible to Parliament.

(17) I am only a [*new* learner]; I took up skating less than a week ago.

(18) Tewkesbury is situated at the [*join*ing-place] of the Avon and the Severn.

(19) The king hid in a [*hollow* place] behind the oak panelling.

(20) This would be an excellent [*first* book] for the infants.

(21) He is a most easy and [*flow*ing] speaker.

(22) Leprosy is now a rare [*ill*ness].

(23) Squares and rectangles are [*four*-sided figures].

(24) The guide book contains a [list in order of *time*] of important events.

(25) The first [period of *ten* years] of this century was known as the Edwardian period.

61. WORDS WITH TWO ROOTS

These questions are similar to those in Set 60, but in each one you will have to look up *two* words in the list of roots.   The answer will be a single word as previously.

EXAMPLE: An imaginary animal like a horse with *one horn*.

In this definition the words **one** and **horn** give us *uni* and *corn*. When these are put together they suggest the word *unicorn*, which can be checked in the dictionary.

CAUTION: Putting the two roots together only *suggests* the right word; the spelling may be different.

(a) An instrument that picks up *small sounds* for electrical transmission.

(b) The singing of the same notes by all voices, so as to make *one sound*.

(c) A person who *loves* to help other *men* and other people.

To find the remaining words you will need to set down the roots in reverse order.

(d) An instrument that *measures* the pressure (or *weight*) of the air.

(e) A speaking-horn that makes the *voice* sound *great*.

(f) A well-known word now means "to make in large numbers," but it used to mean "to *make* by *hand*"; what is it?

(g) To *call back* a decision or a law, and cancel it.

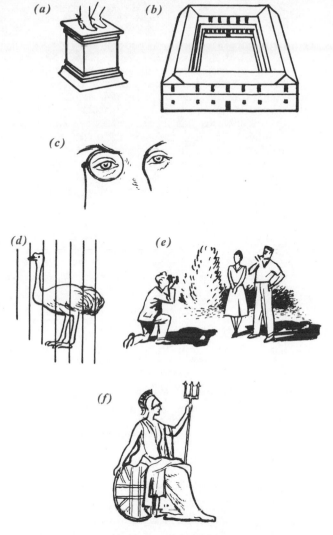

(a)
(b)
(c)
(d)
(e)
(f)

62. FIND THE WORDS

A clue is given below to each of these six pictures. Each clue will give you one root or two roots for the word which the picture represents. Look up the clues in the list of roots on the opposite page.

(a) *foot*
(b) *four*
(c) *single*

(d) *two feet*
(e) *light-writing*
(f) *three teeth*

93

63. WORD FAMILIES

You have seen in previous exercises that when several words are derived from the same root their meanings are alike in certain ways. For example, in Set 60 (15 and 16) you found two related words that come from the Latin word meaning *body*.

In this exercise you will be dealing with other groups of words that can be regarded as belonging to families. First you are given (in bold type) a clue to the root; look this up on page 92, and then use your dictionary as you have previously done. Wherever you find a dash, supply the missing word, but *be sure that all such words belong to the same family.*

1. *From the Greek and Latin prefix meaning* **three**

   (a) A —— is a space enclosed by three straight lines.
   (b) A stand with three legs is a ——, and a cycle with three wheels is a ——.
   (c) Three children born together are ——, and three musicians playing together are a ——.
   (d) France has a three-coloured flag called a ——.
   (e) Father, Son, and Holy Spirit are referred to by a name that means *three joined in one*. What is it?

2. *From the Latin word meaning* **head**

   (a) The head man on board a ship is called a ——.
   (b) The "head" town of a country is called the ——.
   (c) The letter at the beginning or "head" of your name is a —— letter.
   (d) A headland jutting out to sea can be called a ——.
   (e) What does the word *decapitate* mean?

3. *From the Latin word meaning* to **carry**

   A case for carrying official papers is called a ——, and one for carrying clothes is a ——. A typewriter small enough to be carried easily is said to be ——, and a man paid to carry all these things to a train or taxi is called a ——.

4. *From the Latin word meaning* to **hear**

   (a) People who listen to a concert are called an ——; they sit in a hall called an ——, and they are displeased if the singers are not ——.
   (b) People who wish to sing at an important concert or broadcast are given a trial hearing called an ——.
   (c) What does *inaudible* mean?

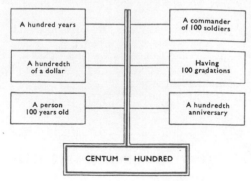

A hundred years	A commander of 100 soldiers
A hundredth of a dollar	Having 100 gradations
A person 100 years old	A hundredth anniversary

CENTUM = HUNDRED

5. Name the six words that are shown here to have grown from the Latin root *centum*.

6. *From the Latin word meaning* **two**

   Two pianists may play a ——; two men may fight a ——; two pupils may sit together in a —— desk; two copies of a letter may be obtained by using carbon paper to make a ——.

7. *From the Latin word meaning* **strong**

   (a) A town made strong against attack is called a —— town; a stronghold can be called either a —— or a ——; strong-willed people who show courage in time of trouble are said to display ——.
   (b) What is meant by the words *effort* and *reinforce*? Use the words *strong* or *strength* in your answers.

8. *From the Latin word meaning* a **doll**

   (a) A doll worked by strings is a ——.
   (b) A young dog small enough to be like a doll or toy is a ——.
   (c) An insect or chrysalis lying like a doll in a cocoon is called a ——.

9. *From the Latin word meaning* a **point**

   (a) A hole made by a sharp point is a ——.
   (b) Putting the points (full stops, etc.) in a written passage is called ——.
   (c) A person who is on the point of time (or "on the dot") is said to be ——.

94

10. *From the Latin word meaning* the **earth**

    (a) What do we call a raised bank of earth?

    (b) What do we call a large area or region of the earth?

    (c) Which dog burrows in the earth for rabbits?

    (d) Find a word that means *concerning the earth.*

    (e) What is the meaning of *interred*? (Look up *inter* in your dictionary, and use the word *earth* in your answer.)

11. *From the Latin word meaning* to **see**

    (a) A distant view between rows of trees is a ——.

    (b) Something seen in a dream or trance is a ——.

    (c) When we call up a picture of something in our minds we are said to —— it.

    (d) Say what these three words mean, using the words *see* or *seen* in your definitions:
        invisible   supervise   evident

12. *From the Latin word meaning* **life**

    Those organs of the body that are absolutely necessary for maintaining life are called —— organs; health-giving and life-giving substances found in foodstuffs are called ——; people who have the strength and power to lead a very active life are said to have great ——.

13. *From the Latin word meaning* **grain** or **seed**

    (a) A storehouse for grain is called a ——, and a country house with outbuildings for storing grain is called a ——.

    (b) Give the name of a very hard rock made up of grains of quartz, etc.

    (c) The modern French word for *apple* is *pomme*, and this is a clue to the name of a fruit that is like a pulpy apple full of grains or seeds; what is it?

14. *From the Latin word meaning* **alone**

    (a) A song sung by one person alone is called a ——; that is to say, the singer is the —— performer.

    (b) A hermit leads a —— life; that is, he prefers to live in ——.

    (c) What does *desolate* mean?

15. *From the Greek word meaning* **lover of**

    (a) A man who loves wisdom and knowledge is a ——, and a man who loves to help other people is a ——.

    (b) What does *philharmonic* mean?

    (c) The Greek word *hippos* means *horse*. Can you suggest the meaning of the name *Philip*?

16. *From the Latin word meaning* to **draw** (or **haul**)

    (a) A machine for pulling a plough is called a ——, and the process of pulling or drawing is ——.

    (b) Give short definitions of these words, using the word **draw** in each one:
        attract   extract   retract   distract   protract

17. *From the Latin word meaning* **pig**

    (a) What do we call the flesh of the pig?

    (b) Give the name of a gnawing animal that is something like a small pig with spines or thorns on its back.

    (c) The name of a fine kind of earthenware is associated with the name of a delicate shell; this shell is shaped like a pig's back. Say what this kind of earthenware is called.

18. *From the Latin word meaning* **great**

    (a) A great and wealthy business-man is called a ——; if he has a home of great splendour we say that it is ——.

    (b) We use a microscope to —— small objects, and a telescope to judge the —— of stars.

19. *From the Latin word meaning* a **cross**

    (a) Christ was ——, and an image of Him fixed on the Cross is called a ——. Wars fought against infidels, under the sign of the Cross, were called ——.

    (b) Many churches are built on a *cruciform* plan; what does this mean?

    (c) Explain, if you can, how it is that the words *excruciating* and *cruise* belong to this word-family.

20. *From the Greek word meaning* **alone**

    (a) Where do monks live alone?

    (b) Who reigns alone?

    (c) Find a word of ten letters that describes speech that is in one tone of voice alone.

    (d) What do we call a pattern of overlapping initials that form one design alone?

    (e) When there is only one firm doing a particular kind of business, what do we call this state of affairs?

    (f) Using the word *alone*, define the words *monologue* and *monosyllable*.

21. *From the Latin word meaning* to **write**

(*a*) Professional writers long ago were known as
——; the handwriting they used is known as
——, and some of their sacred writings are
called ——.

(*b*) Using the words *write*, *writing*, or *written* in your
definitions, give the meanings of the following
words:

> inscribe   transcribe
> description   prescription

22. *From the Latin word meaning* **time**

(*a*) Things that are meant to last for only a short
time are said to be ——; worldly things that are
not eternal but will pass away in time are said
to be ——.

(*b*) What does *contemporary* mean?

23. *From the Latin word meaning* to **look**

(*a*) A sight or a great show is called a ——, and
the people who look at it are ——.

(*b*) A sample for people to look at is called a ——.

(*c*) What do we call the band of colour that is seen
when we look through a glass prism?

(*d*) Give short definitions for these words, using the
word *look* in each one:

> expect   inspect   respect   prospect

24. *From the Latin word meaning* the **hand**

Find words that mean

(*a*) a paper or book written by hand;

(*b*) care of the hands and finger-nails;

(*c*) a kind of handcuff;

(*d*) the skilful handling of a tool or instrument;

(*e*) the controlling and handling of a business.

25. *From the Latin word meaning* to **walk**

Find words that mean

(*a*) to go at a slow walking-pace;

(*b*) a conveyance for sick or injured persons;
> This was once known by a French name that
> meant *walking hospital*.

(*c*) a carriage in which a baby can be wheeled when
one goes out walking;
> This word begins with *per-*.

(*d*) a sleep-walker.
> This word begins with *somn-*.

(1)

(2)

(3)

(4)

Revision. Identify the words represented by the
black pictures, and say how they came into being.

All these words occurred in the exercises of Set 56
on pages 88–9. The red pictures are to remind you
of the words' history.

96

USING AN ETYMOLOGICAL DICTIONARY

UP to this point you have either been told the roots from which certain words are derived, or have been able to identify them on page 92. In the remaining exercises in this section you will have to use an *etymological* dictionary. Almost any etymological dictionary will give you the information you need for most of the questions; if an occasional word is not fully explained in the dictionary you are using, pass on to the next question.

All the exercises in Sets 64 to 71 are concerned not so much with the *definitions* of words as with their *origins*. For example, suppose that you were asked to complete this sentence:

Castanets used to be made from nutshells of the —— tree.

You turn to your dictionary and find something like this:

> **castanets′,** *n.* instruments of wood or ivory, attached to dancer's fingers to rattle in time with dancing. [From L. *castanea*, chestnut.]

The required word is to be found in the square brackets—*chestnut*. No other answer will do, because the purpose of the question is to show you that the word *castanets* comes from the Latin name for *chestnut*. Similarly in all other questions, pay particular attention to the etymology of the given words.

---

64. WORDS FROM MANY LANGUAGES

You have already seen that many of our words are derived from Latin and Greek. The words in this set are derived from sixteen other languages: Arabic, Chinese, Dutch, French, German, Hebrew, Hindustani, Icelandic, Italian, Malayan, Persian, Peruvian, Portuguese, Russian, Spanish, Tibetan.

Using the same abbreviations as those given in your dictionary (e.g., Du. = Dutch, G = German, etc.) say from which language each word is derived.

kaolin	cigar	bungalow	waltz,
bazaar	Hallelujah	cockatoo	yacht
mammoth	jungle	tea	pampas
bandit	poodle	garage	caravan
trek	ranch	lingerie	geyser
sofa	sonata	steppe	lama
loot	jackal	seraph	trousseau
sago	tank	balcony	molasses

When you have finished, think about the words and see how many of them you can associate in your mind with the customs, characteristics, or natural conditions of the countries from which they have come.

65. SOME INTERESTING DERIVATIONS

Before you answer these questions, re-read the instructions above. Remember that the answer to each question must refer to the *etymology* of the given word, which in most dictionaries is enclosed in square brackets, like this: [L. *medicus* physician].

(a) Where does the word *orang-outang* come from, and what does it mean in English?

(b) What does an *umbrella* provide for its user?

(c) What words have been combined to give the word *fortnight*?

(d) Give one adjective that describes the *piccolo*.

(e) The word *alligator* is derived from two Spanish words. What are they, and what do they mean?

(f) Give the meanings of the Latin words from which we derive the word *peninsula*.

(g) What does the prefix *step-* mean in the words *stepchild, stepson*, etc.?

(h) What is *foolscap*, and how did it get its name?

(i) Look up the words beginning with *mill-*, and then give the meaning of the Latin word *mille*.

(j) In two words say what a *cenotaph* is. Where would you expect to find an *epitaph*?

(*k*) A famous German teacher thought of young children as plants that had to be encouraged to grow. Why did he call his school a *kindergarten*?

(*l*) Why is the name *dessert* given to the fruit, etc. that is served after a meal?

(*m*) Say in two words what a *dinosaur* was.

(*n*) The *dodo* was an absurd and clumsy bird, and was very aptly named by the Portuguese. What does its name mean?

(*o*) What evidence have we that the word *canopy* has come to us from one of the hot lands?

(*p*) The word *tandem* (as now applied to bicycles for more than one rider) was once a pun on a Latin word that refers to time, not distance. What does it mean?

(*q*) Some people consider it ridiculous to speak of "pink *blancmange*". Can you say why?

(*r*) It was once thought that there were four "elements" (earth, water, air, fire) and also a highly-refined substance to which the name *quintessence* was given. What does this word mean?

66. PLACES AND PEOPLE

Words from proper nouns. You probably know that sardines are so called because they are caught off the shores of Sardinia, and that it was a man named Macintosh who first produced a waterproof material for making raincoats. The following questions concern other words now in common use that began—like those just mentioned—as the names of places and people. An etymological dictionary will tell you the origins of these words.

(1) A *milliner* sells goods of the kind that used to come from a particular place. Give the name of this place.

(2) How did the flowering tree known as the *magnolia* get its name?

(3) How did the *spaniel* get its name?

(4) Why are *italics* so called?

(5) Explain the derivation of the word *mausoleum*.

(6) Where were some of the earliest *artesian* wells made?

(7) Who was it that showed how to *pasteurize* milk so as to kill harmful germs?

(8) Why is *nicotine* so named?

(9) Some people confuse the words *serial* and *cereal*. You will not make this mistake if you remember that *serial* means *part of a series*, and that *cereal* reminds us of the goddess of corn. What was her name?

(10) The earliest *magnets* were lumps of loadstone. Where did this rock come from?

67. SOME APT COMPARISONS

The *leg* of a table is so called because of its likeness to a human leg; in the same way we refer to a *branch* of a river (as of a tree), the *eye* of a needle, and so on. A similar process has gone on in other languages, as we can easily see by looking at the origins of some of the words that have come to us from abroad. For example, the word *tulip* comes from a Persian word meaning *turban*; think of a turbaned head and then of a tulip flower and you will understand the connection. With this kind of comparison in mind, and remembering that we are concerned with the *etymology* of the given words, complete the following sentences.

(1) *Cirrus* cloud is light and fleecy like a ———.

(2) The function of a *molar* is to grind like a ———.

(3) A *comet* seems to have long ——— trailing behind it.

(4) The *daisy*, which opens in the morning, derives its name from the words ——— ———.

(5) *Khaki* cloth was chosen for soldiers' uniforms because it was so much like the ——— of the desert that it was a good camouflage.

(6) Some of the fat used in the making of *margarine* forms into glistening drops that look like ———.

(7) Someone has described the rippling muscles of a strong man as being "like little rabbits running about under a rug." Look up the derivation of the word *muscle*, and say how it illustrates a fanciful idea of the same kind.

(8) A *stimulus* acts as a ——— to prod a person into being more active.

68. LOOKING BACK

An etymological dictionary reminds us that some words have changed in form or in meaning since they first came into use. It also gives us interesting glimpses into customs and conditions in the past. For instance, we find that the word *furlong* comes from the words *furrow + long*; that is, a furlong was the length of a furrow in the common field in medieval times.

(1) Five hundred years ago the word *good-bye* did not exist in its present form. What was it that people said?

(2) For what length of time did people formerly have to stay in *quarantine*?

(3) How did a *mountebank* originally attract the attention of a crowd?

(4) The word *neighbour* is at least four hundred years old. What did it mean at first?

(5) *Morris* dancing came to England from North Africa, and the Old English name for it reminds us of this fact. What was the original name?

(6) People suffering from madness are called *lunatics* because it used to be thought that insanity was caused by the changes of the ———.

(7) What word did people once use instead of *gaffer*?

(8) What form did a *volume* of historical records take in ancient times?

(9) A *spinster*, nowadays, is an unmarried woman. What did the word originally mean?

(10) The *piano* gives variations in tone that were not possible on the harpsichord, and its original name drew attention to this fact; what was this name, and what did it mean?

(11) In question 24 on page 89 you met the words *naddre* and *ewt* (which we now know as *adder* and *newt*). With these words in mind, explain the derivation of the words *orange* and *notch*.

(12) Thinking about the changes that have taken place in the words given in the previous question will help you to understand how the three divisions of Yorkshire have come to be known as *ridings*. See if you can suggest how the name *North Riding* originated.

69. ADOPTED WORDS

Most of the words that have come to us from other languages have undergone changes. For example, the Hindustani word *jangal* becomes *jungle*, and the German word *pudel* gives us *poodle*. Some words, however, we have adopted in their original form. A few of them are given below, and what you have to do is to look up their etymology and supply their meanings in place of the dashes.

(1) A defendant who says that he has an *alibi* claims to have been ——— when the offence was committed.

(2) A *souvenir* helps one to ——— a past occasion.

(3) An *omnibus* (now called a *bus*) is a vehicle ——— ———.

(4) Strictly speaking, a *café* is a place where ——— is served.

(5) An *opera* is a dramatic ——— in which music is an essential part.

(6) A *nebula* is a patch of light in the sky that looks like ———.

(7) *Neon* gas was so named because it was a ——— gas.

(8) When a governor decides to *veto* a suggestion he says, "———it."

(9) When a judge issues a *fiat* he is in effect saying, "——— ——— ——— ———."

(10) The noun 'table' is of *neuter* gender because it belongs to ——— gender.

(11) A singer is given an *encore* when the audience wishes to hear him ———.

(12) The *focus* of a living-room on a winter's night is the ———.

(13) An *ignoramus* and his stupid companions are likely to answer many questions by saying, "——— ——— ——— ———."

(14) During the *Renaissance*, interest in the arts and in learning was ——— ———.

(15) "Hull *via* York" means "Hull by ——— of York".

(16) A *piccolo* is a ——— flute.

(17) In the earliest kind of *camera*, pictures were made by light in a dark room or ———.

(18) A *tableau* is a group of persons arranged so as to form a ———.

(19) A bride's *trousseau* was originally a ——— of clothes, etc.

70. FIND THE LINK

In the exercise on *Word Families* (pages 94–6) you saw that certain words which at first sight seem to have little or no connection with each other are in fact derived from the same root. For example, *terrace*, *territory*, *terrier*, and *interred* are all associated with the Latin word *terra* (earth). In *Word Families* you were told what the connecting-link was, but in this exercise you have to find it for yourself.

In each pair or group of words say what the root is, and be ready to define the words themselves in such a way that the relationship between them is clear.

> EXAMPLE: A builder's *plumb*-line
> A *plumber* and decorator.
>
> ANSWER: Latin *plumbum*, lead.
>
> If you were asked to define the words, you might say that a plumb-line has a lead weight hanging from it, and that a plumber works in lead.

(1) A highwayman's *cloak*
The town hall *clock*

(2) To *replenish* the larder
Plenty of water

(3) And Moses built an *altar*.
Every valley shall be *exalted*.

(4) To *endorse* a cheque
The *dorsal* fin of a shark

(5) A piece of tin *foil*
The *foliage* of a tree

(6) The *League* of Young Dramatists
A *ligament* in the knee

(7) *Cumulus* clouds rise to great heights.
Stones *accumulate* on the beach.

(8) A *colander* full of boiled peas
A coffee *percolator*

(9) A *corn* on one's foot
Playing the *cornet*
The lion and the *unicorn*

(10) The *calligraphy* of a fine manuscript
Patterns seen in a *kaleidoscope*

(11) A *miracle* in Galilee
A *mirage* in the desert
A reflection in a *mirror*

(12) To *extort* money by blackmail.
To *torture* a prisoner
To *distort* one's features in pain

(13) Tennis-players *congregate* at Wimbledon.
Human beings are *gregarious*.

(14) *Tinsel* glitters.
Diamonds *scintillate*.

(15) A keen and *eager* pupil
Pickled in *vinegar*

(16) The *pile* of a carpet
Capillary vessels in the lungs

(17) A *junior* school
A *juvenile* court
To *rejuvenate* an elderly person

(18) Horses carrying provisions in *panniers*
A *pantry* well stocked with food
A picnic with one's *companions*

(19) Owls and other *nocturnal* creatures
A *nocturne* by Chopin
The spring *equinox*

(20) A *candidate* for election
A truthful and *candid* answer
An *incandescent* lamp-filament

(21) A *disturbance* at a political meeting
A *turbulent* tribe of savages
A *turbid* mill-stream

(22) An amusing *caper*
An unaccountable *caprice*
The tropic of *Capricorn*

(23) A carpenter's *mallet*
A *malleable* metal
To *maul* someone in a fight

(24) Jewels cut and polished by a *lapidary*
A *dilapidated* castle

(25) The *chancel* of a church
A machine to *cancel* the postage stamps on letters.

✓ MARK THESE YOURSELF

The answers are on page 145

1. Can you suggest what the letter *m* stands for in the abbreviation *ml* on a medicine bottle?

2. Mention at least three electrical units that are named after scientists or inventors.

3. In which countries are the places from which these wines take their names?
burgundy, champagne, port, sherry.

4. Use an etymological dictionary to find out why the down-curved points of an arrow are called *barbs*.

Word Families. These pictures are arranged in sets of three. The words they represent are also grouped in threes, just as the words in each exercise of Set 63 were grouped. Identify the words, and say how each group is related.

71. WORD CHAINS

The words in this exercise follow a pattern rather like the links of a chain, one pair leading to another. Each pair of words joined by a curved dash (e.g., two ~ marriage) is a clue to a single word that conveys a similar meaning. To find this word, look up the given words in the table on page 92, and put together the two roots that you find there. This should suggest the required word to you; if not, use a dictionary. Here is an example:

CLUES		ANSWERS
two	~ marriage	bi-gamy
many	~ marriage	poly-gamy
many	~ angle	poly-gon
eight	~ angle	octa-gon
eight	~ foot	octo-pus

(a) well ~ say
bad ~ say
bad ~ wish
well ~ wish
well ~ make
bad ~ make

(b) solid ~ see
small ~ see
small ~ measure
time ~ measure
time ~ word
star ~ word
star ~ law
self ~ law

(c) great ~ mind
one ~ mind
one ~ side
many ~ side
many ~ fold
two ~ fold

(d) between ~ cut
two ~ cut
two ~ year
three ~ year
three ~ fold
four ~ fold
four ~ foot
hundred ~ foot
hundred ~ measure
round ~ measure
round ~ see
far ~ see
far ~ sound
great ~ sound
great ~ stone
alone ~ stone
alone ~ word
life ~ word
life ~ write
light ~ write
light ~ measure
earth ~ measure
earth ~ write
self ~ write

(1)

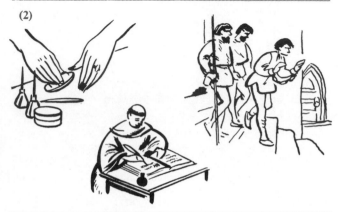

(2)

(3)

Word Families. These pictures, and the words they represent, are grouped in threes as the pictures on page 101 are. Identify the words and say how they are related.

Mention any points of interest you remember about the following words.

breakfast	medieval	cancel	quarantine
canter	unison	fortnight	mountebank
furlong	portfolio	coupon	gaffer
handicap	spinster	alligator	unanimous
journey	piano	foolscap	manufacture
gypsy	transport	cenotaph	lunatic
scapegoat	extract	alibi	kindergarten
gladiator	perimeter	volume	souvenir
carnation	café	tandem	megaphone
salary	conductor	encore	blancmange
calculate	barometer	exalted	quintessence
navvy	predict	milliner	endorse
foliage	intersect	spaniel	costermonger
halibut	cumulus	italics	anniversary
meander	decapitate	pasteurize	unicorn
apron	inaudible	nicotine	kaleidoscope
newt	puppet	cereal	scintillate
bedlam	punctual	cirrus	perambulator
panic	terrier	molar	companion
grotesque	nocturne	stimulus	pomegranate
vaccinate	desolate	comet	candidate
nausea	caper	daisy	philharmonic
tawdry	porcelain	khaki	dilapidated
biennial	crucifix	margarine	orang-outang
microphone	vinegar	muscle	adder
octagon	unique	good-bye	barber

✅ MARK THESE YOURSELF

The answers are on page 145

1. Name and briefly describe the gods of whom we are reminded by these words:

   martial   morphia   volcano

2. Look up the etymology of the word *insect*, and then say which of these three creatures illustrates it best.

3. If the Earl of Sandwich had worn a knitted woollen jacket and the Earl of Cardigan had been fond of meat served between slices of bread we should now be wearing sandwiches and eating cardigans. Explain this.

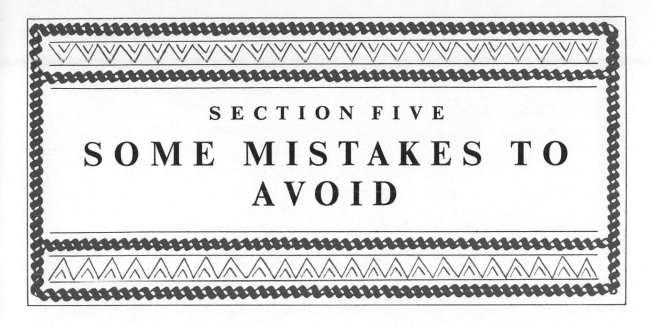

SOME MISTAKES TO AVOID

72. SOME BAD MISTAKES

In each of the following examples you are given in bold type two or more words that are often misused. What you have to do is to choose from these words the correct one to replace each dash in the given sentences.

1. to, too, two

(a) If you run after —— hares you will catch neither.

(b) Eat —— live, but do not live —— eat.

(c) —— eyes can see more than one.

(d) It is —— late to grieve when the chance is past.

(e) It takes —— —— make a quarrel.

2. of, off

(a) Lookers-on see most —— the game.

(b) Never put —— till tomorrow what may be done today.

(c) Two dogs fight for a bone, and a third runs —— with it.

(d) A man —— words and not —— deeds is like a garden full —— weeds.

(e) Better a finger —— than always aching.

3. their, there

(a) Go —— on your way home.

(b) They went with —— parents.

(c) —— are ink-stains on —— clothes.

(d) —— luggage was —— before them.

(e) They handed in —— papers to —— teachers.

4. its, it's

(a) —— my birthday today.

(b) This tree is shedding —— leaves.

(c) When —— melted —— ready to use.

(d) —— breadth is half —— length.

(e) —— possible that the spice has lost —— flavour.

5. theirs, there's

(a) The green towels are ——, not ours.

(b) I shall cover the stool as well, if —— enough material.

(c) —— less than half a loaf left.

(d) These are your sandwiches on the table; Paul and David have taken ——.

(e) —— was the only yacht to finish the course.

6. whose, who's

(a) —— been eating my porridge?
(b) —— slippers are these?
(c) This is the girl —— purse you found.
(d) Go and see —— knocking.
(e) He was a man —— only hobby was reading.

7. learn, learned; teach, taught

(a) Mary wants to —— shorthand, but can find no-one to —— her.
(b) Please —— me to knit; I am anxious to ——.
(c) Boy Scouts are —— to be kind and helpful to others.
(d) Until you have —— how to do something yourself you should not try to —— others.
(e) Last year Mr. Murray —— Peter to play the violin; he said that Peter —— very quickly.

8. lend, borrow

(a) May I —— your pencil, please?
(b) Brenda has lost her rubber; may she —— yours?
(c) David may —— my bat if he will —— me his fishing-rod.
(d) If you —— money you may not be able to repay it.
(e) If you —— money you may not be able to get it back.

73. NOUN OR VERB?

These examples all concern words that are spelt with a **c** when used as a noun, and with an **s** when used as a verb.

> EXAMPLE: We do piano *practice*, but we *practise* the piano.

Choose the correct word from those given in bold type.

1. practice, practise

(a) Are we allowed to —— running in the park?
(b) We have a rugger —— tomorrow.
(c) —— makes perfect.
(d) —— what you preach.
(e) You must —— regularly; an hour's —— a day is the least you should do.

2. licence, license

(a) Must I have a —— for my puppy?
(b) What will it cost to —— him?
(c) They refused to —— the shop for the sale of spirits.
(d) My television —— expires next week.
(e) You must —— the car if you mean to take it out, but no —— is needed while you keep it in the garage.

3. advice, advise

(a) What do you —— me to do?
(b) What —— did you give him?
(c) I —— you to get expert ——.
(d) He likes to —— others, but seldom follows his own ——.
(e) They may —— you to learn Spanish, but I —— you to take French.

4. prophecy, prophesy

(a) For we know in part, and we —— in part.
(b) Blessed are they that hear the words of this ——.
(c) And in them is fulfilled the —— of Esaias.
(d) And he pronounced this —— against me.
(e) He doth not —— good concerning me.

74. SOME FINER POINTS

Choose the correct word from those in bold type.

1. beside, besides

(a) —— hockey she plays netball and tennis.
(b) This wool is too thick; ——, it is the wrong colour.
(c) —— the palace gate stood a sentry.
(d) The dog waited patiently —— his master.
(e) I have other hobbies —— painting.

2. between, among

(a) The bull charged to and fro —— the spectators.
(b) They wondered what use five loaves and two fishes could be —— five thousand people.
(c) The housework can be shared —— the two of us.
(d) The votes were evenly divided —— Mr. Lees and Mr. Horton.
(e) The prize-money will be divided —— the members of the team.

3. **ringed, rung**

   (a) You will find that I have ——— all the mistakes in red ink.
   (b) No-one knew who had ——— the fire-alarm.
   (c) The curfew was ——— at sunset.
   (d) The bull had been ———, and was securely chained up.
   (e) The encampment was ——— about with cannon smoke.

4. **hanged, hung**

   (a) He ——— his head in shame.
   (b) "Beef, sir, is ———; men are ———."
   (c) As well be ——— for a sheep as a lamb.
   (d) He that hath an ill name is half ———.
   (e) Give in? I'll be ——— if I will!

5. **flowed, flown**

   (a) Much water has ——— under the bridges since last we met.
   (b) A stream of lava had ——— to within a few metres of the main gateway.
   (c) The varnish has ——— over the surface much more readily since I warmed it.
   (d) The gaoler unlocked the door of the cell, but the bird had ———.
   (e) Then came the news that Lindbergh had ——— solo across the Atlantic.

6. **all together, altogether**

   (a) We were huddled ——— in the same tent.
   (b) This is ——— ridiculous!
   (c) My time and money have been ——— wasted.
   (d) Keep your tools ——— in one box.
   (e) The guards were ——— unable to withstand the mad rush of prisoners.

7. **principal, principle**

   (a) Regent Street is one of the ——— streets of London.
   (b) The ——— of the college is Mr. Graham.
   (c) That would be dishonest; as a matter of ——— I would never do it.
   (d) The ——— of the telescope was well understood more than three hundred years ago.
   (e) He has already paid fifty pounds in interest on the money he borrowed, and has not yet repaid a penny of the ———.

8. **e.g., i.e.**

   (a) Coal is found in seams (———, in layers).
   (b) Flat-fish (———, plaice and sole) are caught in trawl-nets.
   (c) Kerosene (———, paraffin) is obtained from petroleum.
   (d) Many towns (———, Oxford and Bedford) sprang up at points where the river could be forded.
   (e) Vegetable oils (———, palm kernel oil) are used in the manufacture of margarine.

9. **lightning, lightening**

   (a) The tree was struck by ———.
   (b) You will improve the picture by ——— the background slightly.
   (c) ——— the load on top should make the car easier to control.
   (d) The ——— and thunder continued all night long.
   (e) We could see it ——— in the distance, but there was no sound of thunder.

75. RATHER MORE DIFFICULT

Choose the correct word from those given in bold type.

1. **alternate, alternative**

   (a) I have to work on ——— Saturdays.
   (b) In case the road is flooded we had better choose an ——— route.
   (c) ——— pages of the exercise book are blank paper.
   (d) We are asked to suggest an ——— ending to the play.
   (e) I agree that my plan will not be easy to carry out, but can you suggest an ——— way of overcoming the difficulty?

2. **council, counsel**

   (a) On one side of the square is the ——— house.
   (b) If he is to help you, you must let him ——— you.
   (c) Blessed is the man that walketh not in the ——— of the ungodly.
   (d) ——— for the prosecution then cross-examined the witness.
   (e) Each month we have a meeting of the Prefects' ———.

3. **affect, effect**

(*a*) What will be the —— of this acid?
(*b*) The scarcity of leather will —— the price of shoes.
(*c*) Do the new regulations —— you?
(*d*) This weed-killer will not take —— for about ten days.
(*e*) We expect the new factory to —— a big increase in production.

4. **dependant, dependent**

(*a*) The success of the garden party is largely —— on the weather.
(*b*) A dictionary is a most useful book, but you should not be wholly —— on it.
(*c*) His only —— is his aged mother.
(*d*) If you have a —— you should pay less income tax.
(*e*) I shall want to earn my own living, and not be —— on my parents.

5. **forego(ing), forgo(ing)**

(*a*) The —— instructions should be made known to all employees.
(*b*) I am disappointed at the thought of —— my holiday.
(*c*) The rule for late entries remains as already stated in the —— paragraph.
(*d*) You will have to —— smoking if you want to be a first-class athlete.
(*e*) With all this additional expense I shall have to —— some of my pleasures.

6. **practicable, practical**

(*a*) Men tried to fly by means of wings strapped to their arms, but they found that this was not——.
(*b*) Surely it is not —— to send men to Saturn.
(*c*) The scheme that you suggest is possible but not ——.
(*d*) A lot of electricity would be saved if everyone went to bed at sunset, but is that a —— idea?
(*e*) It would be a good thing if an observatory were built at the summit; what is more, the engineers say that it is a —— proposition.

7. **legible, illegible, eligible, ineligible**

(*a*) I am not —— to join until I am sixteen.
(*b*) Only those who have paid their membership fee are entitled to vote; others are ——.

(*c*) Be sure that your examination paper is neat and ——.
(*d*) How does he expect me to reply? His signature is quite ——.
(*e*) Before you submit your painting make sure that you are —— to enter the competition.

8. **contemptible, contemptuous**

(*a*) To rob a blind man is not only dishonest but ——.
(*b*) He rejected my offer with a —— wave of the hand.
(*c*) It was—— of him to spoil everyone's enjoyment deliberately.
(*d*) He gave a —— laugh when he looked at my drawing.
(*e*) The mob howled and raved, but the duke regarded them with —— indifference.

9. **seasonable, seasonal**

(*a*) Temperatures will be well above the —— average.
(*b*) An umbrella would be a more —— gift than a tennis racket during this wet spell.
(*c*) Among the —— sports, skiing has become very popular.
(*d*) We had snow on Midsummer Day; do you call that —— weather?
(*e*) On special occasions we send our friends —— greetings.

10. **lay, laid, lain**

(*a*) The fallen statue has —— there to this day.
(*b*) I —— down to get my breath back.
(*c*) I —— down my pen with a yawn.
(*d*) The ring must have —— in the drawer unnoticed for several years.
(*e*) They —— down their arms and surrendered.

11. **passed, past**

(*a*) I have not seen her during the —— few days.
(*b*) The Levite —— by on the other side.
(*c*) The —— cannot be recalled.
(*d*) We —— through Rugby at half—— one.
(*e*) The train rushed —— us, and —— out of sight.

106

76. SAME SOUND, DIFFERENT MEANING

1. Confusion sometimes arises when words that are different in spelling and meaning are alike in pronunciation. The pairs of phrases below contain such words. One is already given, and you are to supply the other.

> EXAMPLE: The *kernel* of a nut; the —— of a regiment.
> ANSWER: colonel.

You will realize from the above example that unless you already have a fair idea of the required word the dictionary may not help you very much. To do this exercise quickly and systematically you should refer to a list of words such as that given on pages 163–70 of *A First English Companion*.

(a) The *paws* of a dog; a —— in a song.
(b) A *stair* to an attic; a —— of defiance.
(c) No smoking *allowed*; talking —— is forbidden.
(d) A *draught* from a door; the —— of a design.
(e) The *course* of a ship; —— cloth.
(f) A *sore* place on one's foot; to —— into the air.
(g) A *serial* story; a —— food.
(h) Ripening *maize*; a —— of back streets.
(i) A knotted *cord*; a tuneful ——.
(j) The day of one's *birth*; a ship's ——.

2. For each of the words printed below in bold type find another word pronounced in the same way but spelt differently, and say what it means.

> EXAMPLE: **vale.** A valley.
> ANSWER: **veil.** A cloth to hide the face.

(1) **holy.** Sacred.
(2) **alter.** To change.
(3) **hall.** A large public room.
(4) **hair.** The growth that covers the head.
(5) **pale.** Very faintly coloured.
(6) **stake.** A pointed stick or post.
(7) **ascent.** Upward movement.
(8) **hew.** To cut with an axe, etc.
(9) **roll.** To move along by turning over.
(10) **mews.** A group of stables.
(11) **board.** A broad strip of wood.
(12) **beach.** A sandy or pebbly shore.
(13) **ring.** A hoop or hollow circle.
(14) **gate.** A door in a fence.
(15) **sweet.** Tasting like sugar.
(16) **gild.** To cover with thin gold.
(17) **slay.** To kill deliberately.
(18) **heart.** The blood-pump of the body.
(19) **manner.** A way of doing something.
(20) **team.** A group working together.
(21) **ball.** Something round, like a marble.
(22) **peak.** The pointed top of a mountain.
(23) **rest.** To be still or quiet.
(24) **marshal.** An officer of high rank.
(25) **need.** To want or require.
(26) **beer.** An alcoholic drink.
(27) **muscle.** A part of the body that moves the limbs, etc.
(28) **seed.** A thing from which a new plant grows.
(29) **might.** Great strength and power.
(30) **time.** Duration in hours, etc.
(31) **moat.** A deep ditch around a castle.
(32) **knave.** A rogue or scoundrel.
(33) **canvas.** Strong cloth used for sails, etc.
(34) **plum.** A fleshy stone-fruit.
(35) **bite.** To cut or grip with the teeth.
(36) **rough.** Not smooth or level.
(37) **wave.** A moving ridge of water, etc.
(38) **greater.** Larger.
(39) **slight.** Slender and small.
(40) **slow.** Taking a long time.

📖 LOOK THESE UP

See page 29 for instructions

1. Express these instructions in the passive voice.

49 Ex. 4

(a) You must take this medicine regularly.
(b) You must replace the lid immediately.

2. Complete this invitation in the third person.

32 Ex. 11

Mr. Roy Hale thanks Miss Joyce King for inviting —— to —— birthday party, but regrets that owing to —— recent accident —— will not be able to attend.

3. The sentence given below is badly constructed. Say where the fault lies.   72 **36** Ex. 1

A car with faulty brakes should, in no circumstances, be taken out on the road.

77. PAST TENSE OR PAST PARTICIPLE?

It is a bad mistake to use the past tense of a strong verb when the past participle should be used, or vice versa. This exercise gives practice in choosing correctly between the two.

Replace each dash by the past tense or the past participle of the verb given in brackets, whichever is correct.

> EXAMPLE: The water is ——. (*freeze*)
> ANSWER: The water is frozen.

Pages 172–3 of *A First English Companion* will help you.

(1) She —— to cry. (*begin*)
(2) The money has been ——. (*steal*)
(3) The roof was —— off. (*blow*)
(4) The doctor —— to see me. (*come*)
(5) I —— her yesterday. (*see*)
(6) He has —— me six pence. (*give*)
(7) Were the curtains badly ——? (*tear*)
(8) Crinolines are not —— today. (*wear*)
(9) They all —— home. (*go*)
(10) French is —— in Belgium. (*speak*)
(11) He —— away from me. (*run*)
(12) Have you been —— as vice-captain? (*choose*)
(13) No-one likes to be ——. (*beat*)
(14) Who —— this? (*do*)
(15) This horse has never been ——. (*ride*)
(16) The sun had —— before we woke. (*rise*)
(17) Have you —— your cake? (*eat*)
(18) They —— confetti over us. (*throw*)
(19) Have you —— what I asked you to do? (*forget*)
(20) Several old ships are being —— up. (*break*)
(21) Two bullocks —— a primitive plough. (*draw*)
(22) The bad apples will be —— away. (*throw*)
(23) The generators are —— by steam turbines. (*drive*)
(24) Many pipes are being —— by the frost. (*burst*)
(25) Having —— twice, he retired from the competition. (*fall*)
(26) They —— to win. (*strive*)
(27) Having said this he picked up his hat and —— to the door. (*stride*)
(28) These scarves are —— from pure silk. (*weave*)
(29) Until 1909 no-one had —— across the English Channel by aeroplane. (*fly*)
(30) Have I told you that I —— these tomatoes myself? (*grow*)
(31) I am sure that he —— he was beaten. (*know*)
(32) The Egyptians were —— with a plague of frogs. (*smite*)

See also *Auxiliary Verbs* on page 22.

78. REDUNDANCY

Each of these sentences contains one or more examples of redundancy—that is, needless repetition. Say how the sentences should read with the unnecessary words omitted.

> EXAMPLE: Looking down from the hill-top they saw a forest of trees.
> ANSWER: Looking down from the hill-top they saw a forest.

(a) St. Paul's cathedral was finally completed in 1710.
(b) When did you first begin to feel ill?
(c) The value of π is approximately about $3\frac{1}{7}$.
(d) Countries of the Commonwealth are united together by their loyalty to the Crown.
(e) He is suffering from a nasal infection of the nose.
(f) We revived him to life by means of artificial respiration.
(g) Betelgeuse belongs to the constellation of stars known as Orion.
(h) Draw a four-sided square with equal sides.
(i) The very last pip of the time-signal occurs at just exactly six o'clock.
(j) A short time ago we recently found three medieval coins dating back to the Middle Ages.

See also Exercise 3 on *Collective Nouns* on page 12.

79. HOWLERS AND MALAPROPISMS

A person who says that he is trying to excavate himself from a difficult situation is confusing the words *excavate* and *extricate*. This kind of mistake is called a *malapropism* (after Mrs. Malaprop, in

Sheridan's *The Rivals*). A more glaring blunder is called a *howler*; for example, a pupil who was asked to explain the abbreviation B.Sc. said that it meant *Boy Scout*.

───────────

Point out the errors in the following statements, and say which of them you consider to be malapropisms.

(*a*) When there is something wrong with your eyes you should consult an optimist.
(*b*) The bottom figure of a vulgar fraction is called a detonator.
(*c*) A barbecue is a lot of people waiting to have their hair cut.
(*d*) The lifeboat crew is called out by the firing of a meringue.
(*e*) *To take the veil* means *to get married*.
(*f*) A coroner takes care of the Queen's crown and keeps it polished.
(*g*) A malady is a bad tune.
(*h*) The humerus is the funny-bone.
(*i*) A dodo is an octave.

80. DOUBLE NEGATIVE

If you intend a sentence to have a negative meaning, it is a bad mistake to put two negatives in it.

DO NOT SAY: He did**n't** give me **nothing**.

───────────

Each of the sentences below (*a*)–(*k*) is to be completed *in a negative sense* by inserting a word taken from either list A or list B.

A.* no, none; no-one; nothing; nobody; nowhere

B. any; anyone; anything; anybody; anywhere

EXAMPLES: (*a*) He gave me ——.
(*b*) He didn't give me ——.
ANSWERS: (*a*) He gave me none (or *nothing*).
(*b*) He didn't give me any (or *anything*).

* NOTE. Avoid using a double negative; that is, do not use a word from list A if you are already using one of the following:

not; n't; hardly; scarcely; never.

(*a*) I couldn't hear ——.
(*b*) We spoke to ——.

(*c*) I have never used —— of these tools.
(*d*) They didn't have —— luck.
(*e*) I couldn't hear —— calling.
(*f*) I had —— bacon this morning.
(*g*) There was —— left for me.
(*h*) There wasn't —— for Peter either.
(*i*) There was hardly —— who knew me.
(*j*) He had written scarcely —— on his paper.
(*k*) We have not been —— near the river.

81. AMBIGUITY

These sentences are ambiguous. Explain their double meanings, and—wherever possible—say which meaning is intended, and how the wording could be improved upon.

(*a*) Geoffrey told Michael that his father had been injured.
(*b*) Half of his fortune, which amounted to a million pounds, was left to various charities.
(*c*) The path was very rough, and he slipped and nearly broke his leg in several places.
(*d*) Shakespeare was born and died on his birthday.
(*e*) Pierre was just as anxious to trick the smugglers as the coastguards.
(*f*) Mr. Hale only glanced at Trevor's exercise-book.
(*g*) Do not ruin your watch by tampering with it; let us do it for you.
(*h*) The market hall was built roughly in 1870.
(*i*) My friends; I will not call you ladies and gentlemen—I know you too well for that.
(*j*) Lewis has now won the walking-race three times running.
(*k*) Two million people read this newspaper; they don't know any better.
(*l*) The driver of an Army tank was injured when he jumped from a runaway train carrying the tank.
(*m*) Any person not putting litter in this basket will be fined £5.
(*n*) The name of the rescuer was not published at his own request.

See also Ex. 2 in Set 128 (page 143).

82. ANTI-CLIMAX

Anti-climax produces a humorous or ridiculous effect. If such an effect is not intended, then anti-climax is a fault. But there are times when anti-climax is used deliberately for the purpose of ridicule or sarcasm.

Examples of both these types are to be found in the following passages. There are also examples of the correct use of climax. Say which is which.

(a) They chuckled; they roared; they smiled.

(b) You rascal! You scoundrel! You villain!

(c) After ten hours of unremitting toil in the face of constant danger they struggled at last to the top of the mountain. Then they came down.

(d) They had watched him as a boy, admired him as a youth, and followed him as a man. Today they would see him installed as their chieftain.

(e) Richard Hanslow respectfully informs the nobility and gentry that he can instruct their sons in Mathematics, Latin, Astronomy, History, Geology, Music, etc., etc. Also, chimneys swept.

(f) During the past year this boy has attended school regularly, has spared no efforts to improve his football and cricket, and has talked fluently. With hard work he should one day be able to read and write.

(g) A remarkable man is Mr. Baxter: magistrate, county councillor, mayor, and now winner of the ankle competition at the Church Fête.

(h)   Were the whole realm of nature mine,
          That were a present far too small;
       Love so amazing, so divine,
          Demands my soul, my life, my all.

(i) He spent nearly £500 of his legacy on a long cruise. When he returned to this country he bought a new car for £2500 and a house for about £40 000.
    I understand that he has also given at least £5 to charity.

(j)   Christmas time brings with it
       A host of joys divine;
       Peace on earth, goodwill to men,
       And lots of nuts and wine.

83. ANACHRONISM

An anachronism is a mistake about *time*. It is made by saying something which was impossible at the time spoken about, although the same thing might have been possible many years later.

For example:

One of Pharaoh's slaves struck a match and lit the lamps.

Some of the examples given below are not so obvious, and you may have to turn to encyclopedias, etc., to decide whether they could possibly be true. Say which of them are anachronisms.

(a) The Pilgrim Fathers sailed to America in a steamship called the *Mayflower*.

(b) Thousands of years ago the Egyptians swathed their mummies in linen bandages.

(c) Cromwell, inspired by Napoleon's example, was determined that the king's army should be utterly defeated.

(d) William the Conqueror had Domesday Book printed and a copy placed in every church.

(e) The most outstanding figure in the American Civil War was George Washington.

(f) King Charles II took part in efforts to check the Great Fire of London.

(g) When Nelson had his right arm amputated he refused to have an anaesthetic.

(h) One of Shelley's poems is based on an incident in the Boer War.

(i) Among the dramatists who lived during the reign of Queen Elizabeth I, Shakespeare was the greatest.

(j) Columbus discovered the United States of America.

84. HIGH-FLOWN STYLE

There is an artificial style of writing in which high-sounding words and phrases are used to express simple ideas. You will find it from time to time in newspapers, in official statements, and in some business letters.

The writer tries to make things seem more important than they really are by using a great many long and pompous words, and writing in pretentious and long-winded style. It is always much better to use simple words and say things shortly and clearly.

I will endeavour to assist you. (I will try to help you.)

The council decided to acquire the land for a monetary settlement. (The council decided to buy the land.)

In the first one you see that the words *endeavour* and *assist* have simply been replaced by *try* and *help*. In the second sentence, five words have been replaced by the single word *buy*.

Now try to express the following sentences in a simple and straightforward way. First ask yourself what each one means as a whole, using your dictionary for any words you do not understand, and then put that idea into plain language. (You will seldom get good results by changing only one word at a time.)

(*a*) He was attacked in the vicinity of his place of residence.

(*b*) The termination of his oration was greeted with acclamation.

(*c*) The bricklayers desisted from their labours to partake of liquid refreshment.

(*d*) He was made the recipient of an eight-day time-piece.

(*e*) Six persons were brought to justice for discarding refuse in public thoroughfares.

(*f*) Numerous individuals were precipitated into the icy embrace of the ocean.

(*g*) By means of television, millions of people beheld the nuptial rites in their domestic abodes.

(*h*) Before his decease he had donated large sums to those persons existing in a state of penury.

(*i*) In frigid climatic conditions we should provide our feathered friends with sustenance.

(*j*) Refrain from expectoration.

85. MISUSE OF THE WORD LITERALLY

The word *literally* means *really* or *actually*.

A newspaper once reported that a famous statesman had been *literally glued to his seat* in the House of Commons. The magazine *Punch* remarked that half an hour later he *literally tore himself away*. Explain the point of this joke if you can.

Some people say *literally* when they mean *metaphorically*, *figuratively*, or *in a manner of speaking*. For example, no-one can literally *get blood out of a stone*, so this saying is bound to be metaphorical; but a person can *play with fire* either literally or metaphorically.

Some of the following sentences make sense both with and without the word *literally*: say which they are. Others are nonsense until the word *literally* is omitted; they then become reasonable in a metaphorical sense, as with the example about *blood out of a stone*. Pick out these sentences.

NOTE. An easy test is to try putting the word *really* in place of the word *literally*.

(*a*) After she had heard the good news she was literally walking on air.

(*b*) He looked very ill indeed; he was literally all skin and bone.

(*c*) You may find yourself literally in deep water.

(*d*) He is literally very fond of blowing his own trumpet.

(*e*) She was literally born with a silver spoon in her mouth.

(*f*) He was caught literally red-handed.

(*g*) Having my dog destroyed literally broke my heart.

(*h*) She was literally crying over spilt milk.

(*i*) The sudden fright literally froze her blood.

(*j*) She is literally the apple of her mother's eye.

See also *Speaking Literally* on page 118, and *Hyperbole* on page 129.

86. MIXED METAPHORS

When two metaphors are used in the same sentence, the metaphors should match each other and follow the same line of thought. In all the following sentences there are mixed metaphors which do not match. The effect of mixed metaphors, as you will see, is to make the sentence absurd or nonsensical.

Modify each sentence so that the metaphors match and the sentence makes sense. Either the first metaphor or the second metaphor (whichever is the more convenient) may be altered.

EXAMPLE: Don't put all your eggs in one basket, in case someone upsets your applecart.

SUGGESTED ANSWER: Don't put all your eggs in one basket, in case they all get broken at once.

(1) We are both in the same boat, so we had better stand shoulder to shoulder.

(2) If he pokes his nose into other people's affairs he must not be surprised if he burns his fingers.

(3) You will never surmount this obstacle unless you grasp the nettle boldly.

(4) The community centre was a hive of industry, with everyone working like beavers.

(5) They had an avalanche of applications that nearly drowned them.

(6) She is as changeable as a weathercock; whichever way the stream flows, she goes with it.

(7) We have had a stiff climb during the past few years, but from now onwards it will be plain sailing.

(8) The speaker lost the thread of the argument, and it was some time before he got back on the rails again.

(9) Once you have set your hand to the plough you should keep the ball rolling.

(10) If he kicks over the traces you must make him come to heel.

The answers are on page 145

✔ MARK THESE YOURSELF

"I saw it in print"

There is a mistaken idea among some people that whatever is in print must be right. This is very far from the truth. Newspapers, which have to be produced in great haste, are frequent offenders.

The extracts given below contain examples of common mistakes; see if you can pick them out. Do not mark this book in any way.

(a) es / be | alleged that defendant had never had a wireless license, although he had oper- | wi / me

(b) as | was probably the Council's property, and that if it was not their's it must belong | on

(c) re / or | and greens are most essential. If the baby does not like raw cabbage, boil it. You | hi / th

(d) on | family of great swimmers. His brother swum the Channel last year, and his son | da

(e) av- / rd | asked the Minister of Health if the depend- ents of men killed on active service were | br / fi

(f) or / ly | been thundering and lightning for half an hour before the storm broke over the | Ho

(g) ng / re | that birds rung by his Association in Britain had been recovered in Spain, | Ll / gu

(h) ld. / as | A.A. and R.A.C. have signposted an alternate route that avoids the obstruct- | Me / wr

(i) ss, / ia | injured when a jar of phosphorous fell to the floor and burst into flames. The | th / wo

(j) ng / ax | if diptheria is on the increase, but one salient feature that stands out is that | es / fe

112

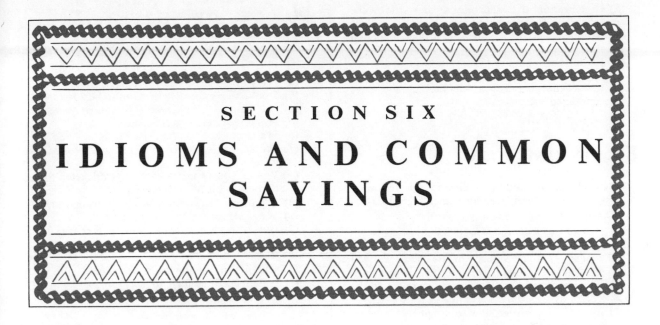

IDIOMS AND COMMON SAYINGS

TO do the exercises in this Section by yourself you will need to be able to refer to a book that contains an alphabetical list of idioms and common sayings. Phrases of this kind are usually given in large dictionaries, but they may be difficult to find. In the following exercises the phrases have all been taken from *A First English Companion*. To look them up, try to decide which are the words under which they are most likely to be indexed. For example, in Questions (a) to (d) of the first Set try *airs*, *cut*, *tooth*, and *pure*.

87. TWO BY TWO

Many common sayings consist of a pair of balanced or contrasting words—for example, *fair and square*, *hue and cry*, *rack and ruin*, etc. All the sentences given below contain such phrases, but one word is missing from each. Supply the missing words and quote the complete phrases.

> **EXAMPLE:** There are difficulties, but we shall find ways and —— of surmounting them.
>
> **ANSWER:** ways and means

(a) Ever since she appeared on television she has put on airs and ——.

(b) Suggestions were not wanted; everything was cut and ——.

(c) They fought tooth and —— to repel the invaders.

(d) Only one thing will get him out of his difficulties: work, pure and ——.

(e) This broken grating is a danger to life and ——.

(f) The junior clerk in our office is at everyone's beck and ——.

(g) Several trouble-makers were thrown out neck and ——.

(h) Would it be a dead heat? The two horses were racing neck and ——.

(i) The Navy will not accept you unless you are sound in wind and ——.

(j) I keep this dress for high days and ——.

(k) Organizations that were plotting to overthrow the king were destroyed root and ———.

(l) No-one is barred; membership is open to all and ———.

(m) Having enough money is not the be-all and ——— of life.

(n) I shall not express an opinion until I have considered the pros and ———.

88. IN ONE WORD

Each phrase printed in italics in the following sentences is to be replaced by a single word that has the same meaning.

(a) Mother was *on pins and needles* until I rang to tell her that I had not been injured.

(b) You say that you will sell me this land; will you put that in *black and white*?

(c) The sound made by the logs as they rolled off the ledge was *for all the world* like heavy footsteps.

(d) I find the typewriter slow to use at the moment, but *in the long run* it will save me a lot of time.

(e) She visits us only *once in a blue moon*.

(f) Mr. Banks gave me a *rap on the knuckles* in my report for not working hard enough in French.

(g) The weather was perfect; the only *fly in the ointment* was that I forgot to take my sun-glasses.

(h) Dick Turpin was hardly the kind of man to *look up to*.

(i) There is only one canoe, so we shall have to use it *turn and turn about*.

(j) Gerald wanted to be a farmer, but his father insisted on his becoming an architect. He now feels that he is a *round peg in a square hole*.

89. SUCCESS OR FAILURE

The following phrases are used by people who intend to make a determined effort to succeed, even though they may ruin themselves in the attempt; complete them.

(a) Kill or ———
(b) Make or ———
(c) Do or ———
(d) Hit or ———
(e) Now or ———
(f) Sink or ———
(g) Stand or ———
(h) Neck or ———

90. YES OR NO?

Answer *Yes* or *No* to each of the following questions. Be prepared to give reasons for your answers.

(a) If a young man is *fancy-free*, is he in love?

(b) Does an *ugly duckling* turn out to be a failure?

(c) Has a man of 75 exceeded his *allotted span*?

(d) Has a *grass widow* a husband?

(e) Is a man who is *on his uppers* to be envied?

(f) Would you be annoyed if someone *cooked your goose*?

(g) Would you expect a first-class cricketer to say that cricket is his *bête noire*?

(h) Are pliers needed for *splicing the main brace*?

(i) Is a *principal boy* usually a woman?

(j) Is it correct to say that an admiral is *serving before the mast*?

(k) Would it be *out of the question* to suggest that all school holidays should be abolished?

(l) Is it an act of courage to *fish in troubled waters*?

91. SAY WHICH

(a) Which of these persons would you expect to be most interested in *still life*—a surgeon, a sculptor, a geologist, or an artist?

(b) Who would be the most likely to *look at the world through rose-coloured spectacles*—an optician, an optimist, a pessimist, or a scientist?

(c) Mr. A *burns the candle at both ends*. Is he deceitful, too industrious, insane, or generous?

(d) If you heard it said of someone that he was *on his beam-ends* would you expect him to be a pauper, a carpenter, a lumberjack, or a builder?

(e) If a person *has his back to the wall* would you expect him to be comfortable, desperate, lazy, or in disgrace?

(f) Mr. B. often *brings the house down*. Is he an auctioneer, a comedian, a landlord, or a demolition worker?

(g) Someone is referred to as *a black sheep*. Does this mean that he is a favourite, a simpleton, a scamp, or an oddity?

(h) Say which of these adjectives you would use in referring to a person who *lives from hand to mouth*: hasty, improvident, unhygienic, uncouth.

92. TWIN SAYINGS

Each of the following statements can be completed in two ways, using either of two sayings that mean the same thing. Using the given words as clues, supply the missing words and write out the sayings in full.

(a) Tom and John had fallen out, but after a time they decided to
  (i) —— —— hatchet.
  (ii) —— —— —— bygones.

(b) Mr. Black was unpopular because he had disgraced himself. He was
  (i) —— —— favour.
  (ii) —— —— cloud.

(c) The teacher told Peter that he would not pass the examination unless he
  (i) —— —— shoulder —— —— ——.
  (ii) —— —— nose —— —— ——.

(d) Advice is wasted on some people. You may as well
  (i) preach —— —— ——.
  (ii) plough —— ——.

(e) When Trevor resumed arithmetic lessons after a year's absence he found that he was
  (i) —— —— —— depth.
  (ii) —— —— water.

(f) Farmers cannot expect every season to be to their liking; they learn to
  (i) —— —— rough —— —— ——.
  (ii) —— —— fat —— —— ——.

(g) He is a traitor, and will ruin us all unless we
  (i) —— —— spoke —— —— ——.
  (ii) spike —— —— ——.

(h) Whichever course he chooses to take, the consequences will be equally disastrous. He is
  (i) —— —— horns —— —— ——.
  (ii) —— —— devil —— —— —— ——.

(i) When Patrick brought home a bad report, father
  (i) —— —— —— —— coals.
  (ii) —— —— —— task.

93. CONTRASTS

Each of the following statements can be completed in two ways, by using one or other of two sayings that have opposite or contrasting meanings. For example, (a) gives us two distinct mental pictures—first a success to be proud of, and then something of which one is ashamed.

Using the given words as clues, supply the missing words and write out the sayings in full.

(a) If you do as you say, it will be
  (i) a feather —— —— ——.
  (ii) a blot —— —— ——.

(b) When Philip was offered a really good job, his headmaster told him
  (i) to strike —— —— —— —— ——.
  (ii) not to —— —— grass —— —— —— ——.

(c) When people guessed what had happened to the money,
  (i) Mrs. Wilkes barked —— —— —— ——.
  (ii) Mrs. Poynton —— —— nail —— —— ——.

(d) When faced with a dangerous situation,
  (i) Carl takes his courage —— —— ——.
  (ii) Raymond has cold ——.

(e) Mr. Knight set the boys a problem in algebra.
  (i) Dennis found it plain ——.
  (ii) Martin thought it was a —— nut —— ——.

(f) When the dog turned on them
  (i) Clive —— —— —— heels.
  (ii) Donald —— —— ground.

✔ MARK THESE YOURSELF

The answers are on page 145

Complete these proverbs:

(a) A drowning man .....
(b) Great oaks .....
(c) Little pitchers .....
(d) Faint heart .....
(e) Take time .....
(f) As you make your bed .....
(g) Discretion .....

94. TRUE OR UNTRUE?

You are told below, as a fact, that Mr. A will have to look to his laurels. You are then given six statements about him; some of them are true, but others contradict what you have been told. Say whether each of them is true or untrue.

1. *Mr. A will have to look to his laurels*

(a) He is in danger of being defeated.
(b) He cannot be beaten.
(c) Unless he is careful, someone will beat him.
(d) His position is unchallenged.
(e) There is a risk that someone may overthrow him.
(f) No-one else is a match for him.

2. *Mr. B does not let the grass grow under his feet*

(a) He spends his time in idleness.
(b) He does things at the earliest possible moment.
(c) He pushes forward with anything he has to do.
(d) He is slothful.
(e) He cannot be relied on to act punctually.
(f) He is prompt and diligent.

3. *Mr. C has put his cards on the table*

(a) He is being deceitful.
(b) He is letting everyone know what course he proposes to take.
(c) He does not mind who knows what he will do next.
(d) He is making no secret of his intentions.
(e) He prevents people from prying.
(f) He wishes to mislead others.

4. *Mr. D runs with the hare and hunts with the hounds*

(a) He tries not to offend anyone.
(b) He does his best to make himself popular.
(c) He speaks his mind openly and fearlessly.
(d) He does not care what other people think.
(e) He is anxious not to be out of favour with anyone.
(f) He does not mind whom he displeases.

5. *Mr. E sticks to his guns*

(a) He refuses to give way when he is attacked.
(b) He wavers when he is criticized.
(c) He gives in when people disagree with him.
(d) He shows firmness in argument.
(e) He is unwilling to alter his opinion.
(f) He is not prepared to stand by his beliefs.

95. WORD CROSSES

In this exercise the idea is to find two five-letter words which have the same letter in the middle (e.g., BLIND and STILE) and which can be arranged in the form of a cross as shown on the right. The answer to each question therefore consists of one word *across* and one word *down*, and these can be found by studying the clues. You will see that the first one has already been answered in the example given above.

```
    S
    T
BLIND
    L
    E
```

(a) *Across:* To this kind of horse it is the same whether you nod or wink.
Down: A lame dog is glad of help when he comes to this.

(b) *Across:* Rome was not · · · · · in a day.
Down: It is a waste of time to cry over this kind of milk.

(c) *Across:* Every one of these is supposed to have a silver lining.
Down: If you wish to be in favour with someone, keep out of his black · · · · · .

(d) *Across:* You will not wander to other topics if you stick to this.
Down: As the crow · · · · · there is no shorter way.

(e) *Across:* Queer this to spoil someone's chances.
Down: Circumstances · · · · · cases.

(f) *Across:* A treacherous person is called a snake in the · · · · · .
Down: The olive branch is an emblem of this.

(g) *Across:* A fool is soon parted from it.
Down: Clip these if you wish to thwart him and spoil his chances.

(h) *Across:* Even a booby can win one.
Down: Pocket this if you decide to put up with conditions that displease you.

(i) *Across:* Do not hide yours under a bushel if you wish to be an example to others.
Down: No harm comes to those who have a guardian · · · · · .

(j) *Across:* One should not expect to find an old head on these shoulders.
Down: In this kind of water one is in difficult circumstances.

(k) *Across:* Tell the truth and do this to the devil.
Down: This adjective suits the pot as well as the kettle.

(l) *Across:* Even when this is made of velvet it may conceal an iron hand.
Down: An eye for an eye is a form of revenge; so is a tooth for a · · · · ·.

When you have finished, cover up your answers and go through the clues again. See if you can complete them from memory, and try to remember the sayings and what they mean.

96. FINISH THE PHRASE

Each of these sentences contains a figurative or idiomatic phrase that is unfinished. Complete the phrases by supplying the missing words.

(a) Let us be quite frank about things, and put all our cards —— —— ——.

(b) The news that war had been declared was a bolt —— —— ——.

(c) We are told that there are no survivors, but we are hoping against —— that this is not true.

(d) Most of this evidence is worthless, but some of it may be reliable; we shall have to separate the wheat —— —— ——.

(e) You should have given us that advice earlier; it is easy to be wise —— —— ——.

(f) The Chancellor has not said how he intends to raise the money, but his recent reference to income tax is a straw —— —— ——.

(g) Gambling has been his downfall. He is a brilliant man, but he has feet —— ——.

(h) The crofters in these lonely islands are the salt —— —— ——.

(i) I shall not visit them more than once a month; I am anxious not to wear —— —— ——.

(j) Swim the Atlantic? Have you taken leave —— —— ——?

(k) His selfish behaviour annoyed me very much, and I gave him a piece —— —— ——.

97. SPEAKING FIGURATIVELY ...

In each of the following sentences replace the words in italics by a figurative or idiomatic expression that has the same meaning. A suitable expression is suggested by the clue given in brackets.

EXAMPLE: Their quarrel soon blew over; it was *a lot of fuss about a ridiculously small matter.* (storm)
ANSWER: Their quarrel soon blew over; it was a storm in a teacup.

(a) He is a pessimist, always *imagining that the worst is going to happen.* (dark)

(b) Arrangements for the festival are almost complete; we have only to *attend to one or two small items.* (dot)

(c) She was willing to *face any risk and undergo any ordeal* to save her child. (fire)

(d) If you are in the wrong I advise you to admit the fact *without being surly or bad-tempered.* (grace)

(e) She has been very ill indeed, but I think that she has *got over the worst of it now.* (corner)

(f) The teams were evenly matched for most of the game, but the serious injury to Miller *settled the issue.* (scales)

(g) What he said about me is not true, and I shall make him *admit his mistake.* (eat)

(h) She *pretended not to notice me, and walked straight past with her head in the air.* (cut)

(i) If you invest all your money in this company you will be *risking everything in a single venture.* (eggs)

(j) Cabinet ministers must expect to be *reported and referred to almost every day in the newspapers.* (eye)

(k) His aunt left him a great mansion, but he soon found that it was *a possession he could not afford to keep.* (white)

(l) You *said exactly what I was just about to say.* (words)

(m) New motor-roads are *completely altering the appearance of* the countryside. (face).

(n) If you imagine that there are no dishonest people around you, you are *being very much too trusting and optimistic.* (rose).

117

98. SPEAKING LITERALLY . . .

In the following sentences the words in italics are not strictly true, but are used figuratively. Replace them by phrases which are literally true and which mean the same thing.

EXAMPLE: You would do better to admit that the situation is serious, instead of *hiding your head in the sand.*

SUGGESTED ANSWER: You would do better to admit that the situation is serious, instead of pretending that all is well.

(a) In the middle of his lecture the speaker *lost the thread,* and had to search among his notes.
(b) Elizabeth's horse is the *apple of her eye.*
(c) You will never get good discipline unless you *put your foot down.*
(d) You are *barking up the wrong tree* if you say that Stephen did it.
(e) I didn't guess; I simply *put two and two together.*
(f) I am anxious that you should not rush into a *blind alley.*
(g) Unless we *get down to brass tacks* we shall never have this carol service ready for Christmas.
(h) If we are to do any good at all we shall have to *sink our differences.*
(i) In the away match they beat us easily, but in the home match we *turned the tables on them.*
(j) The right of way across this field has always been a *bone of contention* between the farmer and the villagers.

99. TRUE OR UNTRUE?

Follow the instructions given in Set 94.

1. *Mr. A cuts his coat according to his cloth*

(a) His expenditure is less than his income.
(b) He lives within his means.
(c) He is wildly extravagant.
(d) He orders more than he can afford to pay for.
(e) He spends recklessly.
(f) His income is in excess of his expenditure.

2. *Mr. B hides his light under a bushel*

(a) He is modest about his achievements.
(b) He is a braggart and a boaster.
(c) He lets everyone know how good he is.
(d) He avoids making a public show of his good deeds.
(e) He prefers to keep quiet about his merits.
(f) He makes sure that all his doings are reported in the newspapers.

3. *Mr. C's word is as good as his bond*

(a) He is undependable.
(b) One can never be sure that he means what he says.
(c) People can safely put their trust in him.
(d) One can depend on any promise he makes.
(e) Anything he undertakes is faithfully carried out.
(f) His promises are like pie-crust—made to be broken.

4. *Mr. D quickly throws up the sponge*

(a) He refuses to give in without a struggle.
(b) His opponents find it easy to defeat him.
(c) He is not easily daunted.
(d) He never even considers surrender.
(e) He does not persevere in the face of difficulties.
(f) It takes very little to make him capitulate.

5. *Mr. E does not like to be in the limelight*

(a) He is shy and retiring.
(b) At any public ceremony he is always at the front.
(c) He likes to make an exhibition of himself.
(d) There is nothing he likes better than to be in the news.
(e) He is not happy unless people notice him.
(f) He detests making a public show of himself.

6. *Mr. F. wears his heart on his sleeve*

(a) He lets no-one know his inner feelings.
(b) He parades his emotions.
(c) He exhibits his deepest feelings to all and sundry.
(d) He conceals from others the things that he feels most deeply.
(e) He keeps his hatreds and affections to himself.
(f) He opens his heart to anyone who will accept his confidences.

100. WORD BOXES

In Set 95 you were asked to arrange pairs of words in the form of crosses. In this exercise you are to find five-letter words that can be set down in the form of hollow squares as shown on the right.

```
T R E A D
H       E
I       A
E       T
F R E S H
```

Notice that the word at the top and the word on the left begin with the same letter (T); the last letter of the word on the left (F) gives you the first letter of the bottom word, and so on.

(a) *Top:* When a horse is a gift it should not be looked at too closely here.
Left: This is the month when hares are mad.
Bottom: This kind of heart is weighed down with sadness.
Right: The Israelites were promised a land flowing with milk and · · · · · .

(b) *Top:* A rose by any other name would smell as · · · · · .
Left: When this is false it leads one away from the right trail.
Bottom: Go at it hammer and · · · · · to be forceful.
Right: A certain kind of 'cat' has nine of these.

(c) *Top:* There is no danger of interference when the coast is like this.
Left: Cut your coat according to this.
Bottom: Many of them make the work light.
Right: It never · · · · · but it pours.

(d) *Top:* The eating of the pudding provides this.
Left: Tune things up to concert · · · · · to be quite ready.
Bottom: Hope deferred for a long time makes this sick.
Right: The finest diamonds are said to be of this water.

(e) *Top:* When the bird has done this there is no sign of the captive.
Left: Wipe the · · · · · with your opponent to defeat him easily.
Bottom: To be healthy, wealthy, and wise you must be an early · · · · · .
Right: This is when to say *die.*

(f) *Top:* Do this to the board to take everything.
Left: In a small caravan there is not room to do this to a cat.
Bottom: Sauce for this is good enough for the gander.
Right: Money is plentiful when this is long.

When you have finished, cover up your answers and go through the clues again. See if you can complete them from memory, and try to remember the sayings and what they mean.

101. WHAT DID THEY SAY?

The persons concerned in the incidents described below used figurative or idiomatic sayings; what were they? Use the words in brackets as clues.

(a) Mr. Plier the plumber tried to mend the kitchen clock, but found when he had finished that he had two wheels left over. His wife's comment was . . . . . (*cobbler*)

(b) Stephen very much wanted a fishing-rod, but complained that if he bought one he would have nothing left in his money-box. His mother said . . . . . (*cake*)

(c) Hilda and Helen had quarrelled, and had not spoken to each other for more than a week. Miss Kendrick took them on one side and said to them . . . . . (*bygones*)

(d) Mr. Hale was well over seventy, but he refused to give up his business. When people asked him when he was going to retire he used to say . . . . . (*harness*)

(e) Mr. Blunder gave up his work because his wages were too low, but was then unable to find any other employment. He was heard to say, with a rueful expression, ... (*frying-pan*)

(f) Charles had done badly in his examination, and for several days afterwards he worked through the papers again and again. His father advised him to put them away, and said . . . . . (*flogging*)

(g) When Miss Love returned to the pavilion after losing her match in the first round of the tennis tournament she shrugged her shoulders and said that the trophy was not worth winning. A bystander who heard this turned to a friend and said . . . . . (*sour*)

(h) For many years Mrs. Proudfoot had collected for the lifeboat fund, and had always regarded Church Street as part of her area. When she found that Miss Sharply was calling on people in that street she said to her . . . . . (*poaching*)

(i) The planning authorities refused permission for a cottage to be built in the valley because the area was scheduled as a National Park, but they allowed a great power station to be put there. People said . . . . . (*gnat*)

102. SAYINGS TO SUIT

In this exercise you are to find sayings to suit incidents and situations that are arranged in groups. In any one group the sayings have a key word that is common to all of them; for example, in the first group each saying contains the word *salt*, and so on.

Give your answers in the form of sentences. In the first group, for instance, one of the answers is *He is worth his salt*.

1. *Key word:* **salt**

(a) Mr. Keen earns every penny he gets.

(b) We always make allowances for the fact that some of Uncle Oswald's stories are rather far-fetched.

(c) Mr. Strutt was delighted to receive an invitation to the Lord Mayor's banquet, but most annoyed when he found that he had been put to sit among the least important people.

2. *Key word:* **red**

(a) When Mr. Dodge is cornered in an argument he tries to change the subject by mentioning something quite different.

(b) When the police opened the office door the burglars were actually taking money from the safe.

(c) Florence Nightingale was refused blankets for wounded men because no-one had the authority to issue them from stock.

3. *Key word:* **water**

(a) When Mrs. Long returned to her native village after an absence of fifty years she found things very much changed, and she knew hardly anyone.

(b) Terence took no notice at all of advice, and simply went his own way.

(c) I made a number of suggestions, but Hazel did not think much of them.

4. *Key word:* **nail**

(a) Some people like hire purchase, but I prefer to put down the money when I buy the goods.

(b) Everybody was wondering why Mr. Dally had been dismissed, but only Judith gave exactly the right explanation.

5. *Key word:* **light**

(a) Mr. Close came to live in the village ten years ago, but has never told a soul that he holds the V.C.

(b) David had always thought poetry dull, but he changed his mind after a few lessons with Mr. Prime.

103. TRUE OR UNTRUE?

Follow the instructions given in Set 94.

1. *Mr. A blows hot and cold*

(a) He is like a weathercock.

(b) Once he has made a decision he does not waver.

(c) People can never be sure of what he really means.

(d) He is always in two minds about what to do next.

(e) He is resolute.

(f) His chief weakness is vacillation.

2. *Mr. B says that he will win first prize by hook or by crook*

(a) He is a fair and sportsmanlike man.

(b) He will cheat if there is no other way of winning.

(c) He would rather be a deceiver than a loser.

(d) He would not stoop to do anything unfair.

(e) He is concerned not so much about winning as about playing fairly.

(f) Dishonourable behaviour is the last thing he would think of.

3. *Mr. C blows his own trumpet*

(a) He is a braggart.

(b) He is reticent about his achievements.

(c) He is not bombastic.

(d) He is averse to praising himself.

(e) He is not bashful.

(f) He does not keep himself to himself.

4. *Mr. D does not set the Thames on fire*

(a) He never does anything outstanding.
(b) He is remarkably successful in all his affairs.
(c) He distinguishes himself in every walk of life.
(d) In his accomplishments he eclipses everyone else.
(e) He achieves nothing of any importance.
(f) He is not an ordinary person.

5. *Mr. E does not pull his punches*

(a) He is a blunt and outspoken man.
(b) He is afraid to say what he really means.
(c) He does not mind who is offended by what he says.
(d) Offend or please, he speaks his mind.
(e) He is careful not to wound anyone's feelings.
(f) He is tactful in all he says.

104. DOUBLE ACROSTICS

If you have done the Word Boxes in Set 100 you will quickly understand these double acrostics. Each one consists of five words of five letters, so arranged that the initial letters on the left make a

1. S P O T S
2. P I A N O
3. A L T A R
4. D R I E R
5. E M P T Y

sixth word (reading downwards) and the end letters on the right make a seventh word.

The clues for the five main words are numbered from 1 to 5, as shown in the example; the clues for the side-words are labelled *Left* and *Right*.

If the main words are done first the side-words can be done as a check. Sometimes it may be easier to begin with the side-word on the left.

(a) 1. This is how a new broom sweeps.
2. This is not right unless it has ninety degrees.
3. Get down to these if they are made of brass.
4. On this part of the wave people are most successful.
5. Argue over fine distinctions, and you will split these.

Left. The hare cannot be cooked unless this has been done first.
Right. Selfish people feather their own.

(b) 1. Some people strain at a gnat but swallow this.
2. When the cart is before this the proper order is reversed.
3. Time and · · · · · it happens repeatedly.
4. Ill-· · · · · ventures are doomed to disaster.
5. They were not made before fingers.

Left. Use something better than this if you wish to catch an old bird.
Right. Distance · · · · · enchantment to the view.

(c) 1. There is no need to do this to the lily.
2. Get the · · · · · hand of someone to master him.
3. People of · · · · · birth are said to have blue blood in their veins.
4. The one belonging to the widow was never empty.
5. Show a clean pair of these to escape.

Left. He is always pleased, it seems.
Right. They sometimes prevent you from seeing the wood.

(d) 1. · · · · · caution to the winds to be wildly reckless.
2. This kind of snake has a reputation for being deaf.
3. A bull is not welcome in a shop where this is sold.
4. Do not trust the crocodile when he sheds them.
5. Have this before midnight if you are in search of beauty.

Left. When these are hard they cannot be disputed.
Right. Do this to the nettle if you wish to face difficulties boldly.

When you have finished, cover up your answers and go through the clues again. See if you can complete them from memory, and try to remember the sayings and what they mean.

✓ MARK THESE YOURSELF
The answers are on page 145

1. Where is your tongue when you are insincere?

2. Where is your head when you are just able to keep out of debt?

3. Where is your heart when you make no secret of your feelings?

105. ...BUT THAT IS ABSURD

The following statements are either absurd or incorrect. Briefly and in your own words say why each one is wrong.

(a) You told me to ask for twelve tomato plants, but Mr. Rootes says that he has only a baker's dozen left. I wonder if that will be enough.

(b) Private Atkins said that he joined the Senior Service because he had always wanted to be a regular soldier.

(c) From Lapley to Dunston is eight kilometres as the crow flies, but only five kilometres if you go through Gailey.

(d) Mrs. Armstrong has always been such a kind and considerate lady that I was most annoyed with Nancy for taking a leaf out of her book.

(e) It happened during the small hours—between one o'clock and two o'clock yesterday afternoon.

(f) I offered him £60, but he wanted £80, so we split the difference and I paid him £65.

(g) I told him to his face what I thought about him, in black and white.

(h) The mayor began his speech with a Parthian shot concerning the newly-elected councillors.

(i) When Mr. Quayle offered to reorganize the business his directors gave him *carte blanche*, so he had to abandon the idea.

(j) He had to choose between losing his house, his money, or his employment; he was on the horns of a dilemma.

106. FOR INSTANCE...

Each set of circumstances outlined below illustrates the meaning of a saying contained in the list given at the end. Find the appropriate saying for each incident.

There are ten incidents but eleven sayings, so one saying will be unused.

(a) Buying a fireguard after a child has been burned.

(b) Giving a farmer a sack of potatoes as a present.

(c) Being a member of so many committees that one cannot attend all the meetings regularly.

(d) Giving customers a small sample in the hope that they will buy more goods of the same kind.

(e) Hesitating for so long about which of two houses to buy that other people buy them both.

(f) Writing an essay for homework that can be used later on as a contribution for the school magazine.

(g) Erecting a scaffolding to paint a small window that can be reached easily with a ladder.

(h) Selling the tools of one's trade so as to pay a debt.

(i) Putting a single litter-basket in a large park.

(j) Telling those boys who have come to school in a blizzard why they ought to make an effort to be present.

Choose your sayings from this list

Having too many irons in the fire
Carrying coals to Newcastle
Shutting the stable door after the horse is gone
Falling between two stools
Using a steam hammer to crack a nut
Casting pearls before swine
Throwing a sprat to catch a mackerel
Killing two birds with one stone
Preaching to the converted
Killing the goose that lays the golden eggs
Stopping one hole in a sieve

107. AS THE PROVERB SAYS...

Each of the ten incidents and situations described below illustrates the meaning of a proverb contained in the list given at the end. Find the appropriate proverb for each incident. (Eleven proverbs are given, so one will be unused.)

(a) A boy may be given all possible educational opportunities, but no-one can force him to make full use of them if he has no wish to do so.

(b) Mr. Proud felt so sure of being chosen as mayor that he sent copies of his photograph to the local newspapers. He felt very foolish when someone else was elected.

(c) Frank had been 'ragged' and teased all day without becoming ruffled, but at last a harmless bit of leg-pull made him lose his temper.

(d) Alan, Brian, and Carl were given a rabbit between them. After a time, each thought that the other two were feeding it, and it died of starvation.

(e) A market salesman once cheated his customers by selling them apples that he knew to be bad inside. He now finds it difficult to sell them even the very best fruit.

(f) Mr. Smith's death was due to the fact that he had worked on high-voltage equipment for so many years that he no longer thought it was dangerous.

(g) Against his father's advice, Neil gave up his studies and went into a blind-alley occupation. He now regrets his decision, but his father tells him that he must put up with the consequences of his own actions.

(h) The students were reminded that although their new building was one of the finest in the country, the college would be judged on the quality of the trained men it produced.

(i) This has been Mrs. Hazzard's unlucky week. She has broken her wrist, had an outbreak of fire in the kitchen, lost her wedding-ring—and now the twins have measles.

(j) Mr. Watts had thought it was impossible to run his business without electricity, but when lightning cut off the power supply he quickly found ways and means of carrying on.

Choose your proverbs from this list

The last straw breaks the camel's back.
Once bitten, twice shy.
You can take a horse to the water, but you cannot make him drink.
It never rains but it pours.
Everybody's business is nobody's business.
Don't count your chickens before they are hatched.
Necessity is the mother of invention.
The proof of the pudding is in the eating.
As you make your bed, so you must lie on it.
He who pays the piper may call the tune.
Familiarity breeds contempt.

✔ MARK THESE YOURSELF
The answers are on page 145

1. Where would you be if you were doing your best not to catch a crab?

2. What is it that the leopard cannot change?

3. Where is the mote usually to be seen?

4. Which has the greater value put upon it—speech or silence? Why?

5. What colour is the town sometimes painted?

★ REVISION

All the sayings given below have already been used in Section Six (Scts 87–107). They appear here in sets of six, each set being followed by a group of six abstract nouns. For each of the sayings there is one noun that expresses its inner meaning. For example, we could say that the meaning of *putting on airs and graces* is conveyed by the single word *conceit*.

Say which noun corresponds with each saying.

1. (a) Having cold feet
   (b) Burying the hatchet
   (c) Blowing one's own trumpet
   (d) Getting the upper hand
   (e) Being under a cloud
   (f) Being a round peg in a square hole

boastfulness	*disgrace*	*cowardice*
unsuitability	*mastery*	*forgiveness*

2. (a) Feathering one's own nest
   (b) Standing one's ground
   (c) Turning the corner
   (d) Turning the tables
   (e) Taking a leaf out of someone's book
   (f) Grasping the nettle

boldness	*selfishness*	*imitation*
reversal	*resistance*	*improvement*

3. (a) Being in the limelight
   (b) Letting the grass grow under one's feet
   (c) Being hauled over the coals
   (d) Being a snake in the grass
   (e) Being on the crest of the wave
   (f) Throwing up the sponge

indolence	*submission*	*success*
rebuke	*treachery*	*publicity*

4. (a) Happening once in a blue moon
   (b) Ploughing the sands
   (c) Looking on the dark side
   (d) Blowing hot and cold
   (e) Shedding crocodile tears
   (f) Putting two and two together

futility	*infrequency*	*hypocrisy*
inference	*indecision*	*pessimism*

✔ MARK THESE YOURSELF

The answers are on page 146

1. Various English words beginning with the letters *tw* have some connection with the number *two*. See if you can make up your own definitions (not copied from the dictionary) for the following words; use the word *two* in each definition.

    (*a*) twice　(*b*) twenty　(*c*) twin　(*d*) twelve

    Now find words (beginning with *tw*) with the following meanings:

    (*e*) String made of two or more strands.
    (*f*) A small branch that forks into two shoots.
    (*g*) The half-light that exists between the two states of night and day.

2. In each of the following, say whether the dash stands for *its*, *it's*, *theirs*, *there's*, *whose*, or *who's*.

    (*a*) Our car is green; —— is grey.
    (*b*) —— a long way to Tipperary.
    (*c*) —— been eating my porridge?
    (*d*) The house stands on —— own.
    (*e*) He was a man —— word I trusted.
    (*f*) —— a breathless hush in the close tonight.

3. The French words for *woman*, *sheep*, *sea*, *bridge*, *door*, *witch*, *bull*, *earth*, and *wine* remind us of other English words that are related to them in meaning. What are they? (See page 21, Ex. 10)

4. Write down these words and show how they are accented. (See page 84, Ex. 5)

    (*a*) latitude　　　　(*d*) laburnum
    (*b*) chrysanthemum　(*e*) vaseline
    (*c*) report　　　　　(*f*) undergraduate

5. From these phrases pick out the ones that should be hyphenated. (See page 71, Ex. 4)

    a swimming bath　a hunting ground
    a flying fish　　　a stumbling block
    a cycling cape　　a faltering speaker
    a bathing cap　　reading spectacles

6. Which is correct .....

    The English *were* defeated at Waterloo
    OR The English *was* defeated at Waterloo?

📖 LOOK THESE UP

See page 29 for instructions

1. The word *record* is accented on the first syllable when used as a noun but on the second syllable when used as a verb. Give eight other words of the same kind.
84 Ex. 6

2. Which of these words are verbs, and which are nouns?
    advise, practice, prophesy, license, advice
104 73

3. Some people make mistakes in the spelling of the following words. Name the associated words that are helpful guides to their correct spellings.

    (*a*) terrific　　(*b*) balloon　　(*c*) secretary
    (*d*) Christmas　(*e*) cigarette　(*f*) bronchial
76 41

4. When are the letters **c** and **g** usually hard? In the words given in Set 46 (*a* to *z*), what letter is used

    (*a*) to keep the **g** hard;
    (*b*) to keep the **g** soft?
78 46

5. In a travel brochure a hotel advertised itself as

    THE SHADIEST HOTEL IN LISBON

    Another hotel, situated on a hill-side, claimed to be

    THE HOTEL THAT OVERLOOKS EVERYTHING

    Most people would regard these statements as being very clumsily expressed. Why?
    Say what name is given to the fault that mars these sentences.
109 81

6. Here are four statements that have actually been made in police courts by defendants or witnesses. Two of them contain *malapropisms*, and two are examples of *euphemism*. Say which is which.
108 79 and 129 111

    (*a*) *I do not think my wife would lie to me, although she might tell me a little fairy-tale.*
    (*b*) *I have always been an optician, and tried to look on the bright side of life.*
    (*c*) *My wife is living under a consumed name.*
    (*d*) *I did not steal it. I took it because I wanted it.*

108. SIMILES AND METAPHORS

If we say that someone is like a donkey we do not mean that there is any bodily resemblance; we are drawing attention to a *similarity* in behaviour—that is, the person's stupidity. A comparison of this kind is called a *simile*.

To be more forceful we may say *You are a donkey*. This seems to go farther than a comparison; it supposes that the person and the donkey are one and the same being. A simile that is shortened or compressed in this way is called a *metaphor*.

The following words and phrases are among those that can be used to introduce similes:

> *like,   as if,   as though,   as . . . as,*
> *much the same as,   seemed,   resembling,*
> *the very image of,   similar to,   -like (as in*
> *snake-like),   in a manner of speaking,*
> *one might have imagined that.*

Here are two comparisons expressed first as similes and then as metaphors:

He is as crafty as a fox. (*Simile*)
He is a cunning old fox. (*Metaphor*)

My feet seemed to be made of lead. (*Simile*)
The prisoners plodded on with leaden feet.
(*Metaphor*)

1. Discovering similes (i). Each of the following passages contains a simile.
Copy out the passages and underline the similes.

> EXAMPLE: Like a bucket from a well,
> Farmer Oak's watch came up
> on its chain from the depths of
> his pocket.
> ANSWER: Like a bucket from a well,
> Farmer Oak's watch came up
> on its chain from the depths of
> his pocket.

(a) Heracles dragged a wild goat after him, for he was as strong as an ox.

(b) She was leaning on a staff, the top of which was like the head of an eagle.

(c) Like scones on a baking-plate we lay that day on the rock in the hot sun.

(d) The plume of wood-smoke, like a blue feather in a lady's hat, curled from the cottage chimney.

(e) The brightly-polished shield shone as though it were the sun itself.

2. Discovering similes (ii). Follow the instructions given in Exercise 1.

(a) Surrounded by sheep, the shepherd looked as though he were an idol in the midst of prostrate worshippers.

(b) A hot breeze, as if breathed from the parted lips of some dragon, fanned him from the south.

(c) Silhouetted against the sunset, the bent figure of the old man resembled a black wick in a candle-flame.

(d) The great aircraft rose bird-like into the morning sky.

(e) The earth around the gateway was trodden hard and bare as a pavement.

3. The following statements are expressed in the form of similes. They can be made more forceful by compressing them into metaphors, shortening each one to the number of words given in brackets.

If any of the sayings are not familiar to you, you will find them explained in *A First English Companion*.

EXAMPLE: We shall find ourselves in difficulties, like a non-swimmer in deep water. (7)

ANSWER: We shall find ourselves in deep water.

(a) I am leading such a monotonous life that I feel as though I am in a groove. (5)

(b) We are both sharing the same risks, like two men in the same boat. (7)

(c) He is a wicked man, and is like an apple that is rotten at the core. (6)

(d) We are wasting our time, like a man flogging a dead horse. (6)

(e) He is so ill that he seems to have one foot in the grave. (7)

(f) The sight was so terrible that I felt as though it had frozen my blood. (5)

(g) Cricket is such a pleasure to Jim that it is like meat and drink to him. (7)

(h) He is afraid to decide and act, like a bather shivering on the brink. (6)

(i) It makes me feel as though my flesh is creeping. (5)

(j) I was so startled that I felt as though my heart was in my mouth. (6)

(k) You have a fine opportunity, like a footballer with the ball at his feet. (7)

(l) He was deceived by our trick just like a fish swallowing the bait. (4)

4. Follow the instructions given in Exercise 3.

(a) Geology means no more to me than a closed book. (7)

(b) You are in a difficult situation, like a snake held down by a cleft stick. (6)

(c) He is as awkward as a piece of cross-grained wood. (3)

(d) Whatever I say to him is forgotten instantly, as though it had gone in at one ear and out at the other. (15)

(e) She is of such a generous nature that one might almost imagine her heart to be made of gold. (6)

(f) He retreated when he was challenged, like a snail drawing in its horns. (5)

(g) He is trying to do too much, like a person who has bitten off more than he can chew. (9)

(h) You must tackle your difficulties resolutely, just as you would take a bull by the horns. (8)

(i) You have things the wrong way round, just as though you were putting the cart before the horse. (8)

(j) He worked until the day he died, like a horse that dies in harness. (4)

(k) He is very clumsy, just as though his fingers were all thumbs. (5)

(l) She is as dependent on her mother as though she were tied to her apron-strings. (7)

5. **Which sentence contains a metaphor?** In each of the following pairs, one sentence means exactly what it says; the other (containing a metaphor) could not be strictly true. Say which one of each pair is metaphorical.

(a) { The disappointment broke her heart.
{ The sudden jolt broke his arm.

(b) { He carried a flaming torch.
{ He was in a flaming temper.

(c) { All night long it rained steadily.
{ The robbers rained blows upon him.

(d) { She was rooted to the spot with fear.
{ The trailing stem had rooted itself in the soil.

(e) { He was greeted with a stony silence.
{ She stumbled along the stony path.

126

6. **Which sentence contains a metaphor?** In this exercise follow the instructions given in Exercise 5.

(a) ⎰ The mother watches the young bird as it flies from its nest.
⎱ At the slightest difficulty Janet flies to her mother.

(b) ⎰ The minutes crept slowly by.
⎱ The cat crept towards the nest.

(c) ⎰ We wrung the cloth and hung it up to dry.
⎱ At last we wrung a confession from him.

(d) ⎰ We must hammer out a solution to this problem.
⎱ We must hammer out the dents in this mudguard.

(e) ⎰ We had a flood of replies to our appeal.
⎱ The flood subsided as the storm abated.

7. **Find the metaphors.** Some of the following sentences contain metaphors, and some do not. Say which ones are metaphorical.

(a) His life is hanging by a thread.
(b) My geography is rusty; I haven't done any for two years.
(c) A red-cloaked trumpeter stepped forward.
(d) She is two-faced.
(e) The whole affair is cloaked in mystery.
(f) For the moment she was speechless with astonishment.
(g) Oliver Twist and his companions suffered the tortures of slow starvation.
(h) The problem bristles with difficulties.
(i) By nightfall the ship had been stranded by the ebbing tide.
(j) He is good-natured but he has feet of clay.

8. **Simile or metaphor?** Each of these biblical quotations contains either a simile or a metaphor; say which.

(a) All we like sheep have gone astray.
(b) Yea, he did fly upon the wings of the wind.
(c) Thy word is a lamp unto my feet.
(d) He maketh the deep to boil like a pot.
(e) My tongue is the pen of a ready writer.
(f) As the crackling of thorns under a pot, so is the laughter of the fool.
(g) Be ye therefore wise as serpents, and harmless as doves.

(h) He was a burning and a shining light.
(i) The love of money is the root of all evil.
(j) As for man, his days are as grass.

9. **Similes and metaphors in combination.** We sometimes find similes and metaphors combined in a single sentence; e.g.

> He cast me aside, like a tool for which he had no further use.

Here we have a metaphor (*He cast me aside*), followed by a simile.
In the following passages see if you can identify all the similes and metaphors.

(a) There were half a dozen specimens of the cactus, writhing round bits of lath, like hairy serpents; another specimen was shooting out broad claws, like a green lobster.
(b) The atmosphere quivered as if the air itself were panting, and the purple sky was set with one great flaming jewel of fire.
(c) In this rat-infested yard was a little counting-house burrowing in the dust as if it had fallen from the clouds and ploughed into the ground.
(d) Through the green tree in the courtyard the sun tossed fragments of light, like coins of silver running through a miser's fingers.

10. **Using words metaphorically.** Choose any eight of the following nouns, and use each of your chosen words metaphorically in a sentence.

EXAMPLE: stepping-stone
SUGGESTED ANSWER: The salary is low, but the job will be a stepping-stone to something better.

iron, forest, spark, cloud, belt, stream, galaxy, veil, tinge, glow, hurdle, sphere.

11. **Using words literally and metaphorically.** Choose any six of the following words, and use each one as a verb in two sentences—literally in the first, metaphorically in the second. The verbs may be used in any of their forms (e.g., *plough, ploughs, ploughed, ploughing*).

EXAMPLE: (i) The farmer ploughed his fields.
(ii) The runaway lorry ploughed through the crowd of shoppers.

rain, jump, drag, wade, gallop, wrestle, pour, fish, poke, bombard, whip, shroud.

127

109. PERSONIFICATION

Some things are often regarded as being either masculine or feminine, although they are in fact not living creatures. We speak of Jack Frost, and of *his* patterns on the window panes; and a motorist may say (in speaking of his car) that *her* engine is running well. There is no rule for deciding which should be masculine and which feminine; we come to know the custom by experience.

This figure of speech, which is a kind of metaphor, is called *personification*.

---

1. In the following quotations, replace the dashes by *his* or *her*. (Towards the end, *he* or *she* will also be necessary.)

   (a) *And all I ask is a tall ship and a star to steer —— by.*

   (b) *Right against the eastern gate*
   Where the great sun begins —— state

   (c) *Slowly, silently, now the moon*
   Walks the night in —— silver shoon.

   (d) *England mourns for —— dead across the sea.*

   (e) *Death lays —— icy hand on kings.*

   (f) *Fortune can take from us nothing but what —— gave us.*

   (g) *Poetic justice, with —— lifted scale.*

   (h) *Love rules —— kingdom without a sword.*

   (i) *Wisdom crieth without; —— uttereth —— voice in the streets.*

   (j) *Accuse not Nature, —— hath done —— part.*

2. The following quotations concern inanimate (lifeless) objects that are referred to as though they were persons. Say what it is that the writer is supposing in each one.

   EXAMPLE:

   The swimming vapour slopes athwart the glen,
   Puts forth an arm, and creeps from pine to pine.

   SUGGESTED The mist is supposed to be able
   ANSWER: to swim, and to stretch out an arm so as to pull itself from tree to tree.

   (a) *The gruff old bell was always peeping slyly down at Scrooge out of a Gothic window in the wall.*

   (b) *At the end of the ally was a dingy, low-browed shop.*

   (c) *The ancient pillars, tired of supporting the heavy oak-beamed town hall, had become bow-legged and knock-kneed.*

   (d) *Scythes, bill-hooks, spades and mattocks jostled with bee-hives and hay-rakes in Jem Carson's shop window.*

   (e) *The red rose cries, "She is near,*
   she is near;"
   And the white rose weeps, "She is late."

   (f) *The Tower Bridge cleared itself of midgets and toy vehicles, and raised its two arms.*

   (g) *When your engine gets tired and run-down, give it a tonic dose of EX-EL to make it fighting fit.*—Advt.

3. In each of the following quotations an inanimate (lifeless) object is referred to as though it were animate (living).

   Write the words *Inanimate* and *Animate* at the tops of two columns, and then choose the appropriate pair of words from each quotation, making sure to put them in the right order.

   EXAMPLE: *Poverty is the mother of health.*
   ANSWER:

Inanimate	Animate
poverty	mother

   (a) *Time, you old gipsy man,*
   Will you not stay?

   (b) *The mountain nymph, sweet Liberty*

   (c) *O sleep, O gentle sleep,*
   Nature's soft nurse . . . . .

   (d) *"If the law supposes that," said Mr. Bumble, "the law is a ass."*

   (e) *For the black bat, night, has flown.*

   (f) *Land of Hope and Glory, Mother of the Free*

   (g) *Life's but a walking shadow, a poor player*
   That struts and frets his hour upon the stage.

   (h) *Virtue and happiness are mother and daughter.*

   (i) *Ol' man River, he jes' keeps rolling along.*

128

110. HYPERBOLE*

Hyperbole is a form of exaggeration that is not meant to be taken seriously. For example, some unkind person may tell you that you have no brains; this is obviously untrue, but you understand full well what is meant by it.

Some of the following sentences are examples of hyperbole, but others could be literally true. Say which are which.

(a) It rained cats and dogs all day.
(b) Our garden is over-run with cats and dogs.
(c) The branch snapped off without warning.
(d) He snapped my head off.
(e) I scalded my hand with boiling-hot jam.
(f) Her forehead is boiling hot.
(g) I have had millions of interruptions this morning.
(h) There are millions of stars in the Milky Way.
(i) He ran me off my legs.
(j) He ran like lightning.
(k) It took me ages to do this jigsaw puzzle.
(l) It has taken ages for the river to carve out this canyon.
(m) A runaway lorry had crashed into a pillar and brought down the roof.
(n) At the fall of the curtain the wildly-enthusiastic audience brought down the house.

* This is a word of four syllables. It is accented on the second syllable, and almost rhymes with the word *verbally.*

111. EUPHEMISM

There are times when it may be desirable to use polite language in referring to something disagreeable or embarrassing. This is called *euphemism.*

EXAMPLE: His clothes have seen better days. (*He is shabby*)

To be euphemistic is often wise and tactful. On the other hand, euphemism can be even more pointed than the outspoken truth. But there are people who can never bring themselves to call a spade a spade; euphemism is then a fault.

EXAMPLE: He passed away. (*He died*)

Express the following euphemisms in plain English.
(a) He is a stranger to the truth.
(b) She departed this earthly life.
(c) Mr. Borrow is financially embarrassed.
(d) My uncle came into conflict with the law for removing property without the owner's consent.
(e) Soap and water would do his collar no harm.
(f) Her reason is under a cloud.
(g) The crossing was so rough that I parted with my breakfast.
(h) Mrs. Grey is not as young as she was.
(i) Mr. Dally will not die from over-exertion.
(j) Mr. Grabb does not let generosity get the better of him.
(k) No-one would accuse Mr. Peacock of hiding his light under a bushel.
(l) She does her best.

112. PUNS

A pun is a play upon words that are alike in sound but different in meaning. For example:

The people of Perth dye for a living.

Puns are not considered to be a very desirable form of humour. Used unintentionally they can create an unfortunate impression. The following samples will help you to recognize puns when you meet them.

(a) A once-popular entertainment at parties was to arrange exhibitions of so-called works of art. The exhibits were in fact nothing more than common household objects, but each one was given an imposing title that contained an amusing pun. See if you can explain the point of the six specimens set out below.

Pillars of Ancient Greece (Old candles)
Relics of the Great (Cinders)
The Colonel's Residence (A nut)
Things to Adore (Hinges)
Glimpse of a Well-known Route (A potato)
The Meet of the Hounds (Dog-biscuits)

(b) Say why these newspaper headlines should have been worded differently:

1. SWIMMER'S GREAT FEAT
2. TRAIN ON FIRE; PASSENGERS ALIGHT

(c) Paul was not very sympathetic about Peter's toothache; he said, *Push your head through the window, and the pain will be gone.* Explain his double meaning.

(*d*) Wedding guests put this notice on the back of the bridal car. Explain the point of it.

> AISLE
> ALTAR
> HYMN

(*e*) The doctor asked the vicar if he thought that life was worth living. The vicar replied, *That depends upon the liver*. What did he mean?

(*f*) These notices appeared in the window of a chemist and photographic dealer. Comment on them:

> 1. WE DISPENSE WITH ACCURACY
> 2. OUR BUSINESS IS DEVELOPING

(*g*) This couplet is taken from a version of the pantomime *Aladdin* that was produced in 1866. Explain the pun.

> *The tree I'll find; with hope my heart is beating;*
> *If it's a yew I'll know it by its bleating.*

(*h*) In a school report the headmaster's comment was *Your son is trying*. Explain how this could be taken in two ways.

113. RHETORICAL QUESTIONS

When a public speaker says to his audience *Can a starving man live on promises?* he does not expect an answer. What he really means is *A starving man cannot live on promises*. A question of this sort is called a rhetorical question.

Re-arrange the following rhetorical questions in the form of statements that do not need question marks.

(*a*) What sense is there in buying a car if you cannot afford to run it?

(*b*) How can one live on two pounds per week?

(*c*) Who wants a world without pleasure and happiness?

(*d*) What use is a fortune to a man if he kills himself in the getting of it?

(*e*) Which of you likes to have government officials prying into your private affairs?

(*f*) What is the value of money on a desert island?

(*g*) Am I expected to shake the rugs without making a dust?

(*h*) We must be prepared. Who can tell when we shall be attacked?

(*i*) Our streets are much too narrow. Is it any wonder that traffic is so congested?

(*j*) Children are roaming the streets until ten o'clock at night. What are their parents thinking of?

114. EPIGRAMS

1. Epigrams are short and witty remarks, often about the follies and shortcomings of men and women. Sometimes they ridicule people and customs by means of satire or sarcasm. Sometimes they make use of paradox—that is, statements which at first sight seem to be absurd or contradictory. Many epigrams are made up of contrasting statements or phrases, which may be evenly balanced about a central point.

With these features in mind, discuss the following epigrams.

(*a*) Duty is what one expects from others.

(*b*) When a man wants to murder a tiger he calls it sport: when a tiger wants to murder him, he calls it ferocity.

(*c*) A learned man is an idler who kills time by study.

(*d*) A life of ease is a difficult pursuit.

(*e*) The less one has to do, the less time one finds to do it in.

(*f*) God cures the ailment; the doctor takes the fee.

(*g*) If you would keep a secret from an enemy, tell it not to a friend.

(*h*) A lawyer is a learned gentleman who rescues your estate from your enemies and keeps it himself.

(*i*) The books that everybody admires are those that nobody reads.

(*j*) Vulgarity is the conduct of those we do not like.

(*k*) The old believe everything, the middle-aged suspect everything, the young know everything.

(*l*) Even the youngest among us is not infallible.

(*m*) Poor men want meat for their stomachs: rich men want stomachs for their meat.

(*n*) He that falls in love with himself will have no rivals.

(*o*) A self-made man is for ever praising his creator.

(*p*) If a man could have half his wishes, he would double his troubles.

(*q*) The only thing experience teaches us is that experience teaches us nothing.

(*r*) We learn from history that we do not learn from history.

(*s*) What orators lack in depth they give you in length.

(*t*) To know what everybody knows is to know nothing.

2. Eight of the epigrams in Exercise 1 are paraphrased below. Taking each of the following sentences in turn, pick out the corresponding epigram.

(*a*) We seldom admit that our own manners are at fault.

(*b*) Idleness is not as free from care as one might imagine.

(*c*) We expect other people to fulfil their obligations to us, even though we may neglect our own responsibilities.

(*d*) Those who have prospered from small beginnings like to sing their own praises.

(*e*) No-one likes a person who is full of his own importance.

(*f*) The more a man has, the more he has to worry about.

(*g*) We refuse to profit from the mistakes of others.

(*h*) Only those with very little experience imagine that they are always right.

115. ALLITERATION

From the following quotations pick out the words that are used alliteratively.

EXAMPLE: *Bed in the bush with stars to see*
ANSWER: bed, bush
stars, see

NOTE. Think of the sounds of the words and remember that a phrase such as *fearful phantom* is alliterative—the initial sound being *f*—although the two words do not begin with the same letter.

(*a*) *Beyond the last lone lamp I passed.*

(*b*) *He stayed not for brake, and he stopp'd not for stone.*

(*c*) *When fishes flew and forests walked*
And figs grew upon thorn

(*d*) *To the gull's way and the whale's way*
where the wind's like a whetted knife

(*e*) *Now air is hush'd, save where the weak-ey'd bat*
With short shrill shriek flits by on leathern wing.

(*f*) *Lord, thy most pointed pleasure take*
And stab my spirit broad awake.

(*g*) *And stand, above the stubble, stiff*
As mail at morning-prime

(*h*) *Sandalwood, cedarwood, and sweet, white wine*

(*i*) *Couched in his kennel, like a log*

(*j*) *Till last by Philip's farm I flow*

(*k*) *I know not where the white road runs.*

116. ONOMATOPŒIA

1. The verbs in the following list refer to various kinds of *sounds*. Some of them (like *cackle*) are onomatopœic; that is, they imitate the actual sounds. Others (like *shout*) show no obvious sign of any such imitation.

beat	boil	bump	burst	cackle
cheep	chime	clank	click	crack
crackle	creak	crunch	cry	dribble
drone	echo	explode	flow	grate
grind	groan	gurgle	gush	hiss
jar	knock	peal	resound	reverberate
ring	roar	rumble	rustle	scream
screech	shout	spit	splinter	split
plop	slap	twang	steam	trill

From this list choose *one* onomatopœic word that in your opinion best describes the sound made by each of the following:

(*a*) Plunging red-hot iron into water

(*b*) Dry leaves blown by the wind

(*c*) Boulders falling in a cave

(*d*) A heavy chain striking a stone wall

(*e*) A person falling heavily on a wooden floor

(*f*) Breaking a dead branch

(*g*) A stream running among stones

(*h*) A plucked bow-string

(*i*) Treading on an egg-shell

(*j*) Burning twigs

(*k*) A rusty hinge on a small gate

(*l*) Newly-hatched chickens

(*m*) A pebble dropped into a pond

(*n*) Small waves striking the side of a boat

2. The poets who wrote the following lines have succeeded in conveying actual sounds. Read the extracts, and then do the exercise that follows them. It is a good plan to say the lines quietly to yourself so that you can feel and hear them.

(i) *Over the cobbles he clattered and clashed.*

(ii) *I heard the ripple washing in the reeds,*
And the wild water lapping on the crag.

(iii)   *How they tinkle, tinkle, tinkle,*
         In the icy air of night!
       Keeping time, time, time,
         In a sort of Runic rhyme.

(iv) *It cracked and growled, and roared and howled.*

(v) *'Neath our feet broke the brittle bright stubble like chaff.*

(vi)   *And even spoiled the women's chats,*
        By drowning their speaking
          With shrieking and squeaking
       In fifty different sharps and flats.

(vii) *Dry clash'd his harness in the icy caves*
      And barren chasms, and all to left and right
      The bare black cliff clang'd round him.

Which of these quotations suggests the following sounds? Pick out the words that are chiefly responsible for producing these effects.

EXAMPLE: Water among bulrushes
ANSWER: No. (ii); ripple, washing

(a) Sea-ice in an Antarctic storm
(b) Sledge-bells
(c) A swarm of rats
(d) Water striking rocks
(e) Horses' hooves on stone paving
(f) Horses galloping over a mown harvest-field
(g) Steel striking rock

3. This exercise follows the same pattern as the previous one.

(i)   *The fair breeze blew, the white foam flew,*
      The furrow follow'd free.

(ii)   *There in the many-knotted waterflags*
      That whistled stiff and dry about the marge

(iii) *You shall see and hear your crackling question hurled*
      Across the arch of heaven while you wait.

(iv)   *The monster grunts: 'Enough!'*
      Tightening his load of links with pant and puff.

(v) *There was never a sound beside the wood but one,*
      And that was my long scythe whispering to the ground.

(vi)   *I watch him striding lank behind*
       His clashing team.

(vii) *Then I heard the boom of the blood-lust song*
      And a thigh-bone beating on a tin-pan gong.

Say which of the above quotations (and which words) suggest the sounds made by the following:

(a) Wind in the bulrushes and lakeside plants
(b) The harness of horses pulling a plough
(c) A wireless message sent in Morse code by means of electric sparks
(d) Grass being mown by a sharp blade
(e) A train drawing out of a station
(f) The bows of a boat cutting through choppy water
(g) A primitive percussion instrument

117. ASSONANCE

In the following extracts from poems, use is made of the poetic device known as *assonance*—the repetition of vowel sounds. Some of these repetitions occur in a single line, and some in consecutive lines. In one of the examples given here there is a kind of delayed echo; that is, vowel sounds are repeated two lines later.

From each quotation extract the words that have identical vowel-sounds. Do not include rhymes such as *whirl* and *pearl*, *lie* and *cry*, etc.

EXAMPLE: *Where the shy-eyed delicate deer troop*
            down to the pools to drink
ANSWER: shy, eyed
         troop, pools

(a)   *He clasps the crag with crooked hands.*

(b)   *Then, the cool kindliness of sheets, that soon*
      Smooth away trouble

(c)   *So strode he back slow to the wounded King.*

(d)   *In a cowslip's bell I lie;*
         There I couch when owls do cry.

(e)   *And a grey mist on the sea's face, and a grey dawn breaking*

(f)   *Yet the light of the bright world dies*
         With the dying sun.

(g)   *Fair daffodils, we weep to see*
         You haste away so soon.

(h)   *The stream mysterious glides beneath,*
        Green as a dream and deep as death.

(i) *Rend with tremendous sound your ears asunder*
   With gun, drum, trumpet, blunderbuss, and thunder.

(j)   *She left the web, she left the loom,*
       She made three paces thro' the room,
       She saw the water-lily bloom.

(k)   *We shall see, while above us*
           The waves roar and whirl,
           A ceiling of amber,
           A pavement of pearl.

118. RHYME

1. Which word does not rhyme? In each of the following groups, all the words rhyme with each other except one; say which this word is.

Remember that rhyme depends on *sound*, not on spelling. You may find it helpful to read the words aloud, taking care to pronounce them correctly.

(a) blown, grown, stone, gone, sewn, lone
(b) over, clover, Dover, drover, lover
(c) pier, brier, dear, sneer, here, weir
(d) smile, style, while, veil, vile, aisle
(e) speak, shriek, cheek, steak, streak, pique
(f) hard, card, stared, starred, charred, barred
(g) tough, dough, rough, puff, gruff, bluff
(h) could, good, hood, would, stood, flood
(i) wood, stud, blood, mud, bud, thud
(j) blade, maid, strayed, plaid, preyed, weighed
(k) fume, noon, June, moon, swoon, tune

2. Rhyming pairs. In this list of thirty words each word rhymes with one other. Re-arrange them so that you have fifteen rhyming pairs.

love,	fate,	now,	done,	height,
dove,	grow,	weight,	feign,	run,
farm,	blue,	plot,	form,	muff,
spite,	chain,	plait,	cove,	yacht,
charm,	flat,	move,	swarm,	prove,
wove,	bough,	rough,	though,	through.

3. Rhyme-patterns. The rhyme-pattern of a stanza of poetry can be set down by letting each rhyme be represented by a letter of the alphabet, starting with **a**. For example:

Gather ye rosebuds while ye **may,**	**a**
*Old Time is still a-***flying,**	**b**
*And this same flower that smiles to***day**	**a**
Tomorrow will be **dying.**	**b**

Using this method, set out the rhyme-patterns of the following stanzas. Do not write them out, but answer in letters only. The pattern of the stanza given as an example is **a b a b**.

(a)   *The sun descending in the west,*
       The evening star does shine;
       The birds are silent in their nest,
       And I must seek for mine.
          The moon, like a flower
          In heaven's high bower,
          With silent delight
          Sits and smiles on the night.

                                    —BLAKE

(b)   *Drink to me only with thine eyes,*
       And I will pledge with mine;
       Or leave a kiss but in the cup
       And I'll not look for wine.
       The thirst that from the soul doth rise
          Doth ask a drink divine;
       But might I of Jove's nectar sup,
          I would not change for thine.

                                    —JONSON

(c)   *Under the wide and starry sky*
       Dig the grave and let me lie:
       Glad did I live and gladly die,
       And I laid me down with a will.

                                    —STEVENSON

4. Internal rhyme. Consider this line from *The Rime of the Ancient Mariner*:

   And the bay was white with silent light.

We have here an example of internal rhyme, because the words *white* and *light* rhyme within a single line.

Another example is to be found on page 69 of *A First English Companion*.

Pick out the internal rhymes in the following lines.

(a) *I am the daughter of earth and water,*
       And the nursling of the sky;
    I pass through the pores of the ocean and shores;
       I change, but I cannot die.

                                    —SHELLEY

(b)   *For all averr'd I had kill'd the bird*
       That made the breeze to blow.
       Ah wretch! said they, the bird to slay,
       That made the breeze to blow!

                                    —COLERIDGE

119. METRE

1. It is possible to represent the rhythm of words by means of a pattern of dots and dashes like that used in Morse code. Dots stand for unaccented syllables,* and dashes for accented ones, thus:

reward	● —	gratefully	— ● ●
startle	— ●	decidedly	● — ● ●
concealment	● — ●	accuracy	— ● ● ●

Make sure that you understand this method. If necessary, say the words aloud and tap out their rhythms with your finger—a light tap for an unaccented syllable and a heavy tap for an accented one.

Copy the above table (including the words) on the left-hand side of your paper or exercise book, and then add the following words on the right, each on its correct line.

lovely	contain	refusal	argument
enjoy	daylight	observe	occasion
marvellous	purpose	horizon	plentiful
community	desirable	intentional	delicacy
memorable	naturalist		

*See Exercises 1–7 of *Pronunciation* on pages 83–4.

2. Copy out the following lines, and then (in another colour if possible) put a dot above each unaccented syllable and a dash above each accented syllable.

EXAMPLE: And the bridegroom stood dangling his bonnet and plume.

(*a*) There's the life for ever
(*b*) Shallow brooks, and rivers wide
(*c*) And now there came both mist and snow
(*d*) Down to the depths of the sea
(*e*) Bound and plumed with scented grasses
(*f*) And green and blue his sharp eyes twinkled
(*g*) How sweet the moonlight sleeps upon this bank
(*h*) And there lay the rider, distorted and pale
(*i*) When the trees in the orchard bend low
(*j*) This is the night mail crossing the border

3. If you look at the metrical index of a hymn book you will see that the metre of each hymn is expressed by a set of figures. These figures tell us the number of syllables in each line of a verse. For example, by tapping out the syllables of the National Anthem (or counting them on our fingers) we see that the seven lines of each verse are constructed like this:

6.6.4.6.6.6.4

Using a copy of your school hymn book, work out the metrical patterns of the following hymns.

(*a*) Blest are the pure in heart
(*b*) All hail the power of Jesus' name
(*c*) Fight the good fight
(*d*) Gracious Spirit, Holy Ghost
(*e*) The Church's one foundation
(*f*) The King of love my shepherd is
(*g*) Now thank we all our God
(*h*) When I survey the wondrous Cross
(*i*) Let us, with a gladsome mind
(*j*) Jerusalem the golden
(*k*) Lord, thy word abideth
(*l*) Rejoice! the Lord is King
(*m*) The day thou gavest, Lord, is ended
(*n*) Thou whose almighty Word

When you have finished you will find that there are two pairs of hymns with identical metrical patterns, which means that a tune that fits either one of them is bound to fit the other. Pick out these two pairs.

4. The following eight lines are taken from various poems and are not related to each other either by sense or by rhyme. Say them over to yourself, and tap out their rhythmic patterns with your finger; then arrange them in four pairs so that the two lines in each pair have the same metre.

(*a*) *As we rush, as we rush in the train*
(*b*) *Up and down the people go*
(*c*) *In a sunset of crimson and gold*
(*d*) *Through the forest vast and vacant*
(*e*) *Out upon the wharfs they came*
(*f*) *They walked beside a hazel wood*
(*g*) *Hid her face but made no answer*
(*h*) *I caught a little silver trout*

5. The following lines are taken from various parts of different poems. The two lines in each pair are from the same poem, but the second one has had the order of its words changed so that the metre or rhythm is not right. What you have to do is to rearrange the second line so that both lines are in the same metre.

EXAMPLE: *And then an open field they crossed*
They stood on a hill at daybreak
ANSWER: They stood at daybreak on a hill

(*a*) *Then did the little maid reply*
So she was laid in the churchyard

134

(b) *The wind hath blown a gale all day*
From the boat Sir Ralph bent over

(c) *Her timbers yet are sound*
And again she may float

(d) *In the pleasant days of Summer*
When in the thickets the birds sang

(e) *His wrath was turned to wailing*
He did discover his child

(f) *And into the midnight we galloped abreast*
In my saddle I turned and made its girths tight

(g) *Have ye left the mountain places?*
Do ye in slumber still sit there?

(h) *And we gazed up the aisle through the small leaded*
panes
A murmur of folk at their prayers came from the
church.*

* In (h), begin with the word *From*.

6. The following passages, which at first sight look like unpunctuated prose, are in fact stanzas of poetry. Write them out correctly, inserting punctuation and capital letters wherever necessary. You are told how many lines there should be in each verse.

(a) (*4 lines*). By this the storm grew loud apace the water-wraith was shrieking and in the scowl of heaven each face grew dark as they were speaking.

(b) (*4 lines*) The wild wind rang from park and plain and round the attics rumbled till all the tables danced again and half the chimneys tumbled.

(c) (*6 lines*) I love the fitful gust that shakes the casement all the day and from the glossy elm-tree takes the faded leaves away twirling them by the window pane with thousand others down the lane.

(d) (*6 lines*) While the ploughman near at hand whistles o'er the furrow'd land and the milkmaid singeth blithe and the mower whets his scythe and every shepherd tells his tale under the hawthorn in the dale.

(e) (*4 lines*) From my wings are shaken the dews that waken the sweet buds every one when rocked to rest on their mother's breast as she dances about the sun.

(f) (*6 lines*) There is sweet music here that softer falls than petals from blown roses on the grass or night-dews on still waters between walls of shadowy granite in a gleaming pass music that gentlier on the spirit lies than tired eyelids upon tired eyes.

(g) (*6 lines*) In his lodge beside a river close beside a frozen river sat an old man sad and lonely and the fire was slowly dying as a young man walking lightly at the open doorway entered.

(h) (*8 lines*) Gloucester that Duke so good next of the royal blood for famous England stood with his brave brother Clarence in steel so bright though but a maiden knight yet in that famous fight scarce such another.

★ REVISION

1. In this exercise you will find two examples of each of the following:

> metaphor,   simile,   alliteration,
> internal rhyme,   onomatopœia.

Say which is which.

(a) *Clang, clang, clang on the anvil*

(b) *Her voice was as harsh as a cinder under a door.*

(c) *And silence falls on flocks and fields and men.*

(d)   *The air was still on crag and hill,*
          On meadow and in valley;
          The sun stared down upon the town,
          In torrid street and alley.

(e)   *All the world's a stage,*
And all the men and women merely players.

(f) *Through the grey light drift of the dust, in the keen*
     cool rush of the air

(g) *Electric motors whirred and hummed; vivid blue*
sparks crackled and hissed; and with a clank of
steel on steel the great machine lurched forward.

(h) *I suspect that she was fishing for compliments.*

(i) *The ungodly are not so: but are like the chaff which*
the wind driveth away.

(j) *The fields breathe sweet, the daisies kiss our feet.*

2. In this exercise you will find two examples of each of the following:

assonance,   **personification,**   **epigram,**
euphemism,   **rhetorical question,**   **hyperbole.**

Say which is which, and express the rhetorical questions as statements.

(*a*) *I was so hungry that I could have eaten a horse.*

(*b*) *We have had our dog put to sleep.*

(*c*)   *The night has a thousand eyes,*
          And the day but one.

(*d*) *Who can say how long the universe will last?*

(*e*) *Round and round the spicy downs the yellow Lotos-dust is blown.*

(*f*) *Gossip is what no-one claims to like but everybody enjoys.*

(*g*) *Scraps of waste paper scrambled to their feet behind the express train and hobbled along behind it as it roared through the station.*

(*h*) *City of mist and rain and blown grey spaces.*

(*i*) *I addressed the parcel clearly enough for a blind man on a galloping horse to see it.*

(*j*) *I am sorry to say that he had had a drop too much.*

(*k*) *A rich man's joke is always funny.*

(*l*) *Does the Government think that we are all millionaires?*

📖 LOOK THESE UP

See page 29 for instructions

1. Correct these sentences:

(*a*) Gerald, with one of his brothers, have gone fishing.   43 Ex. 7

(*b*) Sitting at the back of the church, the preacher could hardly be heard.   54 Ex. 8

(*c*) She was annoyed at me laughing.   54 Ex. 9

2. Rewrite in indirect speech:

(*a*) Father said, "I think the petrol-tank is empty."

(*b*) I said to Peter, "Why don't you use your own bat?"   69 Ex. 7

3. In the *arena* at Rome the ——— was often stained with the blood of the combatants.   99 **69**

✅ MARK THESE YOURSELF

The answers are on page 146

1. Robert Southey wrote a poem called *The Cataract of Lodore* in which he had great fun with pairs of rhyming words that describe the commotion of the falling water. Here is part of it. See if you can supply the missing words; then turn to the answers and see what words Southey actually used.

> *And shining and twining,*
> *And rattling and battling,*
> *And shaking and ———,*
> *And pouring and ———,*
> *And waving and ———,*
> *And tossing and ———,*
> *And flowing and ———,*
> *And running and ———,*
> *And foaming and ———,*
> *And dinning and ———,*
> *And dropping and ———,*
> *And working and ———,*
> *And guggling and ———,*
> *And heaving and ———,*
> *And moaning and ——— .....*

2. When poetic devices are used unintentionally they can produce unpleasant or ridiculous effects. For example:

(*a*) A notice in a railway carriage said

     PLEASE KEEP YOUR FEET OFF THE SEAT.

(*b*) A notice outside an exhibition said

     PATRONS WITHOUT PASSES PLEASE PAY IN THE PORCH.

(*c*) Some people are unfortunate to have names such as

     SHIRLEY HURLEY,   NORMAN WORMAN

Look back over pages 131–3, and then name the features that make the above examples ludicrous.

3. The names of certain tools can be used as puns. See how many you can think of.   129 **112**

4. Many popular similes are alliterative; for example:

> *As hungry as a hunter*
> *As thick as thieves*

Think of others in which the following words are used: good, plain, fit, dull, weak, smooth, blind, sweet, proud, red, bold, dead.   131 **115**

SECTION EIGHT
IN LIGHTER VEIN

THERE are special names for some of the more amusing uses (and misuses) of English. Some of them refer to certain kinds of verse, others to word games and curiosities, stupid blunders, witty remarks, and so on.

In each of the next three exercises you are given several of these special names, followed by one example of each—but not in the same order. To find which is which, look up the given words in any convenient reference book, and then ask yourself which examples fit the meanings of these words exactly.

120. limerick: dialect: anagram: howler: anachronism: Irish bull

(a) The letters in the phrase *no more stars* can be re-arranged to make the word *astronomers*. Now take the phrase *great help* and see if you can make from it the name of a helpful instrument.

What do we call words that can be re-arranged like this?

(b) What special name is given to a nonsense-verse of this pattern?

> *There once was a young man from Crewe*
> *Who found a dead mouse in his stew.*
> *Said the waiter, "Don't shout,*
> *And wave it about,*
> *Or the others will ask for one too."*

Using the letters **a** and **b**, show how the rhymes are arranged.

(c) TEACHER: "What is a polygon?"

PUPIL: "A dead parrot."

What kind of mistake is this?

(d) What mistake does this picture illustrate?

"Why did they build it so far from the railway?"

137

(e) Here is a short extract from a Lancashire tale by T. Thompson:

"Put 'em down," she said acidly. "Them lads'll eat nought but pies if we'll let 'em. Tak' 'em a plate o' bread an' butther, an' then we'll work 'em on to pies through tay-cake. They'll be fit for nowt if tha fills 'em up wi' pies."

What do we call speech of this kind?

(f) Two yokels were making arrangements for an evening excursion. Said one, "If I get to the cross roads first I'll leave a stone on the gate-post to let you know that I've gone on." "And if I get there first," said the other, "I'll take it off."

There is a well-known name that is sometimes used for stupid remarks of this sort; what is it?

121. parody: doggerel: malapropism: pun: repartee: portmanteau word

(a) This verse is taken from a version of the panto-mime *Aladdin* that was produced in 1866. What is the proper name for this so-called poetry?

A feeble widow whom you've treated cruel
Is quite prepared to give you some gruel;
The same weak widow, with unruffled brow
In gentle language asks you, "What's the row?"
Resume your studies, dears, you know my maxim—
The boy who's last in reaching school, I whacks him.

(b) A holiday-maker from the city, who had lost his way in the country, saw a village boy at the cross roads and asked him where the other three roads led to. All that the boy could tell him was that one led to the farm, one to the church, and one to the pump.

"You call yourself a clever lad, I suppose," said the man sarcastically.

"No," replied the boy, "but I'm not lost."

What name do we give to a quick-witted retort like this?

(c) A mixture of smoke and fog is called *smog*, and motorized pedal-cycles have been called *mopeds*. What are words of this sort called?

Suggest a suitable trading-name (a single word) for a firm in which the two partners are named Corfield and Hanbury.

(d) What do we call the figure of speech on which this joke depends?

"That's a queer beast; what is it?"
"A pedigree dachshund. He has two flaws, though."
"Looks more like a bungalow to me."

(e) A man who was a little confused was heard to say that the larch is a *carnivorous* tree. Explain his mistake, and say what name we give to it (the mistake, not the tree).

(f) What name is given to this kind of imitation?

Rumble, rumble, little jet;
How the dickens did you get
Up above the world so high,
Like a blow-lamp in the sky?

122. sarcasm: high-flown English: double negative: spoonerism: redundancy: mixed metaphors

(a) A girl was heard to say that she had learned to ride a two-wheeled bicycle. What error was she guilty of in her English?

(b) A man who meant to say, *I deal at the stores* said *I steal at the doors*. What is a mistake of this sort called?

What did he mean when he said that the destruction of his home by fire was a *blushing crow*?

(c) The following sentence, taken from a newspaper report of a football match, is typical of an artificial style of writing that is not as common nowadays as it used to be. What is English of this kind called?

> *Marriott, the Wanderers' pocket-sized skipper, baffled the custodian with his fancy footwork and banged the leather into the onion-bag.*

Say the same thing in plain English.

(d) Mr. Oddman was an eccentric person, and was for ever making mistakes and getting his facts wrong. An acquaintance said of him,

> *He's a queer fish—always barking up the wrong tree.*

There is a special name for this sort of confused description; what is it?

(e) John said of Tom, *He never has no money in his pocket.* If John really meant exactly what he said, was Tom ever without money?

If John was using English badly, what mistake was he making?

(f) A naval instructor who found one of his cadets completely entangled in a rope said to him,

> *Very pretty! Very pretty! All we want now is a little dab of sealing wax.*

What figure of speech was he using?

123. irony: anti-climax: paradox: ambiguity: palindrome: hyperbole

(a) Introducing a lecturer to his audience, the chairman said,

> *If I tried to tell you anything about the subject of the lecture I should only display my ignorance. I prefer to leave that to the professor.*

The audience tittered. What do we call the mistake that caused their amusement?

(b) Mrs. Gay described Mrs. Weep as *the kind of person who is never happy unless she is feeling sorry for someone.*

Mrs. Gay contradicted herself, but we know very well what she meant. What do we call a self-contradictory statement of this sort?

(c) This is how a boy described a war-time pilot in an essay. The other boys in the class laughed when the passage was read out to them. Why?

> *Andy was the hero of the squadron. He had shot down ten enemy aircraft, and had baled out several times. No-one could beat him at aerobatics. He was also good at darts.*

What name is given to a construction of this kind?

(d) Donald said to Richard, *Eric has tons of conkers in his desk.*

Give the technical name for this kind of exaggeration.

(e) Tired of waiting for the railway station in his town to be modernized, a resident tries to shame the authorities into action by means of an article in the local newspaper. Here are some of the things he says about the station:

> *Unstained by paint, the building has acquired distinctive natural shades of grime-grey and rust-red. The roof of the booking-hall, embellished with an unusual pattern of perforations, affords pleasing glimpses of the sky, and the ventilation leaves nothing to be desired. The oldest inhabitants of the town recall the days when coal was actually burned in the waiting-room grate, and it is stated on reliable authority that the material in the window-frames was at one time transparent. There is as yet no confirmation of the rumour that the building is to be scheduled as an Ancient Monument.*

What name is given to this style of writing?

(f) Read the following sentence backwards, letter by letter, and see what you notice about it.

> *Draw no dray a yard onward*

What is this kind of sentence called? Here is the first half of another sentence of the same kind. See if you can complete it.

WAS IT A C.. . ...?

☑ MARK THESE YOURSELF

AT least ten mistakes have been made in the addressing of the envelopes illustrated below, and at least one of the addresses is entirely correct. See if you can find the mistakes, and then check your opinion against the answers on page 146.

Pages 2 and 3 of *A First English Companion* will help.

124. HOW TO BEGIN AND END A LETTER

When writing a letter to your mother you would begin with the salutation *Dear Mother*. What salutations would you use for the following?

Page 77 of *A First English Companion* will help you.

(*a*) Your cousin Pat.

(*b*) The editor of a magazine.

(*c*) The father of a close friend whose name is Stevenson.

(*d*) A firm trading as Willis and Nesfield Ltd.

(*e*) Your head teacher.

(*f*) An unmarried lady named Fowler who keeps a shop at which you are a regular customer.

(*g*) Your uncle (Mr. Paul Glover) and his wife Susan.

(*h*) The proprietress (whom you have never met) of a boarding-house.

Before signing one's name at the end of a letter it is customary to use a phrase such as *Yours faithfully, Very sincerely yours*, etc. Suggest suitable endings for letters to the persons described above.

125. SUBJECTS FOR SHORT LETTERS

Write a brief letter to each of the following.

You will find useful hints on page 77 of *A First English Companion*.

(*a*) An uncle who has sent you a birthday present.

(*b*) A friend who is spending a birthday in hospital.

(*c*) The mother of a school friend at whose home you have just been staying for a week.

(*d*) A business firm, asking for a catalogue, price-list, or sample.

(*e*) Your head teacher, explaining why you are absent from school.

(*f*) A business firm from which you have ordered goods that have not arrived.

(*g*) A friend who wants advice on where to spend a holiday and where to find accommodation.

(*h*) The manager of your local transport department, inquiring about something that you have left on a bus. Give exact details—including date, time, route, etc.

(*i*) The manager of a laundry, asking about a lost garment. Remember that the laundry is handling thousands of garments every day.

126. ADDRESSING ENVELOPES CORRECTLY

Suppose that you are addressing an envelope to each of the following. For each one draw a rectangle 16 cm by 11 cm, and set out the address in its proper form.

You will find helpful hints on pages 2 and 3 of *A First English Companion*.

(a) Mr. N. Jackson and his wife, who live in the Lincolnshire town of Boston. Their house, in Foxe Road, is No. 117.

(b) A Birmingham firm of builders and contractors whose head office is at 2 Wills Street, which has the post code B19 1PP. They trade as Green and Astbury Ltd.

(c) Two brothers named Fry, whose Christian names are David Robert and William Henry respectively. They live in County Durham at Darlington, and their address is 5 Stockton Road.

(d) Your unmarried cousin Stella, who lives with her parents (Mr. and Mrs. T. E. Edmunds) in Wandsworth, which is in the postal area SW18 2DE of London. Her address is 3 Eglantine Road.

(e) The wife of Mr. Norman John Mills, whose Christian name is Angela. She lives at the Mill House in the Gloucestershire village of Melton.

(f) The two young daughters (still at school) of Mr. and Mrs. R. H. Wardle. Their names are Jill and Rosemary, and they live in the Buckinghamshire village of Steeple Claydon (near Bletchley) in a house called the Grange.

(g) Your uncle John, the father of Brian Ford. He is a clergyman living in Reading (RG1 2SB), and is a Master of Arts. His home, in Church Street, is known as the Manse. Reading is in Berkshire.

(h) The Schools Medical Officer at Newbridge in Northamptonshire. His name is Charles Baker; he is of course a doctor, and is to be found at the Public Health Offices in Rushmore Road.

(i) Your Uncle George and Aunt Mary, who live in Australia. Your uncle, Mr. Hanson, is in business in Queensland, and lives in Hamilton. The address is 284, Kingsford Smith Drive, and the Australian post code is 4007.

127. BRIEF MESSAGES ON POSTCARDS

Write a postcard message to each of the following. Be brief and try not to exceed a total of thirty words; some of the messages can be conveyed in fewer than twenty words. If the messages are to be displayed as though actually written on postcards, draw rectangles 14 cm by 9 cm.

Page 105 of *A First English Companion* will help.

(a) Your parents at home, to let them know that you have arrived safely at your destination after a long journey.

(b) The dealers from whom you have bought a television set, asking them to put right a fault that has developed.

(c) The secretary of a football or hockey club, suggesting (with reasons) an alteration in the time of a forthcoming match.

(d) Your parents at home, asking them to post on to you something that you need urgently in camp.

(e) A friend whom you wish to meet when you visit his or her home town. Give day, time, and place.

(f) A friend who is going on a cycle tour with you, asking if he or she can bring certain items of equipment that you have been unable to get.

(g) A friend who has asked you to give him full particulars of a book that you have, so that he can order a copy for himself.

(h) The secretary of a club or society of which you are a member, explaining that owing to illness you will be unable to help at the annual garden party.

(i) A neighbour, explaining that when you went away on holiday this morning you left your bicycle outside at the back of the house. Suggest what you think is the best thing to do.

(j) A tradesman with whom you placed an order yesterday; you have now changed your mind about the quantity or quality of the goods you want.

(k) A friend to whom you have said that he can have one of your puppies and that you will let him know when he can call for it.

128. TELEGRAMS

1. Choosing the words that matter most. Each of the following messages is to be shortened so as to contain not more than eight words. This can be done by choosing essential words in the order in which they already appear; e.g.:

I have been delayed by thick fog and am staying here overnight. I shall be returning tomorrow.

This can be abbreviated to

DELAYED BY FOG STAYING
HERE OVERNIGHT RETURNING
TOMORROW

Page 137 of *A First English Companion* will help you.

(a) I have left my savings book in my satchel. Will you please post it on to me immediately?

(b) Tuesday is quite convenient for your visit, and I shall be meeting you at the station.

(c) Can you keep goal for us in the match tomorrow afternoon? Atkins has been injured in a car accident.

(d) We left the house unlocked when we ran for the train this morning. Will you please secure all doors and windows?

(e) I very much regret that I shall be unable to sing at tonight's concert owing to an attack of laryngitis.

(f) The sail that I ordered from you recently is required urgently; I need it for a regatta on Saturday.

2. Avoiding ambiguity. Punctuation in telegrams has to be paid for, so short messages are usually left unpunctuated. This can lead to ambiguity—that is, a message may have a double meaning and so cause confusion. There are three such examples below; write out each one *twice*, inserting full stops so as to show that each message has two meanings.

(a) CANNOT LEAVE MOTHER COMING TUESDAY

(b) PLEASE RETURN KEYS WANTED URGENTLY

(c) MATCH PLAYABLE MONDAY IF WEATHER HOLDS WILL WIRE YOU AGAIN

3. Saying much in little. In the circumstances described below it might be considered necessary to send telegrams. Compose a message of not more than eight words (without names and addresses) to suit each occasion.

Page 137 of *A First English Companion* will help you.

(a) Your uncle and aunt are celebrating their silver wedding today.

(b) A friend who has been staying with you returned home this morning. You find that she has left her engagement ring in the bedroom, and you know that she will be very upset if she thinks she has lost it on the train.

(c) On the very day that you expect to return home after a holiday with friends you are invited to stay for a few days longer, and you wish to obtain your parents' permission.

(d) Under the doormat, where it has lain for several days, you find a letter inviting you to join the audience at a circus performance to be televised next week. Today is the last date for acceptance.

(e) Friends who are coming to stay with you will be setting out by car later today. All the main roads in the district are under water after last night's storm, and the only way into the town is by rail.

(f) You are making a long journey home by rail, alone, when the train is held up by a landslide. Sleeping-quarters are arranged for all the passengers, and you wish to let your parents know what has happened.

(g) A fortnight ago you wrote away for a sleeping-bag. It has not yet arrived, and you are due to leave for a camping-holiday in three days' time.

(h) Last night you ordered by post a *Premier* light-weight tent, but you have now changed your mind and would prefer the *Super* model. You wish to let the firm know this before the order is dealt with.

(i) On returning home after a day excursion to London you remember that you have left your new coat on a seat in a museum, and are concerned lest someone else claims it.

(j) You should be taking part in a play tonight, but have developed influenza. Fortunately, there is an understudy, but first the producer must be informed.

ANSWERS *to the Mark These Yourself exercises*

The figures printed in red tell you where to find information or examples that help you to understand the answers given here. For example, 77 **44** Ex. 2 means *Page 77, Set 44, Exercise 2.* You will also find it helpful, when working the exercises, to refer to the main index and look up topics that appear in the questions.

Page 6

(a) 1. A rod. 2. A person from Poland.

(b) 1. A vegetable. 2. A person from Sweden.

(c) 1. A person who damages beautiful things.
2. One of a race of destructive people of the 5th century.

(d) 1. Hawthorn blossom. 2. Name of a month.

(e) 1. Quicksilver. 2. Messenger of the gods.

(f) 1. A garment. 2. One of the Channel Isles.

Page 10

1. (a) Pennies, pence.
   (b) Hoofs, hooves.
   (c) Formulae, formulas.
   (d) Cherubs, cherubim.
   (e) Seraphim, seraphs.
   (f) Aquariums, aquaria.
   (g) Gladioli, gladioluses.
   (h) Brothers, brethren.
   (i) Cows, kine.

2. (a) Although it is popularly called a *dice*, its correct name is a *die*.
   (b) Dice.

3.
In	Out
enter	emerge
intrude	issue
penetrate	discharge
invade	escape
immigrate	evacuate
insinuate	emanate.

4. Accept, bestow; advance, recede; gratify, displease; amplify, diminish; commend, chide.

5. (a) 1. Two public shows.
   2. Eye-glasses.
   (b) 1. Two instruments for indicating direction.
   2. An instrument for drawing circles.
   (c) 1. Medicine.
   2. One of the sciences.

Page 12

1. (a) reptile
   (b) insect
   (c) gas
   (d) shrub
   (e) rock
   (f) instrument
   (g) vehicle
   (h) game
   (i) fruit
   (j) liquid
   (k) grain
   (l) drug
   (m) disease
   (n) boat
   (o) garment
   (p) plant
   (q) clergyman
   (r) coin
   (s) timber
   (t) metal
   (u) alloy

2. Deny.

3. Here are a few of many such names: Barber, Brewer, Butler, Carpenter, Carter, Cook, Cooper, Draper, Fisher, Fowler, Glover, Groom, Mason, Miller, Porter, Potter, Saddler, Shepherd, Slater, Smith, Wright.

4. (a) sings
   (b) fights
   (c) boxes
   (d) eats
   (e) gives
   (f) sells
   (g) owes
   (h) wanders

5. Morgan, Charles; Morgan, J.; Morgan, John; Morgan, J. W.; Morgan, S.; Morgan, Samuel; Morgan, S. J.

6. A large box

Page 38

1. (a) (i) Miner; (ii) minor.
   (b) No. A feint is a sham attack.
   (c) Cockles and Mussels.

2. Sur-name   suit-able
   super-human   under-neath
   un-dress   uni-form.

Page 41

(a) 11	(i) 2	(p) 1
(b) 5	(j) 9	(q) 10
(c) 8	(k) 4	(r) 11*
(d) 7	(l) 6	(s) 3
(e) 12	(m) 7	(t) 12
(f) 1	(n) 3	(u) 11
(g) 3	(o) 12	(v) 2
(h) 10		

* The abbreviation *St.* is indexed as though it were spelt out as *Saint*.

Page 46

(a) 6	(d) 9	(g) 9
(b) 8	(e) 5	(h) 10
(c) 3	(f) 11	(i) 12

Page 56

(a) He says my left eye is the *weaker*. 37 Ex. 4

(b) Olive told us a *far-fetched* story. 71 Ex. 5

(c) Pasteur *benefited* the whole of mankind. 79 Ex. 2

(d) Gwen is a brunette, but Eric is a *blond*. 20 Ex. 3

(e) The *hardiest* of the crew was Bowers. 36 Ex. 2

(f) Neither of the *propellers was* damaged. 42 Ex 4

Page 60

Line

1. Popov was the *funnier*. 37 Ex. 4 . After *funnier*, use either a semi-colon 73 **37** or the word *and* followed by a comma. 25 Ex. 3

2. humorous. 76 **40**

3. You will see from the dictionary definition of *equestrian* that there is no need to say *on horseback.* 108 **78** skilfully.

4. its. 103 Ex. 4
   The chimpanzee clapped, not the trapeze. 45 Ex. 5

5. *But only for a moment* is not a sentence. 2 Ex. 7

6. Neither of us *was* afraid. 42 Ex. 4

7. Didn't. 66 Ex. 1
   my giving him a playful slap. 54 Ex. 9

Page 67

1. (a) Woman's Hour
   (b) Sports Report
   (c) You and Yours
   (d) What's On?
   (e) Gardeners' Question Time
   (f) The Week's Good Cause
   (g) Songs from the Shows
   (h) Bach's Organ Works

2. (*b*) Babies' prams
    (*e*) Gentlemen's outfitter
    (*h*) Buses' radiators.

3. (*a*) Mr. Hughes, the Director of Education, spoke to us. 65 Ex. 5
    (*b*) Breakfast finished, mother washed up.
    (*c*) Stephen replied that he would be as quick as possible. 69 Ex. 7
    (*d*) "If you look in the drawer," he said, "you will find a pair of scissors."
    (*e*) I asked him why he wouldn't let me in.
    (*f*) He took his B.Sc. at Birmingham.

4. These two apples are too small to bake and too sour to eat.

5. HINT — THIN.

Page 73

1. When he re-signs. 72 Ex. 6

2. Gloucestershire, Hampshire, Northamptonshire, Oxfordshire, Shropshire.

Page 74

1. tobacconists, market-gardener, chiropodist, hairdresser, smallholder, signwriter, metal merchants.

2. Microphone, preparation (homework), association football, refrigerator, veterinary surgeon, mathematics, general purposes vehicle (G.P.), operation, mackintosh, high fidelity, cinematograph, pianoforte, repertory, locomotive, amperes, fanatic.

3. An F.R.C.S. is a surgeon, and an F.R.C.O. is an organist, so take your choice.

4. (*a*) Reverend   (*b*) Revelation
    (*c*) revolution.

5. Alfred, Bertram or Herbert, Christopher, Daniel, Donald, Frederick, Geoffrey, Joseph, Kenneth, Leonard, Leslie, Michael, Patrick, Philip, Raymond, Reginald, Ronald, Samuel, Sidney, Stanley, Stephen, Thomas, Anthony, Wilfred.

6. (*a*) 9   (*b*) 4   (*c*) 11
    (*d*) 4   (*e*) 9

7. The farmer.
    Bob, the farmer's dog.

8. Jill, says Jane, is good at hockey.
    66 Ex. 9(*c*)

9. Did you say, "How old is she?"?

Page 76

1. All the five vowels occur in alphabetical order.

2. It's a minute or two to two two.

Page 80

The following words are among those that are acceptable.

    (*a*) Chameleon, chaos, character, chasm, chemist, chlorine, chloroform, choir, cholera, chord, chorister, chorus, christen, chromium, chronic, chrysalis, chrysanthemum.
    (*b*) Chagrin, chalet, chamois, champagne, chandelier, charade, chassis, chateau, chauffeur, chef, chiffon, chivalry, chute.
    (*c*) Wrangle, wrap, wrath, wreak, wreath, wreathe, wreck, wren, wrench, wrest, wrestle, wretch, wriggle, wring, wrinkle, wrist, write, writhe, wrong, wroth, wrought, wry.
    (*d*) Knack, knapsack, knave, knead, knee, kneel, knell, knife, knight, knit, knob, knock, knoll, knot, know, knowledge, knuckle.
    (*e*) Gnarled, gnash, gnat, gnaw, gnome, gnu.

Page 82

(*a*) offer   (*f*) check, dam
(*b*) chief, principal   (*g*) tart, sharp, acid, bitter
(*c*) flinch
(*d*) tear   (*h*) mound, grave, tumulus
(*e*) rob

Page 87

1. (*a*) 2   (*c*) 2   (*e*) 2
    (*b*) 3   (*d*) 2   (*f*) 4

2. On the first syllable.

3. It rhymes with *hurt*.

4. Z (as though the word were spelt *zylophone*).

5. Fish.

Page 100

1. Milli (a thousandth).

2. Ampere (after Ampère), farad (Faraday), joule (Joule), ohm (Ohm), volt (Volta), watt (Watt).

3. France, France, Portugal, Spain.

4. Because they are like a man's beard (Latin *barba*, beard).

Page 102

1. Mars, the god of war.
    Morpheus, the god of dreams.
    Vulcan, the god of fire.

2. The first, because its body is nearly *cut* in two. (Latin *secare, sectum*, to cut)

3. Knitted woollen jackets would have been called sandwiches (just as they are now called cardigans, after the Earl of Cardigan), and meat served between slices of bread would have been called cardigans.

Page 112

(*a*) Licence (*license* is the verb). 104 **73**
(*b*) Theirs (*ours, yours, hers, theirs* have no apostrophe).
(*c*) To avoid complaints from the N.S.P.C.C., say *Boil the cabbage if the baby does not like it raw.* 30 Ex. 2
(*d*) Swam (use *swum* after *has, had,* etc.). 108 **77**
(*e*) dependants (*dependent* is an adjective). 106 Ex. 4
(*f*) Lightening (*lightning* is a noun). 105 Ex. 9
(*g*) Ringed (bells are *rung*). 105 Ex. 3
(*h*) Alternative (look these words up in the dictionary). 105 Ex. 1
(*i*) Phosphorus (*phosphorous* is an adjective, as in *phosphorous oxide*).
(*j*) Diphtheria.
    Salient means *standing out noticeably*, so there is no need for the words *that stand out.* 108 **78**

Page 115

(*a*) A drowning man will catch at a straw.
(*b*) Great oaks from little acorns grow.
(*c*) Little pitchers have long ears.
(*d*) Faint heart never won fair lady.
(*e*) Take time by the forelock.
(*f*) As you make your bed, so you must lie on it.
(*g*) Discretion is the better part of valour.

Page 121

1. In your cheek.

2. Above water.

3. On your sleeve.

Page 123

1. In a rowing-boat. (To catch a crab is to get the oar jammed deeply in the water.)

2. The leopard cannot change *his spots*.

3. In someone else's eye.

4. Silence, because "Speech is silver, but silence is golden."

5. Red.

Page 124

1. (*a*) Two times   (*b*) Two tens
    (*c*) One of two that make a pair.
    (*d*) Two and ten   (*e*) Twine
    (*f*) Twig   (*g*) Twilight.

2. (*a*) theirs   (*b*) It's   (*c*) Who's
    (*d*) its   (*e*) whose   (*f*) There's.

3. The following are among the answers that are acceptable.
    Female, feminine; mutton; mere, mermaid; pontoon; port, portal; sorcerer, sorceress; toreador; territory, etc. (See Ex. 10 on page 95.); vine, vintage.

4. (a) lat'itude
   (b) chrysan'themum
   (c) report'
   (d) laburn'um
   (e) vas'eline
   (f) undergrad'uate

5. A swimming-bath   a hunting-ground
   a cycling-cape   a stumbling-block
   a bathing-cap   reading-spectacles.

6. The English were *not* defeated at Waterloo.

Page 136

1. Quaking, roaring, raving, crossing, going, stunning, roaming, spinning, hopping, jerking, struggling, cleaving, groaning.

2. (a) Assonance and internal rhyme
   (b) Alliteration
   (c) Rhyme.

3. The following are examples:
   Auger, awl, brace, die, drill, file, plane, saw, vice.

4. As good as gold
   As plain as a pikestaff
   As fit as a fiddle
   As dull as ditchwater
   As weak as water
   As smooth as silk (satin)
   As blind as a bat
   As sweet as sugar
   As proud as Punch
   As red as a rose
   As bold as brass
   As dead as a doornail

Page 140

(a) *Mr.* and *Esq.* must not be used together.

No county or post code given. (There are twelve places named *Sutton* in the United Kingdom.)

(b) *Messrs.* should not be used where there is no personal name.
No street-number given.
No post code given (e.g. M15 5AL).

(c) *To* and *Local* should not be used.
No name of town given.

(d) Address written too high; the cancellation-mark will obliterate part of it.
No post code given.

(e) *Mr.* should be *Messrs.*
No road or street given.
No post code given.

(f) Correct. (It is correct to address the wife of Mr. John R. Handley as *Mrs. John R. Handley.*)

INDEX

The first part of each reference is the page-number; figures given in bold type refer to sets of exercises; individual exercises are indicated as such. For example, 77(**44** Ex. 2) means *Page* 77, *Set* 44, *Exercise* 2. Where several references appear under one head, the first is normally to be regarded as the most important.

INDEX